Blaming Teachers

New Directions in the History of Education

Series editor, Benjamin Justice

The New Directions in the History of Education series seeks to publish innovative books that push the traditional boundaries of history of education. Topics may include social movements in education; the history of cultural representations of schools and schooling; the role of public schools in the social production of space; and the perspectives and experiences of African Americans, Latinx Americans, women, queer folk, and others. The series will take a broad, inclusive look at American education in formal settings, from pre-kindergarten to higher education, as well as in out-of-school and informal settings. We also invite historical scholarship that informs and challenges popular conceptions of educational policy and policy-making that address questions of social justice, equality, democracy, and the formation of popular knowledge.

D'Amico Pawlewicz, Diana, *Blaming Teachers: Professionalization Policies and the Failure of Reform in American History*

Steele, Kyle P., *Making a Mass Institution: Indianapolis and the American High School*

Blaming Teachers

Professionalization Policies and the Failure of Reform in American History

DIANA D'AMICO PAWLEWICZ

Rutgers University Press

New Brunswick, Camden, and Newark, New Jersey, and London

Library of Congress Cataloging-in-Publication Data

Names: D'Amico Pawlewicz, Diana, author.
Title: Blaming teachers : professionalization policies and the failure of reform in American history / Diana D'Amico Pawlewicz.
Description: New Brunswick, NJ : Rutgers University Press, [2020] | Series: New directions in the history of education | Includes bibliographical references and index.
Identifiers: LCCN 2019045977 | ISBN 9781978808423 (paperback) | ISBN 9781978808430 (hardback) | ISBN 9781978808447 (epub) | ISBN 9781978808454 (mobi) | ISBN 9781978808461 (pdf)
Subjects: LCSH: Teachers—United States—Social conditions—20th century. | Public schools—United States—History—20th century. | Educational change—United States—History—20th century.
Classification: LCC LB1775.2 D43 2020 | DDC 371.10973—dc23
LC record available at https://lccn.loc.gov/2019045977

A British Cataloging-in-Publication record for this book is available from the British Library.

A portion of chapter 3 was previously published as Diana D'Amico, "'An Old Order Is Passing': The Rise of Applied Learning in University-Based Teacher Education during the Great Depression," *History of Education Quarterly* 55, no. 3 (August 2015): 319–345. The author is grateful to the journal editors and publisher for their permission to reprint it here.

∞ The paper used in this publication meets the requirements of the American National Standard for Information Sciences—Permanence of Paper for Printed Library Materials, ANSI Z39.48-1992.

www.rutgersuniversitypress.org

Manufactured in the United States of America

To Rob, for all time

Contents

Blaming Teachers

Introduction

> School-teaching is the most beggarly profession in the United States. No other calling that is presumed to require anything like the same amount of training and ability is so ill-paid. No other calling that is presumed to require a considerable mental discipline and development is held in such low regard or is so little supported by public admiration. No other learned calling except the ministry is pursued under conditions that involve so much humiliation.
> —"School Victims," *Saturday Evening Post*, April 6, 1918

In January 1891, readers of the *New York Times* learned that even "the most reactionary and unprogressive members" of New York City's Board of Education agreed with rising public sentiment that the school "system is drifting the wrong way, and, instead of improving, really losing what little life and upward tendency there was in it."[1] In response, local leaders assembled the Committee of Seven, a group of school commissioners charged with examining the problems facing the city's public schools. Commissioners placed the blame for the city's faltering schools on teachers, reporting that "the evils and defects of the system are due to lack of intelligence and efficiency on the part of teachers." One commissioner dismissed the city's teachers as "educated ninnies" and another pointed to a "decrepit old woman" as indicative of the city's fundamental school problems. "It is perfectly clear to my mind," a committee member and school commissioner noted, "that the greatest need of reform in our school system is the quality of the teachers."[2] With little recourse, a dismayed teacher, identified only as "One of Them," penned a letter to the newspaper's editor. "The New-York public-school teacher is what the New-York public-school system has made her," the anonymous teacher lamented. Though teachers shouldered the blame, in the estimation of this letter writer, the city's teachers "never had a chance."[3]

Since the expansion of publicly supported education and rise of municipal school systems in the mid-nineteenth century, policymakers, educators, and taxpayers looked upon public education with mixed emotions. On the one hand, filled with hope, Americans identified public schools as powerful social institutions capable of safeguarding and encouraging national goals. For example, Caroline LeRow explained to readers of the *Ladies' Home Journal* in 1890 that "all civilization is but the outgrowth of education."[4] Arne Duncan extended this premise into the twenty-first century during his tenure at the helm of the Department of Education when he characterized public schooling as the "civil rights issue of our generation."[5] In a resounding chorus, Americans have maintained that through the education of individual children, local public schools could serve national aims ranging from Americanization to economic security to social justice. On the other hand, tempering that optimism, members of the public from parents to pundits also expressed frustration, arguing that public schools have fallen short of their lofty mission. In 1949, one critic fretted, "American education is so defective in theory and practice as seriously to threaten the long continuance of the way of life to further which this nation was founded."[6] Frederick Hess of the American Enterprise Institute ruminated on the state of public education in 2001 and urged "unchaining the bulldozer."[7]

At the nexus of this history of hope and frustration sits the nation's public school teachers. Commissioner of Education John Eaton observed in 1870 that "teachers make the nation." Therefore, he continued, "all educational improvements" ought to "concentrate themselves upon the work of the teacher." This framing charted the course for a national policy discussion about local public school reform in the United States that has persisted for more than a century. In Eaton's estimation, "the character of the American teacher . . . most deeply concern[s] the body politic."[8] President Franklin Delano Roosevelt extended that fundamental policy narrative in the spring of 1938 when he extolled, "the teachers in America are the ultimate guardians of the human capital in America, the assets which must be made to pay social dividends, if democracy is to survive."[9] Throughout the history of the public schools, Americans of all stripes have concurred that teachers are essential to the success of the public schools and nation. They have also concurred that public school teachers are to blame for the failures of the nation's public schools. As one social commentator bemoaned in 1879, in spite of "all the advances made in the theories and methods of education, and all the elevation of educational standards, it is, and remains, true, that the poorest work done in the world is done in the schoolroom."[10] Duncan echoed that sentiment in 2012, explaining to a crowd of educators that too often, "bright, young people don't even consider teaching" as a future occupation and, in another initiative, called for "a sweeping transformation of the [teaching] profession."[11] Somewhat more bluntly, speaking at a rally in El Paso, Texas, Donald Trump Jr. warned his audience to beware of "loser teachers."[12]

As public support of basic schooling spread from its New England strongholds, teachers came to stand at the nucleus of education policy both as targets of reproof and objects of reform. Dating back to the mid-nineteenth century, social commentators, educators, and reformers traced national problems to underperforming public schools and the problems of underperforming public schools back to the nation's teachers. In this historical loop, teachers were to blame and professionalization was the solution. More than reform for the sake of the schools, though, education policy and social policy entangled from the start as reformers heralded teacher professionalization measures as means to improve the nation's schools in the name of national security, economic solvency, and international competition. The discourse of blame gave way to policy stories that shaped America's unique brand of education reform. Rather than factual certainties, the problems attributed to teachers are historical artifacts. Reflections of a particular time and place, the definition of problems along with the policies and reforms designed to redress those troubles emerged from manmade stories intended to make sense of and simplify complex circumstances.[13] As Bennett and Edelman explained, "narratives create a particular kind of social world, with specified heroes and villains, deserving and undeserving people, and a set of public policies that are rationalized by the construction of social problems by which they become solutions."[14] This book tracks the history of the creation and maintenance of these policy stories rooted in blame, the professionalization reforms they generated, and their consequences.

American public school teachers have existed in a perpetual state of blame and reform. Of course, the irony is that if the persistent discourse of blame is any indication, this legacy of reform never gave way to a sense of improvement, much less accomplishment. Instead, negative appraisals of teachers persisted over this long history and professionalization measures cloaked as novel undertakings abounded. In this book, I historicize the professionalization policies applied to teachers and the debates that surrounded them over a landmark period from the rise of municipally supported public school systems in the mid-nineteenth century through the development of the modern teachers union into the 1980s. *Blaming Teachers* unearths a Sisyphean irony with historiographical and contemporary significance: the historic language of professionalism applied to public school teachers generated reforms that subverted professional legitimacy. Superficially, professionalism connotes authority, expertise, and status, but public school teachers never gained these from the so-called professionalization initiatives that surrounded them. This book explains why they did not.

The 1890 census coded twenty occupations under the category of professional services, marking them as distinct from work in agriculture, fisheries, and mining; domestic and personal service; and trade and transportation. Census takers grouped actors and architects, journalists and lawyers, physicians and professors, teachers and veterinary surgeons, as well as twelve other fields together as professionals: this select group represented just 4 percent of all occupations and teachers comprised more than one-third of that entire corps.[15] By the 1970 census, eighteen more fields including librarians, nurses, and airplane pilots joined the ranks of professional occupations alongside teachers and together they represented 15 percent of all employed workers; teachers constituted close to one-quarter of all professional workers in the United States.[16] Theorists have long defined the professional through a functionalist framework and identified university-based preparation, expertise, autonomy, and authority as the critical markers that separated professionals from other workers.[17] These same definitions have led other scholars to conclude somewhat definitively that teachers are, in fact, not professionals but instead semiprofessionals, a paradoxical turn, indeed, as teachers are the most numerous among all professional occupations.[18] Moving beyond taxonomic sociological definitions, historians have explored the social dimensions of profession revealing that the aura of professionalism carries with it cultural and economic prestige that goes beyond the workplace: expertise grants cachet in the broader community. Since the nineteenth century, professional identity has sprung from gendered and racialized ideas of objectivity and rationality that pivoted on White, middle-class manhood and created boundaries that kept women and other minoritized groups on the fringe.[19] Even as the female-dominated field of teaching remains the largest professional occupation, teachers have historically found professional credibility and respect just out of reach.

It follows, then, that professionalization is an aspirational process about improvement and stature in the workplace and beyond it. In the historical development of some occupational groups, members professionalized their fields by coming together to define the terms of work, establish a shared body of esoteric knowledge, create barriers to entry, and rid their field of meddlers. Members of the field directed these internal processes that transpired in universities and professional associations. Professionalization for teachers, however, never unfolded this way; rather, it was an exogenously directed process fueled by blame in which others identified teachers' shortcomings and proposed policy solutions. In this formulation, professionalization, still an aspirational process about improvement and stature, was also a contest for power as others motivated by discrete institutional interests jockeyed for the controlling voice.

Teacher professionalization has remained the central preoccupation of reformers over the long history of the American public schools. In 1917, local school leaders in South Carolina echoed concerns of their colleagues around the nation when they reported, "the status of the teaching profession is of all educational concerns the greatest."[20] Yet the policies and initiatives levied in the name of teacher professionalization bore little resemblance to scholars' theories, much less the practical realities of what other professional occupations experienced. For public school reformers, the vocabulary of professionalization built consensus as something fundamentally positive that offered cultural and social rewards. In substance, though, policymakers, school leaders, and others understood professionalization measures for teachers as efficient and effective ways to bolster the growing bureaucratic order of the public schools through regulation and standardization. Jal Mehta argued that in the case of teachers "failed professionalization breeds external rationalization."[21] Historically, though, teacher professionalization and rationalization, rather than two opposite poles, were one and the same from the start. The shared vocabularies of profession, professionalism, and professionalization engulfed teachers as they did doctors, lawyers, and other similar occupational groups. But professionalization was not a singular, uniform process. The rhetoric of professionalization generated consensus as it carried popular positive connotations, but when reformers, school leaders, and others thought about the needs and goals of the public school workforce—a female-dominated workforce—they crafted reforms and policies that bore little resemblance to the professionalization processes that granted status, expertise, and authority to male-dominated fields. By design, the history of teacher professionalization is the history of rationalization.

Local educators around the country participated in a national discussion as they sought to define teacher professionalism through policy and created codes to discourage unprofessional behavior. For instance, in December 1916, school leaders in Marion County, Oregon, developed a code of ethics "to establish professional ideals, to dignify the profession, to standardize professional conduct, to elevate the professional spirit, and create in the minds of others a deeper respect for the profession." The code warned teachers of disloyalty and characterized negotiating pay and criticizing superiors as "undignified, unprofessional, and dishonorable conduct."[22] School leaders in Boston developed a similar code in 1927. According to school superintendent Jeremiah E. Burke, "It is for the pupils, not for the teacher, that the schools exist" and, thus, "teachers are not justified in publicly expressing an adverse opinion of a school official."[23] Historically, formal and informal school policies defined teacher professionalism as compliance.

Teachers, to be sure, did not sit idly by. Aware of the consequences for speaking out, many teachers penned anonymous letters to local newspapers and boards of education to fight against practices they deemed unfair. However, as New York City teacher Emma L. Daly learned in 1922, anonymity promised no protection. On two occasions, Daly sent city Superintendent William Ettinger an anonymous letter to express concerns about her principal and the leadership of her school. She signed one letter "Teacher of P.S. [public school] 38" and another "Teachers' League of P.S. 38." Ettinger dispatched District Superintendent Joseph J. Taylor to locate the author. After interviewing teachers at P.S. 38 and gaining no information, Taylor solicited the services of two handwriting experts who identified Daly. When confronted with their findings and charged with forgery, an offense punishable by imprisonment, Daly tearfully admitted that she was the author, avoiding jail time but facing public ridicule.[24]

Long-standing rules about professional conduct combined with public sentiment about the importance of public schools left teachers vulnerable and open to blame from multiple fronts, just as this chapter's epigraph described. In his 1949 critique *And Madly Teach: A Layman Looks at Public School Education*, Mortimer Smith asserted that all citizens had a stake and therefore a say in public schooling. "There is something condescending and faintly derogatory about the term 'laymen,'" he offered. Even as a "coterie of experts" claimed supremacy, Smith demanded, "education is not so mysterious that it will yield its secrets only to the specialist. After all," he continued, "practically every adult has been subjected to some amount of formal education."[25] The following year Mary Holman observed, "the teacher must serve at least five masters." "Society sets up a situation," she argued, "which, instead of helping the teacher make a total adjustment, tends to tear her apart."[26] In 1946, Lois MacFarland explained to readers of the *Saturday Evening Post* why she quit teaching: "The teacher is considered community property. Everyone has a right to speak sharply to her, criticize her and tell her wherein she is not doing her job right."[27] Concurring, another teacher wrote anonymously in 1977 to the editor of the *Chicago Tribune*, "I am tired . . . of columnists taking cheap shots at the teaching profession for all the woes of the world."[28] The simultaneous discourses of blame and professionalization engulfed teachers, sapping them of authority and relegating them to a history of reform.

Even as the concept of teacher professionalization evoked broad support and appeal over the long history of the public schools, this book reveals another critical part of the story: stakeholders including taxpayers, politicians, school leaders, teacher educators, union leaders, and teachers understood the notion of the professional teacher in terms that often competed. Reformers and critics began local conversations that resonated nationally from similar starting places: teachers are not yet professionals, but they ought to be and much would be improved as a result. The consensus, however, ended there as Americans from across the educational landscape defined the barriers to and benefits of professional stature in opposing terms and in ways that often bore little resemblance to theoretical constructions. These disparate versions of the professional teacher stood as metaphors for power and authority in the education policy milieu.[29]

In important regards, ordinary classroom teachers stand somewhat voiceless in this history. Their absence reflects both the nature of historical evidence and, more importantly, school reform. Policies were applied to teachers; debates occurred around them. Perhaps counterintuitively, the size of the occupation disempowered the individuals within it and reduced them to members of a faceless legion, indistinguishable and replaceable. This book documents how policymakers created and applied professionalization reforms in a top-down fashion, but this book also documents something else: rarely did those initiatives go uncontested. Members of other groups—unionized teachers and teacher educators, for instance—spoke on behalf of teachers, motivated by their own institutional interests. These stakeholders contributed to policy debates and offered modifications to and critiques of professionalization reforms. Driven by discrete institutional pressures ranging from financial obligations to desires to assert their own authority, however, the nature of these responses often contributed in equal measure to teachers' deprofessionalization. This book tells a story about historical change in which shifting economic, social, and political contexts yielded different ideas about who professional teachers were, the cultural rewards at the base of the demarcation, and how such a cohort might be created.

At the same time, *Blaming Teachers* also reveals a story about continuity. Four critical factors—structure, ideology, gender, and race—have been historical constants and informed the policy stories around professionalization and ensuing reform initiatives. The institutional structure of public education generated barriers and boundaries that shaped teachers' work lives. Bureaucracy delimits nearly all occupations; for some, that structure preserves privilege and for others it yields disempowering managerial control.[30] The history of teachers helps to account for these divergent outcomes. The institutional development of the nation's public schools followed a different trajectory than other established professions. Doctors, for one, existed and worked independently before the advent of hospitals.[31] Unlike in teaching, the cornerstones of the profession—including, most importantly, university-based preparation—were in place before medicine was institutionalized. The institution of public schooling predated the occupation of public school teaching and thus set the parameters around teachers' work lives. To be sure, teachers existed before the mid-nineteenth century. They worked in homes as private tutors, in dame and charity schools, in loosely organized common schools and one-room schoolhouses, and in private schools. However, in salient regards, the institutionalization of public schooling that came with the rise of municipal school systems changed the nature of that work, making teaching before and after the rise of public schools similar in name only. Early school leaders recruited teachers for the public schools who would fit the needs of the institution, ushering in a new cohort of school workers. This book tracks the historical development of the institutional structures of public education over time—the local K–12 school, higher education, and unions—and the ways those organizations shaped the discourse of teacher blame and reform.

Public schools stand among the nation's most important social institutions, but their value does not rest alone on teaching children fundamental academic skills. Instead, embedded in professionalization policies are ideologies about the purpose of public education and the social value of schooling. Though they shift from one era to another, these ideologies constitute the hidden curriculum of the schools. Historical professionalization reforms sought to cultivate a teacher corps that conformed to shared ideals around assimilation, global competition, and national security, among others, rather than the taxonomic elements of professional identity. The ideologies of public schooling at once vested teachers with deep social significance and superseded their professional authority. Policymakers and the broader public never doubted the significance of teachers' work; at the same time, members of those groups never trusted teachers to determine what that work was or how it ought to be conducted. The history unearthed in this book casts light on how national ideals ranging from aspirations of democracy to national security transformed into local policy.

Finally, the structural and ideological underpinnings of professionalization cannot be understood in neutered or color-blind forms ignoring the fact that the majority of teachers were White women and the majority of those controlling their work were White men. From the rise of municipally supported public education systems in the mid-nineteenth century and into the present, teaching has not only been a female-dominated occupation but more women have taught than have worked in nearly any other single field. Moreover, public school teaching has been a field dominated by White women, in spite of long-standing efforts of people of color to make their way into the nation's public schools. Deeply entrenched formal and informal policies and practices sustained by implicit and explicit gendered and racialized assumptions created barriers to entry that make the history of teaching in the nation's public schools, and particularly in large urban school districts like those in New York City, at once the history of institutionalized racism and White women at work.[32] Gendered and racialized perceptions bolstered the structural and ideological foundation of the institution of public schooling. Early school leaders identified stereotypical feminine traits of pliability and docility as indicators of teacher quality and conflated racialized ideas of Whiteness with notions of quality and Americanism. Not only would White women be inexpensive, early policymakers reasoned, but they would follow the rules of the organization and stand as apt role models for a diversifying population. Since the mid-nineteenth century, women's social, political, and economic status has changed, as have some racial dynamics, but the historical structures that sprang in part from sexist and racist perceptions nevertheless remain in place as does the imperative to cultivate a large cohort of practitioners who unwaveringly and uniformly support the goals of the public schools. The four factors of structure, ideology, gender, and race did not appear uniformly in each era over this long history, but together these dynamics formed the subtext of the discourse of blame, teacher reform, and ideas about teacher professionalization.

Professionalization has often been understood as a historically bounded process that applied to the "educational elite"—policymakers and education researchers—and unfolded in tandem with the bureaucratization of the schools during the early years of the twentieth century.[33] The professionalization of school leaders undoubtedly had deep implications for teachers, but that process was also separate from the professionalization of the nation's public school teachers, a project that began as early as the mid-nineteenth century and continues into the present. Reflecting dominant functionalist frameworks derived by sociologists, historians of professions and professionalization have paid teachers little attention. Historians of education, of course, have offered a range of in-depth analyses of teachers. However, reflecting the same functionalist frameworks, these scholars have taken teachers' lack of professional authority as a given and focused on the resultant status strains. Some historians, for instance, have focused on teacher education and the place of education schools within universities.[34] Others have called attention to the gendered norms and hierarchies that shaped the school space.[35] Another group of scholars has examined how pedagogical and bureaucratic reforms shaped teachers' work lives.[36] And still others have explored the tensions between association, unionization, and professionalism.[37] To date, however, no work has examined the historic professionalization reforms and policies targeted at teachers; the debates that surrounded those initiatives; and the interplay of faculty in schools of education, union members and leaders, school administrators, policymakers, and members of the public. Professionalization reforms may have had the façade of unanimity, but policymakers, teacher educators, and unionized teachers wrangled over details and often understood both the initiatives and the fundamental problems those initiatives addressed in competing terms, informed by their own institutional interests.

The history recounted in this book unfolds across the New York City urban landscape. In some ways, it is an eminently local story that reveals the idiosyncratic nature of school reform. Local school leaders together with local politicians, reformers, teacher educators, union leaders, and the public sought to improve the city's public schools by improving their teachers, guided by discrete political, economic, and social circumstances. At the same time, these local conversations did not transpire in isolation. As the largest city containing the largest public school system in the country, New York City has long drawn the eyes of the nation. A model of centralized bureaucratic control, a trailblazer in teacher unionization, and home to a variety of teacher training institutions, New York City has been a theater for national policy debates and a harbinger of reform nationwide. Municipal public school systems developed and matured earlier in New York City and other large cities in the urban north like Boston and Philadelphia than they did elsewhere, a reflection of local immediacies more than anything else.

Embedded in this local history of teacher professionalization reform is a broader story about the nature of national education policy and the interplay of federal and local contexts. Following the passage of the Elementary and Secondary Education Act in 1965, the federal government became a fixture in local public education, both incentivizing and mandating various reforms. But, as *Blaming Teachers* reveals, the history of the federal role in education predates the typical mid-1960s origination story and the common trope around top-down interventions. The early history of education policy reveals a two-way street and highlights the saliency of big city school systems in creating national educational priorities. Systems like New York City's functioned as testing grounds for reform and garnered national attention. Beginning as early as the turn of the twentieth century, policymakers had begun to transform local school experiments like teacher certification, municipal partnerships in teacher education, and tenure reform, among other initiatives, into national education policy.[38]

Certainly, the New York City story was not the national story in all regards. For instance, before the landmark *Brown v. Board of Education* ruling in 1954, Black teachers were prevalent across the American South in a way that they were not in the North and especially not in New York City. Discussions about the importance of Black teachers and reforms around recruitment and salary equalization for Black teachers that unfolded elsewhere did not do so in New York City. Instead, New York State legislation that prohibited segregation positioned school leaders to frame teacher and education policy as if they were color-blind. Beneath that façade, formal and informal practices and policies meant that Black children attended separate and under-resourced schools and prospective Black teachers found a pathway into the city's schools mired with barricades and difficult to traverse. From the start, teacher policy in New York City was implicitly about White women. After the *Brown* decision and the mass firings of Black teachers across the South, this New York City approach to school reform nationalized as well. During the second half of the twentieth century, as federal intervention increased and national organizations like the

American Federation of Teachers gained prominence, the distance between New York City and the rest of the country closed and the discourse of teacher blame and the reforms it generated became more similar than different.

Organized chronologically to recover points of continuity and change, each of the following chapters explores the discourse of blame, the policy stories that gave way to teacher professionalization reforms, and the debates around and consequences of those initiatives within the context of shifting and complex historical circumstances. Chapter 1 traces the creation of the entwined policy narratives of blame and professionalization to the mid-nineteenth century and the rise of big-city publicly supported municipal school systems. Although local public education was a chaotic and disorganized affair that had been around in one form or another for several decades, guided by leaders like Horace Mann, Catharine Beecher, and Henry Barnard, appreciation for the social significance of public schooling swelled in urban areas, gradually spreading across the country and giving way to centralized municipal school systems. Reformers were adamant that these new institutions demanded a new type of school worker, and they were equally clear about who that ought to be: young White women. School leaders grounded their vision of the public school teacher in Victorian ideals of White feminine propriety and reasoned that White women, perceived as naturally maternal and docile, were biologically—if not supremely—made for the schools. However, the mounting hope around the potential of public education to serve as a social salve combined with the practical realities of schooling in growing and diversifying cities gave way to concerns that the schools were faltering, all because of teachers. Social critics and reformers called for professionalization, echoing the same language that lent credibility to doctors and lawyers of the day, but devised reforms for teachers that were similar only superficially. In the name of professionalization, reformers implemented three different initiatives intended to improve teachers and, by extension, the schools and society: municipal teacher preparation partnerships, hiring standards and certification exams, and testing. Far from the stature and expertise professionalization promised other professional occupations, teacher professionalization, inextricably rooted in deeply held gendered perceptions of the character and intellect of women, centered on systematization and regulation and entrapped early teachers in the thrall of a quickly developing bureaucratic structure.

Chapter 2 centers on the development of the modern school bureaucracy and the rise of tenure policies during the Progressive Era. Against the backdrop of immigration, World War I, and the rising mantra of 100 percent Americanism, critics once again lambasted public schools in New York City and around the nation for falling short of their mission and argued that the consequences of their failure were dire and far-reaching. This chapter identifies the rise of the modern school bureaucracy as a teacher professionalization initiative. Guided by a faith in scientific efficiency, school leaders promised that the new public school system would raise standards for teachers, but this escalating organizational hierarchy fixed teachers on the lowest rungs where they were voiceless and vulnerable. Extending the policy story set in motion during the formation of municipal public school systems, education reformers blamed teachers for a host of school and societal problems. Pointing to the rising number of immigrant school workers, teacher reform for school improvement entwined professionalization with Americanization. The centerpiece of this project was teacher tenure. Teachers, to be sure, supported tenure initiatives and women of the elementary schools were among the first to raise the issue. However, teachers did not speak with a singular voice and understood the rewards of tenure and professionalism differently over time. Regardless of internal fissures, policymakers and local school leaders implemented tenure policies for their own reasons, none of which resonated with teachers' calls. Indeed, tenure policies flourished during the Progressive Era, starting in cities on the East Coast, making their way into state policies, and spreading across the nation. However, tenure, as enacted by policymakers, bore little resemblance to the scenario for which teachers advocated. For policymakers, teacher tenure was for the benefit of the system. In name, tenure initiatives offered teachers the illusion of status and authority, but in practice, those reforms were components of the historical policy story that identified teachers as the problem and regulation via professionalization as the solution.

By the Depression years, social commentators once again concurred that public schools in America were failing and placed blame on teachers, this time focusing critiques on the nature of teacher preparation. During the early years of the twentieth century, two discrete models of professional preparation existed in New York City: the normal college offered an education rooted in practical skills designed to prepare young women to work effectively in public school classrooms; elite university-based schools of education at Columbia University and New York University situated their work within the liberal traditions of the academy and offered advanced studies in the science of education to school leaders and others. As chapter 3 explores, following the economic collapse, market forces, exogenous policies, and gendered assumptions converged in schools of education, causing those once stark differences to melt away. Even as normal schools faded from the educational landscape as the twentieth century pressed on, university-based teacher education programs adopted the forms that characterized the normal approach, discarding the science of education in favor of applied learning. The turn toward practical knowledge produced school workers who fit the needs of the school system but also deprived teachers of the type of esoteric knowledge in which other professional fields grounded their expertise. Instead, teachers framed their professional identity against the backdrop of the Great Depression and grounded their authority in the gendered and racialized norms of the American middle-class home.

By the post–World War II years as the discourse of merit engulfed the nation and its public schools, no problem felt more pressing to school leaders and social commentators than the era's teacher shortages. Population growth, diversification, and redistribution, including the great migration and suburbanization, combined with the heating of the Cold War, brought long-simmering issues of race to the fore, complicating teacher hiring in urban schools. As chapter 4 chronicles, even as policymakers agreed that the answer to shortages centered on hiring more teachers, they disagreed about the causes of the shortages as well as about who ought to be hired and how they could best be recruited. Out of those various definitions of the problem arose an array of competing policy solutions including emergency licensure and certification, salary reforms and merit pay, and revision to teacher preparation. Bound up in each initiative were different visions of merit and teacher professionalism; far from the color-blind formulation each concept implied, racialized ideas of quality took center stage in national policy debates. Beneath the façade of shared vocabulary, policymakers, union leaders, and teacher educators articulated the central discourse of teacher blame differently, crafting competing ideas about the professional teacher. Even as some reformers called for professionalization through the broadening of teachers' professional preparation and increased competition, the fundamental structures that regulated and standardized teachers' work lives remained in place. These highly managed and routinized work environments created a climate in which teacher unionization flourished.

The rise of collective bargaining in the 1960s and an array of demonstrations of teacher militancy in New York City and around the state and country marked the ascendency of the modern teachers union. Union leaders concurred with social commentators and policymakers and called for school improvement through teacher professionalization. However, as was the case for teacher educators, union leaders identified the pathway to professionalism as well as what was best for teachers through their own institutional and organizational interests. As discussed in chapter 5, teachers unions in New York City and around the country gained visibility and notoriety during these years, earning a seat at the proverbial policymaking table. As the union grew, teachers, spoken about rather than on behalf of, navigated a new educational bureaucracy in which they once again inhabited the lowest rungs. The merger of the High School Teachers Association and the Teachers Guild created the United Federation of Teachers in New York City and highlights the paradox of unionization: in the name of teacher power and collective action, individual teachers, in this case the women of the elementary schools, lost out. For labor leaders like Albert Shanker, teacher professionalism and union power—understood through gendered and racialized perceptions of authority and success—were one and the same. However, in the name of professionalism and union power, increasingly teachers also found themselves isolated and set apart from school leaders, the communities of color they served, and teacher educators.

The discourse of teacher blame powered the historic policy stories that produced education reform, locally and nationally. At the heart of *Blaming Teachers* is an essential historical dilemma: teacher professionalization initiatives were never about improving the stature, working conditions, or general circumstances of individual teachers but instead were meant to support the goals and functioning of the institution of local public schooling in the name of the national good. The fate of teachers was no mere historical accident. Instead, as *Blaming Teachers* chronicles, the problems confronting these women workers were manufactured, slowly but surely, from the earliest days of municipal public schools systems. Many agree that schoolteachers lack voice and work in isolated conditions; this book helps us understand why as it reveals the barriers to professional authority as they were created and maintained through policy and reform.

Beyond casting a narrow light on schools and education policy, the history of teachers is central to understanding the experiences of working women in the United States and the gendered dimensions of workplace reform. Historically, more women worked as teachers for the nation's public school systems than any other single employer. Neither shop floor laborers nor members of the traditional professions, teachers have existed in a tenuous middle ground. The nebulous nature of their identity as neither workers nor professionals combined with the gendered composition of the occupation and the social significance of their labor gave way to workspaces that were both highly regulated and contested. Social commentators, policymakers, union leaders, and university-based faculty each sought to exert a controlling voice and together engulfed teachers in the discourse of blame. Inherently gendered, those historic criticisms set these working women adrift in a sea of reform. Professionalization may have been a beacon, but rather than bringing these workers closer to shore, the nature of the reforms acted like a rip current. At its core, *Blaming Teachers* is a labor history of working women and an exploration of the gendered limits of professionalization.

At the same time, *Blaming Teachers* is also a history of the racialization of school reform and teacher policy, demonstrating in equal measure the racialized limits of professionalization. School leaders in New York City rarely spoke explicitly about race when it came to teachers. As one city superintendent explained in 1903, "there is no race question in the public schools."[39] Instead, they adopted a discourse of reform that was color-blind only superficially. Over this long history, public school teaching has been a White-dominated profession, but not because White women were the only ones interested in this line of work. Instead, as this book chronicles, implicit and explicit policies and practices made public school teaching in New York City and around the nation the work of White women by thwarting the entry of people of color. Conflating Whiteness with quality, success, and Americanism, reformers envisioned White teachers as respectable role models, professionals uniquely suited to help manage the diversifying city and country. On the reverse side of this calculation was a vision of Blackness grounded in inferiority and otherness. The history of public education is the history of American society, and this history of school reform in New York City is a lens that magnifies the distribution of power and the preservation of inequality through policy in American history.

1

"A Chaotic State"

The Rise of Municipal Public School Systems and the Institutionalization of Teaching

Upon his election to the U.S. Congress in 1848 when he assumed John Quincy Adams's historic seat, Horace Mann issued his *Twelfth Annual Report* on the conditions and importance of common schooling in Massachusetts and, indeed, the nation. In clear and certain terms, he declared, free public schools "will solve the difficult problems of political and economical law." For Mann and a growing legion of leaders at local, state, and federal levels, "improved and energized" public schooling would accomplish far more than the diffusion of basic arithmetic and literacy to children. Rather, these social institutions could serve as the "the most effective and benignant of all the forces of civilization."[1] Equally clear to public school advocates was who ought to staff these new institutions of national significance. Departing from previous arrangements where men were schoolmasters, Mann offered emphatically in 1853 that public school teaching was "woman's work; the domain of her empire, the scepter of her power, the crown of her glory."[2] Victorian notions of femininity and ideas of Whiteness as superiority were central to reformers' vision of the ideal teacher.

Embedded in this history is also a broader story about the rise of municipal public school systems and the role of big cities in creating national education policy. By the mid-nineteenth century, the idea of publicly supported education was not a new idea. Figures like Thomas Jefferson and Benjamin Franklin had long extolled the virtues of public schooling, but in a society wary of big government and taxation, early common schools received tepid support and attention.[3] Public schooling first emerged in New York City in 1805 with the formation of the Free School Society, an endeavor to bring education to the city's destitute children, but it was not until 1826, with the rise of the Public School Society, that free schooling began to reach more of New York City's children. Even then, however, public schools remained unregulated, poorly attended, loosely organized, and mired in debate as Catholic New Yorkers argued that public education infringed on their religious rights. The key turning point in the development of municipal public schools systems came in 1842 when the New York State Legislature created the Board of Education of the City of New York. Over the next fifteen years, board members and politicians gradually consolidated the organization and management of single schools and small districts into a unified city school system. New Yorkers continued to debate who ought to control the schools—taxpayers, through ward elections and trustees, or the mayor, though political appointments—but the organization of the public schools into a single system had become a foregone conclusion. Spurring support for the municipal systemization of public education were a host of local and national social and political changes, including the end of the Civil War, westward expansion, the documentation of rising illiteracy rates, and the population growth and diversification that came with immigration and emancipation. By 1898, as part of a continuing effort to increase uniformity and efficiency, city and state leaders consolidated the schools of New York's five boroughs—Manhattan, the Bronx, Brooklyn, Queens, and Richmond (later named Staten Island)—into a single system under a central Board of Education. Much was exceptional about New York City and its public schools during the second half of the nineteenth century, making it more different from than similar to the rest of the nation, particularly its rural areas. However, the brand of education reform in New York City was a catalyst rather than an outlier; within decades similar projects spread to localities across the country as leaders at the state and federal level kept a watchful eye on schooling in the city and incentivized the spread of similar initiatives.[4]

As consensus around the social value of public education and White women as teachers mounted across the urban North, so too did another point of agreement: the schools were not living up to their potential and the quality of the nation's teachers was to blame. "Whether America is to lead or fall behind in the march of human progress," U.S. Commissioner of Education John Eaton explained in 1870, depended on teachers, and often, "the work of teaching among us has been too much a mere makeshift, something to be resorted to when nothing else could be done."[5] Social critics and reformers turned to male-dominated fields like medicine and law for emulation and identified professionalization as a panacea. "The greatest fault in the schools of our country lies in the professional weakness of our teachers," well-known education reformer Joseph Mayer Rice cautioned. "Raising the standard of our schools," Rice and others maintained, depended on "increasing the professional strength of the teachers."[6] Education reformers adopted the language of professionalization that transformed the work and preparation of doctors and lawyers at the time, but they suffused that vocabulary with different meanings. For school leaders in the city and around the nation, the gendered composition of the public school workforce, combined with the civic responsibilities of public schools, made teaching fundamentally different from other fields and, as such, teacher professionalization would necessarily follow a different path. Breaking from the individualistic orientation of traditional forms of professionalization that were grounded in esoteric university-based knowledge that extended status, authority, and autonomy to members of the occupation, during the second half of the nineteenth century, the professionalization of the nation's schoolteachers was a primary way for reformers to bolster the new and tenuous system of public schooling. The discourse of blame ignited professionalization initiatives and in this incarnation, the professional teacher was one suited to the needs of a rapidly growing but highly disorganized social institution. The so-called professionalization of teachers and the early institutionalization of municipal public school systems unfolded in tandem, one project supporting the other.

Divided into three parts, this chapter begins with "The 'Depraved Classes': Local Public Schools, White Women Teachers, and National Public Policy," which explores the intersections between, on the one hand, local and federal policy discussions that cast public schooling as a social institution of national significance and, on the other, gendered and racialized calls for schoolteachers. Profession and professionalization, buzz words of the day, implied quality, standards, and a cohort of trusted practitioners. The next section of this chapter, "'The Teacher Makes the School': City Schools and Concerns about Teacher Quality," chronicles how education reformers in New York City and elsewhere adopted the rhetoric of profession in response to mounting criticisms of public education even as they envisioned the women who populated the schools as fundamentally different from professional men. The result was a durable policy narrative of blame that placed the cause of and solution to social and educational problems directly at teachers' feet. The final section of this chapter, "The Rise of 'Red-Taperism': Teacher Reform for School Improvement," traces three key teacher professionalization reforms that were part and parcel of the institutionalization of public school teaching and set teachers on a course separate from the one followed by other professions: municipal partnerships in teacher preparation, hiring standards and certification, and the rise of testing. During these formative years, gendered expectations and racialized assumptions, growing ideologies about the social significance of public schooling, and nascent but quickly developing education structures converged to create the bedrock policy stories that defined public schooling and the nature of teacher reform in the United States.

The "Depraved Classes": Local Public Schools, White Women Teachers, and National Public Policy

During the second half of the nineteenth century, New York City was both a harbinger and a mirror of teacher reform nationwide, shaping educational practices and conversations but also responding to national calls for change.[7] The urban landscape developed at a rapid clip, and New York City garnered national attention as the largest city in the country. With a population of nearly four million, the city counted close to one million *more* inhabitants than second runner-up Philadelphia.[8] The population growth, topographical expansion, and architectural modernization unfolding across the city and others like it were the backdrop and motivation for the institutional development of municipal public school systems and gave rise to the modern profession of public school teaching as well as calls for women to enter the field. The goals and nature of New York City's public schools were simultaneously local and idiosyncratic and refracted through a national lens that cast municipal school systems as a salve for far-reaching social issues.

Commentators around the country argued that publicly funded education could ease class tensions, assimilate immigrants, and spur economic growth, and local level school leaders agreed. The very same impulses that sparked the spread of municipal public school systems also gave rise to public hospitals and municipal sanitation, police, and fire departments. In his address to the graduates of the city's normal schools in 1855, longtime New York City Board of Education president William H. Neilson explained that the tasks of the schools went far beyond teaching fundamental literacy and arithmetic. Instead, he advised prospective teachers that "the first instructions given to our children are obedience to law, respect for constituted authority and moral and religious accountability." In Neilson's estimation, "the only anchor which can keep our ship of state from drifting to destruction before the wild gale of popular passion, is a liberal, enlightening, humanizing, Christianizing system of public education."[9]

By 1860, nearly half of New York City's population was foreign born.[10] The surge of immigration exacerbated existing infrastructure problems and nativist sentiments, and around the city and nation, policymakers and taxpayers looked on with a mix of fascination and fear. Wanting to see the new realities of urban life firsthand, increasing numbers of wealthy residents and tourists from elsewhere embarked on "slumming tours." To one touring alderman, the hordes of immigrants spilling from the tenements were reminiscent of "ants from a hill." Exposed to the "sweltering humanity" and "depraved classes" that filled the city, "slummers" returned home disarmed and anxious.[11] As people worldwide watched the growth of the metropolis, wealthy New Yorkers envisioned themselves as part of an elite vanguard.[12] The harsh realities of urban life destabilized both the modernity and standing they claimed.

A widely circulated cartoon by Frederick Opper printed in the satirical magazine *Puck* in 1883 encapsulated long-standing concerns through contrasts in femininity (figure 1). On the right side of the image stands an Irish domestic servant: a mannish woman with bulging muscles and simian-like facial features reminiscent of widespread Jim Crow caricatures of the day. With her fist clenched and raised like a pugilist and the buttons on her clover-covered dress threatening to burst, she stands aggressively, according to the caption, making "the Irish declaration of independence that we are all familiar with." Meanwhile, the dinner she has presumably prepared for the family boils over on the stovetop and burns in the oven. Juxtaposed to this figure is the delicate and piously covered yet curvaceous woman of the house. A visual representation of the Victorian feminine ideal that fused race and gender, buttoned up from head to toe with red lips and doe eyes, she cowers in fear, her hands pleading for mercy. The image resonated with viewers because it captured an essential fear. Immigrants, the majority of whom were Irish Catholic, were not merely numerous. To native New Yorkers, the new immigrants were racially, culturally, morally, and religiously at odds, and those differences threatened the existing social, political, and economic order.[13]

The American home served as a key front for social policy tracing back the nation's deepest roots as mothers assumed responsibility for imparting the skills, morals, and virtues necessary for citizenship. With this wave of immigration and the first generation of emancipated slaves, faith in the ability of the home and the ideals of Republican Motherhood to preserve national norms eroded.[14] As Mann warned, "In a republican government, legislatures are a mirror reflecting the moral countenance of their constituents." Attempting to maintain American democracy without a "well-appointed and efficient means for the universal education of the people," Mann prophesized, would be nothing short of "the most rash and fool-hardy experiment ever tried by man."[15] Writing not to the parents of those who would attend the public schools but instead to those who would fund them through tax dollars, Mann explained these children would grow into the adults their parents trained them to be, unless society interceded. Echoing similar sentiments in 1855, Ira Mayhew, an advocate of universal education, wrote that public schools could care for "the children of a whole neighborhood" more effectively and "at less expense . . . than in their respective families."[16] Agreeing, the superintendent of New York City's public schools explained in his annual report of 1856 that teachers would stand in loco parentis.[17] Increasingly, policymakers and social reformers envisioned public schooling as a social necessity that would fill the void left by many contemporary

FIG. 1 Frederick Burr Opper, "The Irish Declaration of Independence That We Are All Familiar With," *Puck*, May 9, 1883. (*Source*: Library of Congress, LC-DIG-ppmsca-28386.)

homes and mothers and, in doing so, set in motion a policy narrative that attributed problems to individuals and families rather than to poverty, inequality, or social structures.

Before the expansion of public education, men dominated the teaching force, using it as a stepping-stone into law, medicine, and the ministry or as temporary seasonal work.[18] Faced with increasing demand for public schools, population growth, diversity, concerns about the new American home, and limited funds, by the mid-nineteenth century, policymakers and reformers amplified calls that had begun to surface over the previous decades that new teachers were needed: women. Historians have tracked the economic forces that pulled women into the schools and pushed men from them to account for the feminization of the field, but other forces were also at play.[19] The ways in which policymakers defined both the social problems of the day and the necessity of public schools explicitly beckoned women to the schools.

Conserving rather than disrupting the Victorian myth of separate spheres, reformers like Horace Mann, Catharine Beecher, and many others across the nation turned to that trope and contended that native, White women—mavens of the home—were perfectly suited to teach in the schools. Erastus C. Benedict, Esq., proudly noted upon his re-election as president of New York City's Board of Education in 1855, "Our system of public instruction has, indeed, opened to them [women teachers] a career—if such a word be not inappropriate—in the direct line of their natural sympathies and peculiar instincts—the care and education of children."[20] Not only were women available in large numbers as very few employment opportunities existed for educated females outside of teaching, but by virtue of their presumed feminine temperament they would be well suited for work in the schools, institutions increasingly cast as stand-ins for deficient homes. The state superintendent of California concurred, reporting that women "are the natural educators of the young."[21] Drawing on other educational thinkers, in his annual report for 1856, New York City Superintendent Randall observed that the natural characteristics of women and successful teachers were "alike." "Nature has marked her out for this great work," he alerted school leaders around the nation. "Outside of the family, she nowhere seems so truly to occupy her appropriate sphere. All her attainments and powers can here be actively and earnestly employed. The work is adapted to her mental and moral constitution. No occupation harmonizes better with her character, or yields her more genuine pleasure."[22] Affirming a vision of teaching as mothering, Catharine Beecher explained that joining the ranks of paid laborers would not detract or distract women teachers from their natural responsibilities, but instead that it would enhance them. "*Every* woman ought to be trained to act as an educator," she explained in *The True Remedy for the Wrongs of Woman*. Continuing, she reasoned, "No woman ever ought to be considered as qualified to become the head of a family till she has been *practically exercised* in this her highest professional duty."[23]

With mother-teachers at the front of the room, expanding municipal public school systems would serve as the nation's guardian, a stabilizing force in a chaotic time. The curricular content students would spend their days attempting to master in the public schools, one local school administrator assured, would "uplift the intellectual and moral culture" of the city and country and help maintain an established sense of order.[24] During the Civil War years, local school leaders in New York City cast the public schools as an emblem of national strength. In his monthly report to the Board of Education, school superintendent Randall noted that several teachers left the city's schools to join the war effort as soldiers and nurses, and students and teachers alike "exerted themselves in every practicable matter for the advancement of the great cause of the Union against its reckless and treasonable assailants." However, even as the war unfolded across the South, Randall proclaimed that "amid the din and clash of arms . . . the work of popular education and public instruction has gone uninterruptedly on." Beyond merely persisting, Randall reported that during this time the schools thrived. In his estimation, public education in the city organized under a single municipal system represented an enduring national identity. Not only were the schools untouched by the "ignorance" that spawned "the hydra-headed standard of rebellion," but they were the nation's first line of defense against it in the future.[25]

The establishment of the Department of Education in the spring of 1867 illuminates growing sentiments that schooling could function as a powerful vehicle for public policy at the local and national levels, as well as the interplay between urban locales and national policy. Earlier that year, members of the National State and City Superintendents Association met in Washington, DC, and unanimously agreed that "the interest of education would be greatly promoted" by a federal bureau. As these local and state school leaders imagined it, a federal Department of Education would gather statistical information from across the nation and highlight the important work occurring in various localities. More than merely distributing information, the department would also "contribute to the discussion of educational problems" and "provide a potent means for improving and vitalizing existing systems." A corrective to dangerous local idiosyncrasies, a federal bureau for education would provide the "general diffusion of correct ideas" and, more importantly, "respect the *value* of education as a quickener of intellectual activities; as a moral renovator; as a multiplier of industry . . . and finally, as the strength and shield of liberty."[26] Nevertheless, policymakers remained ambivalent about the role of the federal government in local schools. Even as calls for centralized information and recordkeeping garnered support, fears of an oversized influence of the federal government persisted. Just one year after President Andrew Johnson established the Department of Education as a cabinet-level agency, in 1868 it was downgraded to an office within the Department of the Interior.

In spite of concerns over the size and authority of the federal government, by the second half of the nineteenth century, local and national policymakers concurred that something much larger than the individual child was at stake in public schooling. As the century pressed on, consensus surrounding the social value of schooling only increased, with one commentator noting that "the public school . . . has become the palladium of our liberties."[27] For education reformers like Henry Barnard, public schools targeted children not for their own individual betterment but for the good of society. In an endeavor to carve out space for the federal government in local education, in his first report as commissioner of education, Barnard included a lengthy section titled "What Is Education?" in which he quoted dozens of thinkers from Kant to Cicero all highlighting the deep and broad impact of schooling.[28] Concurring with his predecessor, in 1870, Commissioner of Education John Eaton wrote that education promised "each interest the grand instrument for the solution of its difficulties."[29] Young children would be the target of education, but the value of education centered on how those lessons would reverberate through families, across neighborhoods, and over generations, shoring up the nation's social, political, and economic footing.

Race, of course, was central to the existing power arrangements municipal education systems were meant to preserve, and ideas about Whiteness as superiority coupled with deficit views of non-White populations suffused the public schools and were implicit to musings about the ideal female teacher. Over the second half of the nineteenth century, the population in New York City along with other urban areas not only grew but also diversified. And yet, the demographic composition of the teacher workforce remained nearly all White, even as Black families in the North and South pressed for education and community leaders advocated for the importance of Black teachers. According to the 1890 census, of 4,383 teachers in private and public schools in New York City, only 16 were Black. Of 1,486 teachers across all schools in the Boston area, only 3 were Black. Los Angeles and Chicago had no Black teachers anywhere to be counted by the 1890 census.[30]

Rather than a lack of interest on the part of the Black community, structural and ideological barriers prevented Black teachers from entering northern public schools. In 1883, Miss Susie B. Hopper, a teacher in training, made her way into public school (P.S.) No. 13 to fill in for a sick teacher. According to an article in the *Chicago Daily Tribune*, "her appearance at the teacher's desk was the signal for a stampede." In many regards, Hopper should have been the ideal teacher. According to the paper, she was young, she had earned a high school degree, and she was at the time embarking on a normal college education. She made her way to P.S. 13 that spring morning following city-mandated protocols; she was "next in line" for promotion. Hopper was also Black. Angry parents called on the school commissioner to remove Hopper immediately and Hall complied. However, "through a misunderstanding," Miss Hopper showed up at school again the next day only to be met by "another uproar" by "indignant parents." This time, "Miss Hopper was told that her services as a substitute were not required" and she was dismissed.[31] Rather than being exceptional, stories like Hopper's unfolded across the North time and again.

Nationwide, census takers counted more than 15,000 Black teachers, the vast majority of them in the South.[32] Publicly supported education in the South spread rapidly for White and Black children following the Civil War as the political activism of Black leaders and the promise of reconstruction opened a policy window for change. Even as that window slammed shut shortly after as the *Plessy v. Ferguson* decision dashed the hope for reconciliation and justice, the value placed on education with the Black community persisted. Throughout the South, Black families and community leaders banded together to press for Black teachers for Black children. In Baltimore, for instance, Frederick Douglass stood alongside local parents and argued, "It is fifteen years since the war, since freedom came to us, and it is not too soon to ask for a share of the educational fund or the positions of dignity and influence it gives. . . . The School Board cannot have peace until they give us colored teachers."[33] From the start in the nation's largest city, racist sentiments converged with the cover of northern liberalism. The result was an array of school and teacher level reforms and policies that would take root nationally and preserved teaching as the work of White women. Ideologies about race and gender were inextricable from the rise of municipal public school systems and formed the bedrock of discussions around teacher quality and professionalization reforms.

"The Teacher Makes the School": City Schools and Concerns about Teacher Quality

By the second half of the nineteenth century, mounting ideological support for public education offered little help when it came to the practical realties of schooling in the nation's largest city. During these years, New York City's public schools faced endemic student attendance problems and high teacher attrition as well as competing ideas about the purposes of public schooling. In addition, city leaders struggled to break free from ward politics and localism that made each school and community an entity unto itself, in spite of the creation of a unified municipal school system. Looking beyond these vast and significant challenges, commentators and reformers blamed teachers for the schools' troubles and identified professionalization as the solution. Even as critics agreed that teachers were the root cause of a range of problems, they disagreed about how to define, measure, and encourage teacher quality.

In 1858, Andrew Green, president of the Board of Education, noted there were more children in the New York City school system than in that of any other city.[34] Compounding the complexities inherent in size was instability. By 1867, over 190,000 children were enrolled in the city's public schools at the grammar and primary levels, but the average daily attendance was just 81,916.[35] Based on daily attendance averages, the teacher-student ratio in primary schools was 1:50; in grammar schools it was 1:35.[36] On a given day, approximately 40 percent of the children enrolled came to school but the composition of that group changed daily, confounding instructional plans and classroom routines for the city's 3,351 teachers.[37] In an attempt to increase regular attendance, in 1874 the board passed an act requiring parents to send their children to school for at least fourteen weeks a year and eight weeks consecutively, or to provide documented proof of education at home under threat of a penalty beginning at one dollar for the first offense and rising to five dollars per week.[38] Ultimately, because of the difficulties associated with accurate record keeping, the legislation had a negligible impact and attendance remained uneven and low until the early twentieth century.

Students were not the only transient population; teachers were, too, as attrition rates soared. Teachers described working in spaces that forced them to huddle with children "in classrooms like sheep in a pen" and to stand "in the closet, on the table—anywhere they can get."[39] Across the city, teacher's salaries varied widely and depended on the number of students enrolled, attendance statistics, and the whims of ward leaders. According to one committee report, the result was a "great disparity in salaries paid to persons holding the same relative position in different schools."[40] Teachers complained to one another and to the public through city newspapers that salaries were far too low. According to one anonymous teacher, "Ladies who hold positions in the public schools and depend on them for a living are not paid as much as the average servant girl."[41] In response, school leaders justified women teachers' low pay by turning to the gendered logic that established schools as appropriate spaces for women in the first place. New York City, like many other school districts, strictly enforced marriage bann policies in an attempt to ensure that only single women would teach. The policies represented a way to preserve propriety and family structures in the city, as school leaders reasoned that women could teach and offer their maternal skills to the city's children until they had their own families to care for. As single women, their financial needs were minimal, local leaders surmised, and furthermore, as good women, teachers ought to be self-sacrificing: should schools deny children services and resources to pay teachers more?

As the century progressed, wanting love and a career, many women teachers married surreptitiously and, in an endeavor to keep their jobs, neglected to report their changed marital status. The practice had become so alarming to local school leaders who fretted over impropriety and insubordination that by 1883, the Board of Education resolved that "any female teacher marrying shall report in writing her married name and address to the Clerk of this Board and chairman of the Board of Trustees of the ward in which she is employed; and any teacher failing to comply with this within 30 days after her marriage shall thereby forfeit her position as teacher, and all salary that may be due her from the time of her marriage."[42] Meanwhile, across the city and from Philadelphia to Chicago to Washington, DC, teachers worked without pay for various periods of time as school district leaders maintained that money was simply not available.[43] The result, one teacher anonymously reported in the *New York Times*, was "Every year we notice a new set of names and faces, and learn, upon inquiry after their predecessors, that they have gone to teach elsewhere, have been engaged by private seminaries, or perhaps are trying the pleasanter path of independence on a small but profitable scale in their own name."[44]

Board President Neilson, one of Green's successors, highlighted another element of complexity that school leaders faced. Neilson understood that the public school system was "deservedly dear to all citizens" of the city. But he also understood that beneath that basic fact was an entangled reality: the residents of the city valued the public schools, but not for the same reasons. In his 1874 inaugural address celebrating his re-election, Neilson explained that "the poor regard [public schooling] as the greatest boon to their children; the rich in it recognize the security of their persons and their property; the patriot values it as the greatest prop and defense of the institutions of our country; the philanthropist loves it because it refines, cultivates, humanizes, elevates and renders useful and happy his fellow man."[45] Stakeholders across the city held different expectations of their publicly supported schools. Some expected that the schools would grant access as a beacon of meritocratic justice, while others expected these municipally funded institutions would conserve existing social, political, and economic arrangements.

Adding to the complex and at times contradictory purposes of public education in the city was the deep local variability of schooling across the city's wards. In the early 1850s, city politicians voted to consolidate two school systems in favor of the single Board of Education in an attempt to bring uniformity to the city's schools. But the ward system and local politics continued to shape individual schools for much of the century. For Board President Green, the local boards and school officers that comprised the city's schools each moved "within its own orbit."[46] In 1856, the total school budget was just under $1 million, but per pupil spending ranged from $20.48 in the Nineteenth Ward to $10.18 in the Eighteenth Ward.[47] Further, even as city residents and national politicians rallied around public schooling, the basic infrastructure had yet to be formed. Across the city, students went to school in church basements, hallways, and other unsuitable settings, and teachers and pupils alike complained of health ailments from the dank and unventilated environments. In one of his monthly reports from the 1855 school year, Superintendent Randall cautioned, "the health both of pupils and teachers is and must be seriously endangered by their constant confinement in these gloomy, unwholesome and uninviting localities."[48]

Considered as a whole, New York City's wards tell a story of ethnic, religious, and class diversity, but within wards, homogeneity reigned, yielding variable contexts within the single municipal school system. For instance, in the winter of 1883, the board met to discuss a group of eight teachers with high rates of student absenteeism. City administrators sought to measure teachers' efficacy through an array of questionable indicators, including the regularity of student attendance. During the month of October, one group of teachers from the district's Sixth Ward came to the attention of the school examiner who, in turn, brought the matter to the board. Each of the teachers had more than 20 percent of their students absent during that month. Why, board members wondered, would so many students be out of these classrooms; were these teachers delinquent? Upon investigation, board members learned that many Jewish holidays fell during the month of October and that 60 to 90 percent of the students in each teacher's classroom were Jewish. The teachers were absolved of responsibility and the cases were fully documented "in order to prevent a false impression" of their work.[49]

The lofty rhetoric of hope that surrounded public education as a social salve also led to biting criticisms of the institution, further complicating the real infrastructure and human capital issues facing local schools. For policymakers and social commentators, economic recession, political turmoil, and continued social unrest all traced to public schools that were falling short of their mission. In 1855, New York City Board of Education president E. C. Benedict outlined improvements the city's schools had made in his annual report. However, he also noted that "so far as the public is concerned," the public schools were "much behind" where they should be.[50] In 1872, P. R. Burchard's essay in *Scribner's Monthly*, a popular national magazine, struck a similar chord while dispelling notions of American dominance. "The traditional vanity of the American people," he wrote, led to the mistaken assumption that "we are superior." "Among other fallacies into which this habitual self-conceit has led us," he blasted, "is the conclusion that our educational system is as good as any in the world, if not the best, and that we rank first among educated nations."[51]

Policymakers and education leaders at the local and national levels maintained that the success of the schools depended on teachers, looking past the myriad practical realties that made urban schooling a complex affair. In 1879, Commissioner of Education Eaton explained, "The assertion that 'the teacher makes the school,' trite though it be, is nevertheless so true that in any inquiry as to the quality of the country schools we should seek first to ascertain the character of the teaching force."[52] If teachers, in the general sense, were the schools' hope, it was teachers, in the specific sense, that were the schools' downfall, according to school officials and commentators. Assistant Superintendent Henry Kiddle warned as early as 1856 that schools could only be improved "by increasing the efficiency and elevating the character and accomplishments of the teacher," but this would prove difficult given the teacher corps.[53]

Policymakers concurred with Kiddle's assessment but disagreed about the precise problems plaguing teachers. For Kiddle, the problem was one of experience and teachers simply did not have enough of it.[54] For Randall, the problem was slightly different and centered on maturity: most teachers were just too young.[55] Others highlighted preparation, with some arguing that teachers needed more practical training in normal schools and others calling for an expanded education in the liberal arts. Yet other policymakers and reformers called attention instead to dispositions, suggesting that what teachers really needed and as a group lacked were habits and temperaments like "cleanliness," "gentleness of manner," and "a cheerful spirit."[56] Still others linked the deficient teacher corps to a lack of job commitment. One New Yorker described public school teachers as self-interested "sleepy souls" who taught just "for a salary."[57] Pointing to rising illiteracy figures and employment statistics, commentators like Burchard cried out for reform and pointed directly at teachers, whom he believed had flocked to the schools "because they are too lazy to work at other employments."[58]

This burgeoning policy story positioned school leaders, social commentators, and policymakers to lay the blame for school problems on teachers rather than on any number of other issues including the lack of uniform curricular resources and adequate school facilities or the problems of child labor and public health. "It is obvious," Commissioner Barnard explained in 1868, "that neither constitutional provisions, legislative enactments, nor the existence of the most perfect school-houses, will secure the right education of the children of the nation, without a body of teachers devoted to the work of public instruction, possessing in a sufficient degree the requisite qualifications of character attainments, and skill."[59] The consensus was clear: school quality depended on teacher quality. But what was teacher quality?

Education leaders and public officials offered a variety of definitions, very few of which centered on tangible markers. For Jacob Gould Schurman, an educator who would become president of Cornell University later in the century, the essential principals of good teaching centered on "love" for the child but also, as another author explained, "love for the business" of education.[60] In a different formulation, one writer suggested that teacher quality centered on refinement and "personality," proposing that if teachers "were people of real culture themselves" many school and instructional problems could be solved.[61]

Disagreeing, Rice, along with school leaders in New Hampshire, Rhode Island, and New York, offered that teacher morality formed the bedrock of teacher quality.[62] Even as many agreed that some knowledge of pedagogical principles mattered, critics remained steadfast that more salient to teacher quality were a host of intangible characteristics ranging from "tact," "good judgement," and "power to stimulate and magnetize," to "refined and ladylike manners," a "mellow and winning voice," "enthusiasm," and a "beaming" face.[63]

Even as policymakers and the general public disagreed about the precise problem beleaguering the corps of public school teachers, they agreed that collectively these individuals were "the anchor" that "drags on the bottom," impeding progress and achievement in the public schools.[64] One author wondered in the *Atlanta Constitution*, "As teaching is such grand work, why not make it a profession?"[65] Perhaps, as reformers like Rice and others advocated, professionalization was the solution. Schurman attempted to cast light on the situation. "The present day is witnessing splendid improvements in medical instruction," he wrote in *The Forum* in 1896. "The custom" of professionalization was "rapidly spreading" across other professions, Schurman explained, but teaching in neither "ideal" nor "practice" came close to attaining similar standards.[66] "What would become of lawyers and doctors if any greenhorn could try his hand at a case whenever he wished?" Burchard asked *Scribner's* readers years earlier.[67]

For many school leaders and education reformers in New York City and across the nation, however, teaching was not simply a profession populated by women but instead a woman's profession. "All women will be educated," Catharine Beecher maintained, "and, what is more, they will be educated for their profession, as the conservators of the domestic state."[68] Even as women of the time demonstrated that the Victorian spheres ideology was little more than a myth as they worked outside of the home, joined organizations, and exerted influence, the gendered and racialized ideal nevertheless continued to shape perceptions of women as they moved between private and public spaces.[69] Echoing Beecher's sentiments, Horace Mann explained, "God created the race, Male and Female, on the principle of a division of labor. . . . As a general law, the man surpasses the woman in stature, in physical strength and in . . . intellectual facilities . . . ; but the woman surpasses the man in beauty, in taste, in grace, in faith, in affection, in purity." In teaching, women would not become like men or step into male domains like the professions but instead join their "proper rank." To clarify his views even further, writing as the first secretary of the Massachusetts Board of Education, Mann explained, "I revolt at the idea of our wives and sisters mingling promiscuously with men in the varied affairs of life, industrial, social, and political." Women belonged in the "empire of Home," of which school teaching was a natural extension.[70] To professionalize teachers as if they were doctors and lawyers seemed preposterous.

Education leaders and reformers agreed: women belonged in the nation's public schools; however, they also agreed that women's place in the schools was limited. Women, surely, could be trusted to handle the education of young children. As Superintendent Russell noted, "In all elementary instruction, the very structure of her mind fits woman for the task." However, "in our high schools where mind, in its maturing state and fuller development, is stimulated by the strongest incentives to study, and subjected to the severest discipline, and led onward into the higher departments of literature and science," Russell alerted educators to a different situation that necessitated different teachers. "Obviously," he explained, it is "better to employ permanent male teachers."[71] A temporary workforce at the bottom of a developing educational hierarchy, for school policymakers and reformers around the country, women teachers—even as they outnumbered all school workers—were professionals in name only.

On a stormy evening in the spring of 1858, New York City Board of Education president W. W. Smith convened a meeting to assess the state of the city's public schools. As one speaker pointedly explained, "Our city school system, as it is, lacks nearly every requisite of organization . . . it has no systematic and organized official management based upon principles of action."[72] The city's Committee on Teachers agreed, reporting, "No other considerable department of the public service is left in such a chaotic state, where system is possible."[73] The solution, education leaders in the city and elsewhere concurred, centered on systematization and rationalization. "The best is the best everywhere," John Philbrick wrote in his assessment of city school systems across the nation in 1885. "The essential elements of a good school system are the same" everywhere and the goal must be to create "uniformity of excellence" and make "progress toward the ideal standard."[74] Heeding Commissioner Barnard's call to root school reform in teacher reform, school leaders in New York City and around the nation regulated, systematized, and institutionalized teachers' work in the name of teacher professionalization for school improvement, igniting a process that would ensnare generations of the nation's teachers and bore resemblance to other professions in name only.

The Rise of "Red-Taperism": Teacher Reform for School Improvement

In the name of teacher professionalization for school improvement, education leaders in New York City launched three entwined reform initiatives during the second half of the nineteenth century: municipal partnerships with normal schools, hiring standards and certification tests, and the rise of testing. Each measure stemmed in a different way from the discourse of blame and each fit hand to glove with the growing formalization and institutionalization of the city's municipal public school system. In the name of professionalizing teachers, these reforms systematized and regulated teachers' work lives. New York City school leaders were among the first to experiment with such measures, but they were far from the last. In short order, federal-level incentives that tied funding to reform transformed what started as local experiments into national education policy priorities, gradually spreading urban education initiatives to small cities and rural outposts alike.

Normal schools and colleges represented an important educational intervention for women across the nation; before their creation, little beyond grammar schooling was available to girls. Akin to a secondary or high school curriculum, the normal experience provided generations of women with an opportunity to expand their education through their teenage years, democratizing the landscape of higher education.[75] Samuel Read Hall created the first normal school in the country in 1823 in Concord, Vermont, and over the next decades, state-sponsored normal schools cropped up around the country. According to historian Christine Ogren, by 1870, eighteen of thirty-seven states had at least one normal school; by the final decades of the nineteenth century, the total number of normal institutions had climbed to more than one hundred.[76] In addition to state normal schools and a smaller number of private institutions, during the 1860s municipally supported normal institutions opened their doors in New York City, Boston, Philadelphia, Baltimore, St. Louis, and San Francisco.[77] Education reformers seated the professional preparation of teachers in normal schools; however, in form and function, these institutions differed from the universities that housed the professional preparation of doctors, lawyers, ministers, and others.

In 1840, decades before members of New York City's Board of Education voted to establish a formal, free-standing normal school within the city in 1869, prospective teachers received varying degrees of municipally sponsored preparation. However, reflecting the decentralized, ward-based organization of public education in the city during these years, options available to teachers varied. Some teachers took brief extension classes offered through local grammar schools; others enrolled for varying amounts of time in the Saturday or daily programs offered by the Board of Education.[78] Despite these variations, local education leaders agreed that an "absolute and pressing necessity" was finding appropriate teachers and that a normal preparation was key mechanism for "adequately prepar[ing] such young ladies" for the city's public schools.[79]

The explicit ties between the Board of Education and teacher's professional preparation lent a strong vocational orientation to the professional preparation of female teachers. Upon admittance to one of the board-sponsored programs, all students signed a pledge in which they promised "to submit to all the rules and regulations prescribed for the government of the Schools."[80] Even as ward leaders expressed concerns over centralized teacher preparation, members of the Board of Education told of the efficiency to be gained from close partnerships with normal schools. "Those employed in our schools who are skillful and efficient, have only become so after the experience of years," but many teachers did not make it that long and why waste time, board members questioned. "How much better to avoid this," city school leaders proposed, than "by imparting to those who design to teach, the theoretical principles and practical rules of teaching"?[81] The faculty and leadership of normal schools oriented their work around a single, shared goal: to "make her [future teachers] an ornament to the school and society."[82]

In the fall of 1853, the Board of Education proposed sending all of the city's teachers below the rank of principal back to one of the board-sponsored Saturday or daily normal programs for additional training, arguing that a uniform sequence of courses was a primary mechanism to improve school quality. Teachers turned to the editorial pages of local newspapers, responding that they were "not a whit less capable than their principals of managing the schools [and] have families that deserve some little attention."[83] Later in the year, board members additionally proposed "grading the salaries of teachers according to the amount of knowledge they possessed." Teachers made their plea to the public in the city's papers once again, arguing that such a measure "would be degrading and humiliating to the whole body of teachers of New York."[84]

As school leaders linked municipally sponsored normal school learning with teacher quality, many teachers understood the nature of their work in different terms. Writing anonymously to the *New York Daily Times* under the pseudonym "A. Teacher," one author demonstrated her opinion through the juxtaposition of two individuals. "Miss A," educated in the city public schools and "having only a passably fair education," knew "nothing of 'biquadratic equations,' but fairly posted up in the principles of the 'Rule of Three' . . . perfectly innocent of any knowledge of French, but quite at home in the grammar of English language." "Miss A." worked her way up through the teacher ranks, now earning a high salary but if re-examined on the basis of knowledge, as the board proposed, would neither earn the high ranking "nor receive one-third her present salary." In contrast, "Miss B.," "perfectly indoctrinated with all the necessary and unnecessary theoretical learning, knowledge of French, &c., &c., but entirely wanting in the qualities of a disciplinarian, no faculty to communicate to others the knowledge possessed by herself, but who under the new classification, would perhaps rank with the highest, and, perhaps receive double the pay received by Miss A." "Which of the two," the author posed, "would render the most real and acceptable service to the pupil and the public, and which should receive the most money?"[85] In spite of their opposition, teachers had no real leverage to speak of as few other employment opportunities existed for educated women and many lacked the means to relocate beyond city limits for work. In 1856, members of the Board of Education approved new rules that required all teachers, except those who already possessed a certificate, to return to the normal schools or a board-sponsored supplementary program. Not doing so, the bylaws stated, would lead to the teacher's termination and the forfeiture of all salary.[86]

In 1869, in recognition of the importance of teachers and the need for uniform preparation, the New York City Board of Education voted to establish the Female Daily Normal and High School of the City of New York, the first formalized high school or higher education opportunity available to females in the city. That same legislation also mandated that the new municipal normal school would be the only pathway into the city's schools for teachers, except in cases where special exceptions were granted.[87] Opening the next year in rented quarters and with a new name, the Normal College of the City of New York was the utilitarian counterpoint to the all-male, liberal arts–oriented Free Academy, founded in 1847 and later renamed The City College of New York. Twenty-five years after its dedication, school leaders celebrated that more than three-quarters of the city's teachers traveled through the Normal College.[88]

For a time, the Normal College democratized the landscape of public education not only by carving out a space for women but also by carving out an inclusive space for African Americans. In 1873, the New York State Legislature prohibited discrimination in public education on the basis of race, prompting New York City to close its four segregated public schools. That year, eight African American women entered the Normal College. However, by 1881 only one woman of color was admitted out of 808 accepted students. This drop-off and lack of representation, historian Linda Perkins has observed, could have been a result of multiple factors. Perhaps, as city schools integrated, the demand for Black teachers dropped. Admittance to the Normal College was contingent on examination; it is also possible that, as discussed later in this chapter, those exams created barriers that inhibited teachers of color. Additionally, it is plausible that the promise of teaching in the new reconstruction schools lured teachers of color south. Even as the Normal College remained a haven for working-class women of immigrant families over the next several decades, the integrated institution welcomed only a small number of Black students.[89]

In 1873, the Normal College of New York moved into what contemporary observers described as an impressive building on Lexington Avenue (figure 2). As memorialized in the dedication to New York Normal College's new campus, the institution "had its origin in the imperative necessity of providing a sufficient corps of trained teachers to meet the increasing wants of a rapidly growing metropolis."[90] The new quarters embodied the formalization of teacher professionalization and were celebrated as a beacon of modernity for public schools and the city alike. Writing to a national audience, James Richardson described the new building and transformation of the city with wonderment.

FIG. 2 The New York Normal College, 1874. (*Source*: The Miriam and Ira D. Wallach Division of Art, Prints and Photographs: Picture Collection, The New York Public Library, New York Public Library Digital Collections.)

"Ten years ago," he reflected, the east side of the city was marred by "shanty-covered rocks," "unfinished streets," "cattle-yards and similar abominations." In his estimation, the construction of the Normal College represented a stunning metamorphosis. "The former site of unmitigated ugliness" had been completely transformed, he wrote. The "elegant" building spanned "32 full size city lots." For Richardson and other onlookers, the architecture of the college "correspond[ed] with the importance" of the institution and "satisfied every reasonable demand as to beauty, solidity, convenience, and durability." Justifying the great cost of constructing the Normal College to his readers, Richardson explained, "the future of the public schools is in their hands; and in the schools, to a great extent, lies the destiny of the city."[91] The building symbolized the growth of the metropolis, the institutionalization of public schooling, and, most important of all, that those projects were bound together.

As the Normal College's first president, Thomas Hunter, noted, a chief aim of his institution was the development of teachers with "prompt and cheerful obedience" to school rules.[92] "The amount of evil which an inexperienced teacher can do in six months, while learning the art of governing," Hunter explained in 1873, "is almost incalculable." A normal preparation would prevent such problems by "supplying the city schools with superior teachers," a contribution that would "be felt throughout every vein and artery of the whole system."[93] As Kiddle explained in 1873, the foundational and enduring purpose of normal schools in the city was "education of the inexperienced and untrained teachers employed in the schools under its management and control."[94]

Prospective teachers continued their basic education in the city's normal schools and, most important of all, learned how to fit themselves into the burgeoning public school system. Setting teaching apart from the other developing professions, Hunter maintained that more important than any academic learning for prospective teachers was "natural aptitude." Without certain natural characteristics such as "a good voice, a pleasant manner and inborn tact, quickness of perception, inexhaustible patience and great love for children," there was no amount of learning that could prepare prospective teachers, identifying a range of attributes that correlated little to the cornerstones of professionalism as defined by male-dominated fields: expertise, authority, autonomy.[95] As Rice noted, future teachers needed "earnestness, conscientiousness, and enthusiasm." But, as he also explained, those characteristics, "favorable as they are," pertained little to real expertise and professional authority, particularly as compared to "medical and legal qualifications."[96] Rather than evidence of a shortcoming in teachers' normal school preparation, for Rice, the different measures of efficacy for teachers and doctors simply highlighted that teachers were a different sort of professional.

As the century progressed, the city's normal schools became an arm of the Board of Education, enabling school managers to have a direct hand in cultivating their workforce. In 1881, for instance, when the supply of teachers exceeded the city's demand for them, members of the Board of Education turned to the Normal College, calling on faculty to "reduce the number of graduates as nearly as possible to the number required to fill the vacancies in the schools."[97] Thomas Hunter, the Normal College's president, complied even as faculty members struggled to identify a scholastic basis for the decision. Faculty at the Normal College reduced the size of the graduating class by adding an extra year to the required sequence of coursework but also complained that the extension was academically unnecessary. "With the exception of greater attention to mental and moral philosophy as the right basis of correct teaching, and more extensive practice in the Training Department, very little was added to the curriculum," Hunter expounded. Furious with the last-minute change, students' parents who wanted their daughters to "earn salaries as soon as possible" appealed to Hunter, who could do little.[98]

From the start, school leaders in the city turned to the professional preparation of teachers to create a workforce that would match the needs of the nascent institution of public education. Beyond merely bringing qualified teachers to the schools, Commissioner Eaton also contended that normal schools, nationwide, could serve as a powerful filter, "exclud[ing] from the profession unworthy and incompetent members."[99] An example of the powerful role of cities in national education policy, school leaders in urban centers like New York City set these municipal partnerships in motion. In 1888, the federal government solidified the relationship between teacher preparation and public schooling when officials linked grants from the U.S. Treasury Department in support of the establishment of common schools to specific normal school coursework.[100] In response, New York State passed "An Act to Encourage and Promote the Professional Training of Teachers" in 1895, mandating that "no person shall be employed or licensed to teach" who did not have an approved education background, and extending the policy to schools in small cities and rural areas.[101]

Nevertheless, even as public school leaders looked to the Normal College to regulate the quality and supply of the city's teachers, many agreed that in spite of these efforts, too many poor teachers continued to populate the schools. As one social commentator reported to readers of the *New York Daily Times* in the spring of 1856, schools included many teachers "who are unfit for such calling." Too often, the author continued, "persons having physical defects, or persons who were unfortunate in business, or failed in other professions," secured jobs as teachers. In this author's estimation, "a higher standard of attainment is now demanded."[102] But teacher hiring was a complex affair. Reflecting on the task, Superintendent Randall characterized the selection process as one of the most "delicate and embarrassing" duties of school leaders.[103] Not only did many building-level leaders fail to hire the right sort, Randall assessed, but no standard protocol existed. As the century advanced, school reformers in the city and across the nation called for a uniform system cutting across district and state boundaries. "Candidates rejected in one township may be certified in the next," B. G. Northrop explained in his 1880 book on teacher hiring. "Hence," he continued, "many of our schools suffer greatly from the incompetency of teachers. This evil arises not so much from the scarcity of good teachers, as from vicious method of selection."[104] For many, the solution was standardization and regulation. "There is only one best way of securing and retaining efficient teachers," Philbrick reasoned.[105] In New York City, as elsewhere, school leaders identified certification exams and licensure as the mechanisms to streamline teacher hiring practices and increase teacher quality, thereby improving schools, writ large.

In spite of widely divergent definitions of teacher quality and the lack of consensus surrounding the sort of knowledge teachers needed to be successful in the classroom, education reformers placed their faith in assessments as a way to quantitatively and objectively identify the best teachers. Gradually increasing the minimum age to teach in the city's schools, by 1879, school leaders established that "no person shall be examined for a teacher's license who has not attained the age of eighteen years," unless the individual in question had graduated from the Normal College. Offering exams on the third Friday of every month in the Hall of the Board of Education, prospective teachers submitted to oral and written exams on "Reading, Spelling, English Grammar, History of the United States, English Literature, Arithmetic, Algebra through Quadratic Equations, Plane Geometry, Descriptive Astronomy, Physics, Zoology or Physiology, and Principles and Methods of Teaching."[106] Over the next years, school leaders added an additional requirement: "No license shall be issued unless the candidate shall present a certificate of a physician of the City of New York, in good and regular standing, certifying that he has examined the candidate, and finds him or her to be in sound bodily health."[107]

Notwithstanding the transparency standardized exams and regular announcements purportedly offered, many prospective teachers remained befuddled by the new practices. In 1881, 206 individuals presented themselves for the teacher certification exams and scorers at the city's Board of Education rejected 101.[108] Unsure of precisely what the examinations would cover, how they related to normal school curricula, or how they would be graded, the standards gave rise to a new education industry: test preparation. Isaac Stone, an author of one test preparation book and a former examiner, explained in the third person that "nine-tenths of all the teachers he had examined failed in greater or less degree" and offered his book as an "an errand of benevolence."[109] Other manuals offered sample questions and reviewed fundamental information ranging from algebra to physiology.[110]

Teachers were not the only ones confused by the exams: school leaders were, too. Even as they were armed with seemingly objective data and the practices spread from the local level across the nation, school leaders in New York City and elsewhere gave little credence to the new information and circumvented the standardized hiring measures, defaulting to other criteria to determine the teachers most suited for their schools. A school commissioner from Long Island, New York, outlined one key problem with the assessments: from his experience, passing the test had little correlation with ability in the classroom. "Every year a large number of girls come for certificates; they pass examinations well enough, perhaps, but very few teach properly; they have no teaching gifts or power whatever, to model the mind."[111]

Reflecting the lack of consensus surrounding definitions of teacher quality, some school leaders eschewed the results because they revealed nothing about teachers' morality and deportment. Board President Neilson implored school leaders to "look to something beside mastery of the subjects they are required to teach: graces should be considered as well as gifts, and no person of bad manners, trifling disposition or unsettled moral views should be admitted to our corps of instruction."[112] Similarly, Randall called on those hiring teachers to employ "reasonable discretion" in assessing the "qualifications of candidates" and to look beyond "scientific attainment" to the "moral culture" of the applicant.[113] "The mere ability to pass a satisfactory examination in the various branches of study required to be taught," Randall affirmed in 1861, "constitutes in reality a very small portion of the conditions requisite for the successful administration of the responsible duties devolved on the teacher."[114]

Throughout the second half of the nineteenth century, city officials envisioned certification tests and standardized hiring practices as ways to curb the tide of nepotism that shaped local schools and city politics. Contending that the increasing insider-ism of the schools made them difficult to manage and even harder to regulate, members of the board approved bylaws mandating that "No teacher shall be employed in any Ward School . . . who is within four degrees of relationship, either by blood or marriage, to any school officer already elected or appointed."[115] In spite of the rules, school leaders continued to hire teachers according to individualized and idiosyncratic criteria. Newspapers chronicled ensuing school skirmishes with vivid detail as they exemplified the broader dynamics of political privilege and favoritism unfolding across the city and its expanding municipal government. In the winter of 1888, for instance, newspapers regaled city readers with the details of Miss Fitz Gerald's open teaching position in the Tenth Ward, which she relinquished upon marriage. Fitz Gerald's brother-in-law, George Hall, a lifelong politician, was the "Tammany leader in the Eighth Assembly District." Described by the *New York Times* as "a typical ward politician [who] keeps a sharp outlook for himself and his relatives," Hall "pull[ed] wires" to ensure that Fitz Gerald's open position went to Miss Brennan, "either a relative or a very intimate friend" of the recently married Fitz Gerald. For local reporters, the case was just another example of how politics infiltrated the schools. For education leaders, the situation was evidence of the barriers to institutional development and standardization.[116]

Even as local leaders doubted the information they could glean from certification tests and sidestepped those initiatives in various ways, by the late 1880s, federal-level officials once again transformed big-city practices into national praxes. According to a bill approved by the 50th Congress, "no school district shall . . . be entitled to a share in the national grant," a total sum of $25 million to be dispersed over ten years, "which has not maintained school in a suitable premises under a legally certified teacher."[117] Across the nation, local newspapers alerted prospective teachers of forthcoming tests. "An examination will be held in the basement of the court-house . . . for colored applicants for teachers' licenses to teach in the public schools," the *Atlanta Constitution* advised readers. "A small lunch should be brought as no intermission may be given. A fee of $1 will be charged to cover expenses." White applicants, the newspaper informed, would sit for the exam in the office of a board member.[118]

For some prospective teachers, school leaders argued that certification exams and hiring standards were irrelevant and cumbersome, and that they only obscured the information about what made an individual fit for the schools; for these candidates, school leaders regularly bent rules and implemented informal practices. But for other would-be teachers, certification exams represented a powerful barrier that prevented them from ever entering the schools. In 1884, the *New York Times* reprinted a story from the *Newberry South Carolina Herald* that highlighted incorrect answers from Black candidates on the "Theory and Practice of Teaching" portion of the teacher certification exam. In response to "What are the principal objects of a recitation?" one candidate wrote, "Stand erect and be submissieve. Know they lesson perfect. Stan correct and be perfec submissive." In response to "What works on teaching have you ever read?" another candidate responded, "Astonamy, philosophy, Shakpeare, &c.,

Philosiphy, theology." According to the article's author, "these are specimen answers taken from the papers of some six or eight applicants who were not the most successful."[119] The implicit function of the article was twofold: not only did it celebrate the exam as a gatekeeper, but it ridiculed the very idea of Black teachers. Policymakers cast these tests, like other education reforms, as objective, color-blind measures of teacher quality, but all aspects of the exams, including their questions and answers, the nature of scoring and administration, and access to preparation, were a reflection of a deeply unequal society.

In addition to regulating the preparation of teachers and standardizing hiring practices, city school leaders, again in the name of teacher reform for school improvement, also attempted to systematize teachers' work in the classrooms. With a limited budget, school officials in New York City could not afford to purchase classroom resources such as textbooks for all public school pupils. As a result, by midcentury, most children brought their own books to school, not only making a uniform curriculum nearly impossible to achieve but also subverting teachers' ability to deliver uniform content. If popular support for public schooling rested on the institution's ability to conserve a national order and train the next generation of citizens, then the "diversity of books," as Board President Benedict explained in 1851, was "an evil of the greatest magnitude."[120] As purchasing uniform textbooks remained financially out of reach, school leaders in the city instead urged the creation of uniform curriculum guides for teachers. Assistant Superintendent William Jones, for instance, called for detailed "outlines" that would describe to teachers with precision what they must teach.[121] Education leaders, Kiddle implored, must "enumerate, but with more explicitness" precisely what teachers must teach, for they could neither be expected nor trusted to do this on their own.[122]

Even as school leaders assigned the "faithful teachers" of the city's schools to impart a standard curriculum, how could they be sure that all teachers would follow the guides with fidelity?[123] For Kiddle, the only way to measure "whether the instruction given has extended to all the pupils of each class" was to test students.[124] Even as the new tests assessed students, education leaders used the results as a metric for teacher efficacy: a reflection not of what a student learned but instead of what a teacher taught. Through test results, Kiddle offered, school leaders could derive information about the nature of instruction, for instance, whether the teacher delivered the curriculum "by rote . . . and without proper cultivation of understanding," as well as classroom management, such as "whether the influence of the teacher upon the class, with respect to discipline, has been effective, and such as to give correct habits of deportment." Too many teachers, Kiddle noted in 1860, "seemed still to misapprehend the objects of these examinations," thinking that "the extent of [student] progress" mattered when really the focus was on "thoroughness of acquisition"—that is, the extent to which teachers taught what they were supposed to.[125]

To affirm the purpose, education policymakers linked student test scores to tangible consequences for teachers. For instance, in 1881, Miss M. E. Neary of the Primary Department Grammar School No. 58 was "degraded in rank and fined $170 a year because, it was alleged, the general average of her class had not during the year of 1880 come quite up to the standard."[126] Test results, "disheartening in the extreme," only confirmed education leaders' concerns. As the *New York Times* reported in 1891, "the evils and defects of the system are due to the lack of intelligence and efficiency on the part of teachers." Carefully created uniform curriculum guides could only accomplish so much; standardized, paper-based tests on the required aspects of the graded curricula, reformers reasoned, was the only way to evaluate if *teachers* had accurately imparted the material. "I asked one class one of the simplest questions in geography I had selected from the lesson of Monday. This was on Wednesday," one examiner explained to a *Times* reporter. Not one student offered an answer and even when the question was repeated, "the scholars sat dumb," the incredulous examiner recalled. Continuing, "I turned to the teacher and said, 'Miss Blank, you answer it for them,' but she was as dumb as her pupils." For this examiner and other school leaders in the city, occurrences like this one provided evidence not only that too many teachers were "incompetent and unfit for service," but also that if they could not be removed due to supply concerns, even more stringent regulations would be necessary.[127]

The solution to the nation's public school problems, education reformers concurred, centered on teacher reform. The professionalization of teachers was integral to and inseparable from the institutional development of municipal public school systems and the outcome was what one author described as "red-taperism," a broad range of policies and regulations intended to standardize the teacher's work and fit her to the needs of the growing school system.[128] During the mid-nineteenth century, the teacher-student ratio in the primary schools hovered around 1:50. By the late 1800s, the teacher-administrator ratio across the city was just 1:13.[129] As one social commentator described, the "elaborate schools systems" of "our great cities" "set a thousand machine-moved teachers in the schools."[130] The nature of early professionalization reforms fit teachers to the schools as efficient workers and rule followers but also led to their disempowerment. "The class teacher has lost his sovereignty and has become a private in a great army ruled by 'educators,'" William Desmond offered in *The Century Magazine*. "Teachers in large cities," he continued, "having the matter and method of their work thought out and prescribed for them, are ceasing to be *thinkers* in a professional way."[131] According to another commentator, "red tape has wound itself so closely about the public school system, that teachers and pupils alike suffer from the ill effects of constriction. Under its baneful influence teachers have become automatons, capable of imparting only cut-and-dried information."[132] Teachers complained that they were forced to submit to a "system of pains and penalties such as might answer (although imperfectly) to govern small children," but, placed at the lowest levels of a quickly developing school bureaucracy, they had little recourse.[133]

The institutional development of unified, municipal public school systems during the second half of the nineteenth century proceeded from the shared sentiments that even as these new institutions were socially valuable they were also failing, in large measure because of the teachers. Looking to other developing fields like medicine and law, education reformers highlighted professionalization as the antidote to the school's problems. However, the same reformers also understood the teachers of the nation's public schools as fundamentally different from the men who occupied the burgeoning medical and legal fields. For education leaders who envisioned schools as extensions of homes, women, recruited for their stereotypically feminine capacities, were natural teachers. As such, from the start, the professionalization of teachers took on new forms and centered on regulation and systematization. The structural development of the nation's municipal public school systems and the creation of the teaching profession occurred simultaneously and were inseparable from broader ideologies about the purpose of schools in a diversifying society and derogatory and deeply held gendered and racialized perceptions.

In many regards, the history of New York City school reform during these years was exceptional. However, as appreciation for the national significance of local public school systems swelled, big-city practices dictated a national education policy agenda. Additionally, out of this era sprang a series of highly durable and interwoven policy narratives that infused how education leaders defined school problems and the ensuing reforms. First, public schools emerged as salves for social problems that commentators attributed to deficit homes. Second, teaching was not merely an occupation in which women predominated but it was distinctly a woman's profession infused with racialized notions of Victorian feminine docility. And third, the success and failure of the schools rested on teachers' collective shoulders.

2

To "Raise Teachers' Profession to a Dignity Worthy of Its Mission"

The Development of the Modern School Bureaucracy and Tenure Policies during the Progressive Era

As the 1906 school year drew to a close, New York City's Board of Education commissioned doctors to remove infected adenoids from public school pupils at the municipality's expense. Rumors of the procedures spread throughout the city's immigrant neighborhoods and sparked riots. Though school officials insisted that all of the student-patients returned signed parent-consent forms to teachers weeks earlier, many of the parents who lived in the city's lower east side could neither speak nor read English. Convinced that teacher-assisted doctors were brutalizing their children, parents took to the schools. "Tearing their hair," the *New York Times* reported, "and talking wildly in Yiddish, the parents stormed a dozen public schools at once and mourned for the little girls and boys whom their maddened fancy pictured already slain." "Easily excitable," the report continued, "the Jews who have migrated here from Russia are prepared to believe any tale of violence they hear, and so there seemed nothing implausible in the rumor that teachers paid by the city were engaged in cutting the throats of innocents."[1] After learning what had happened in the nearby schools, the following day Italian parents surrounded their public school. According to another *Times* article, "the same wild rumors that the teachers were cutting the throats of their pupils, which stirred the women of the east side to frenzy on Wednesday, maddened the mothers who come from Sicily and Calabria." In a moment full of unintentional symbolism, as the mass of Italian parents tried to squeeze through the school entrance, "the teachers piled up against the door inside and with a long, steady heave managed to slam it shut."[2]

Policymakers and commentators touted the far-reaching benefits of public education during the latter half of the nineteenth century, but by the Progressive Era the ideology of local public schools as social institutions of national importance had gained such broad appeal and consensus that it had become a foregone conclusion. One author happily chronicled "a most significant sign of the times": the "crude conception" of public education as "charity" or "opportunity" so that "the young" may "equip themselves for the battle of life," he explained, had finally been "superseded by the somewhat more adequate view that social security and economic prosperity must depend more and more largely upon the education of the people, and that the schools, accordingly, are requisite to the preservation and extension of the nation's most important interests."[3] By the turn of the twentieth century, "popular education," another author noted, had reached heights "such as even Horace Mann never dreamed of."[4] Reflecting on the war years, education officials from the Department of Education explained that "the schools had become an essential part of the very machinery of modern war."[5] Though locally controlled, big-city educators defined the goals of the public schools through a federal lens and understood the education of the individual child as a project in support of national cohesion and strength, translating national ideals and aspirations into local education policy.

Even as a series of explicit and implicit racialized barriers prevented some candidates from entering the public schools, solidifying teaching as the province of White women, administrators remained disenchanted by the pool of available applicants and wondered to each other and to the public why they could not attract a finer sort. A research brief produced by the National Education Association encapsulated policymakers' concerns: "The racial and family background of many teachers is such that they are not prepared to transmit the best American political and cultural ideals to the children under their care. In some States such a high percentage of normal school students come from homes which, although in America, are entirely foreign in language, customs, and ideals."[6] The remedy for school problems, policymakers and education reformers around the country concurred, centered on manufacturing a corps of professional teachers who were thoroughly Americanized and sympathetic to the broader social goals of the institution. Drawing on the progressive reform impulses of the day, education leaders pointed to bureaucratic organization as the most efficient route to teacher professionalization.

The policy stories that blamed teachers for underperforming public schools and highlighted professionalization as a salve were not new, but the specific ways school leaders attempted to reform teachers reflected the social landscape of the day. Though typically understood as separate processes, during the Progressive Era, Americanization and professionalization entangled, one project fueling the other as education leaders reasoned that teachers' collective "professional weakness" stemmed from their nativity and racial backgrounds.[7] Historians have vividly documented the growing bureaucratization of the schools, and the new organization is often depicted as having developed around teachers, separate from them.[8] Indeed, teachers had little voice in the developing school system, but reformers manufactured the structures that defined public education with teachers in mind. The highly routinized environments teachers found themselves in were no unintended consequence of the rise of the modern school system. The structural development of the modern school system, ideologies about the national role of public teachers as Americanizers, and gendered and racialized assumptions about the nature of women workers and Whiteness as Americanism converged to yield a brand of Progressive Era professionalization reforms that, on the surface, promised stature and order, but in practice degraded teachers and their work.

This chapter begins with "To 'Muzzle' or 'Bridle': Teacher Reform as the Search for Order," which explores the interconnections between Americanization, ideas about race and quality, teacher professionalization, and the rise of the modern school bureaucracy. Education reformers held up the new system of schooling as a way to Americanize teachers and students, increase efficiency, and create a professional corps of public school teachers. This system, offered in the name of teacher professionalism and sustained by the language of blame, also inhibited teachers of color from entering the city's public schools and left teachers sapped of voice and authority, paid unevenly, and vulnerable to unexplained firings and finings. Discussions of tenure sprang from this context and highlight the contradictory ways people across the educational landscape understood and defined teacher professionalism. Even as school leaders and education reformers were initially cool to the idea, as explored in the next section, "'The Ordeal of Annual Election' and Early Tenure Policies," teacher tenure quickly became part of the broader professionalization through Americanization and bureaucracy projects. Policymakers complained of the costs and inconveniences associated with high teacher turnover rates. For them, tenure represented a way to ensure a stable, Americanized corps of public school teachers. Tenure policies, however, represented something altogether different to teachers. Women teachers of the urban elementary schools around the country, the most numerous of all school workers, advocated for tenure rights first, as the next section, "City Teachers and the Fight for Marital and Maternal Rights," chronicles. Without the right to vote and with little social authority, they envisioned tenure as a fundamental workplace protection. As enacted by policymakers, however, tenure initiatives never gave teachers the security they craved. Linking their fight for workers' rights with the broader suffragist project of women's rights, these teachers looked beyond the schools to the legal system for marital and maternity rights.

The first teacher unions in the United States were local organizations run by women of the elementary schools and trace back to 1902. By 1916 and the rise of the American Federation of Teachers, the nature of teacher unionization shifted as men of the high schools claimed leadership positions; with them came a new definition of the professional teacher. As examined in the final section, "Tenure and the Quest for Academic Freedom," male union leaders fought for a vision of tenure that aligned teachers with university professors and sought to flatten the increasingly hierarchized order of the schools. Their efforts were met with opposition and were largely unsuccessful. On the surface, the language of teacher professionalism that motivated school reform in New York City and elsewhere during these years connoted security, authority, and respect for school workers but, in reality, it promised nothing of the sort.

To "Muzzle" or "Bridle": Teacher Reform as the Search for Order

Through the first decades of the twentieth century until the 1924 National Origins Act, hundreds of thousands of non-English-speaking immigrants disembarked upon a city unprepared. According to Superintendent William O'Shea, from 1904 to 1924 the number of students enrolled in New York City's public elementary schools increased by more than 60 percent. During this same period, the city's public high schools witnessed a growth of 422 percent, jumping from 20,948 students in 1904 to 109,370 in 1924.[9] The inundation of the public schools underscored the same troubles in housing and health care that besieged immigrant cities during these years; with the largest immigrant population of any city in the country, New York City epitomized this expansion.[10] By 1908, nearly half of all children enrolled in the city's public schools had foreign-born fathers.[11] And by 1920, over three-quarters of the city's population was either foreign-born or born of foreign parents.[12]

As the war mounted and the mantra of 100 percent Americanism rang out, the shifting demographic composition of the nation's cities assumed new saliency. Across the United States' urban centers, administrators fretted over students' perceived problems, which school leaders nationwide attributed to alien birth, and agreed that filling the schools with teachers who embodied the *American way* was the only remedy.[13] In a speech delivered to city public school teachers in the fall of 1918, New York City superintendent William Ettinger insisted that "it is imperative that every teacher within our system shall be aggressively patriotic in word and deed . . . [and] shall interpret history so as to reveal the enduring Anglo-Saxon principles of personal liberty."[14] The most revealing and basic measure of loyalty to the country, school leaders concurred, was the quality of one's English. As William Vlymen, a city school principal, argued, "it is necessary that the pupils be trained to use correct English . . . because the English language is our Mother Tongue, and teachers should show proper affection for it for that reason if for no other."[15]

Across the United States in 1918, over twenty million children made their way through neighborhood public schools. Together, local public schools employed nearly 770,000 teachers and spent over $800 million on educational expenses.[16] The growing magnitude of the schools amplified the sentiment that public education was accountable to the public. Prominent education leader Nicholas Murray Butler explained that the "deep interest" in the nation's public schools was a result of the "the newly roused municipal conscience" and that "taxpayers" demanded "efficiency."[17] These growing expectations also accelerated other concerns that the nation's public schools were falling short of their mission. "I feel at times that we are farther off the right path than ever, as if our whole system were a failure," Frederick Harrison lamented to readers of *The Forum* in 1891. "There are hours," he continued, "when I feel about education nothing but this,—wipe it out, and let us begin it all afresh."[18] Calling attention to the "transcendent importance of the teacher's work," policymakers and the broader public once again set the schools' collective shortcomings at teachers' feet.[19] "The greatest obstacle to better and more rational teaching," Butler professed, "is the teachers themselves," a group both "untrained" and "uninspired." Thinking "first of their personal ease and comfort," in Butler's analysis, school problems traced back to teachers who clung "with passionate ignorance to that which is usual and familiar."[20] Concurring with Butler's assessment, Rice insisted that the nation's public school teachers represented "the greatest problem" and the barrier to school improvement.[21]

Beyond affecting who sat in the nation's school desks, this wave of immigration had a profound impact on the urban public school teaching population. According to the 1900 census, 30 percent of teachers nationwide were foreign-born or born of foreign parents.[22] But in New York, that figure was a striking 50 percent higher, with 45 percent of teachers either first- or second-generation Americans.[23] In pockets of the city, these numbers were even more pronounced. One study of the city's teachers-in-training reported that although over 90 percent were born in New York City, nearly 70 percent were first-generation Americans and more than 90 percent of that group had at least one grandparent born outside of the United States.[24] According to Verne McGuffey's study of the city's prospective teachers, twice as many student-teachers spoke a language other than English as opposed to just English alone, and nearly half of these new teachers' grandparents spoke no English at all. "It is evident," McGuffey speculated, "that three-fourths of the students are more likely to speak with a foreign accent than in an Americanized English."[25]

New York City's corps of public school teachers diversified in terms of ethnicity during the turn of the twentieth century and Progressive Era, but Black teachers continued to encounter barriers as they tried to make their way into the schools. Even as the number of Black teachers employed across all schools in New York City increased from just 16 teachers in 1890 to 214 in 1920, they constituted just 0.67 percent of the local teaching force.[26] In the late 1890s, the New York State Legislature passed antidiscrimination laws that opened civil service exams to everyone, regardless of race, and in 1900, Governor Theodore Roosevelt officially abolished separate schools for Black and White children, ending what one reporter characterized as "a long battle against them by the colored population."[27] In terms of policy, the pathway into the public schools should have been clear, but practice was a different matter altogether. Not only did Black children continue to attend deeply segregated schools due to neighborhood organization and housing patterns, but White parents, schoolchildren, and teachers actively fought against the hiring of Black teachers in schools with significant concentrations of White children.

In 1899, William L. T. Buckley, PhD, the former vice president of Claflin University in South Carolina, moved north and sought out work in the city's public schools. Buckley earned a position in New York City Public School 11 only to be greeted by "threats on the part of the corps of White teachers in the school to resign in a body if the appointment is not recalled." City leaders agreed: "There is no doubt to the qualifications of Mr. Buckley. His color is the only objection found to him. The other teachers declare they will not teach with a colored teacher." Far from exceptional, episodes like this one were commonplace across the urban north. In 1903, John S. Brown was "the only negro who has risen to the requirements of the examiner since the new charter placed control of all the greater city's schools under their present central management in February, 1902." White children in the class threw "paper wads and other missiles" at him in "disapproval of his color and presence." Brown scolded the children for their behavior, sparking "an outcry of indignation among parents" who complained he was too severe and demanded his removal. When responding to questions from local reporters, Superintendent William Maxwell dismissed concerns, saying, "there is no race question in the public schools." Instead, school leaders transferred Brown to another school in the city "where his color would not be likely to create a prejudice among the pupils."[28] A mixture of formal and informal policies and practices cast teaching in the urban north as the work of White women.

If the influx of immigrants early in the century roused existing concerns about the erosion of a cohesive national identity, then the nation's entrance into

World War I elevated these fears to a fever pitch and added to the mix new anxieties encircling loyalty and national security.[29] In the spring of 1919, the federal Bureau of Education for Americanization sponsored a four-day conference. In his opening remarks, Fred C. Butler explained the purpose of the symposium: "We are on the way to having not a unified country, but as Roosevelt phrased it a 'polyglot boarding house.'"[30] As another example of big cities as a harbinger of national school reform, federal officials invited leading educators from the nation's urban centers to provide tangible details that would "help us to answer the question, 'How can I do this thing?'"[31] As Commissioner of Education Philander Claxton explained to the audience, "We are fully convinced that [Americanization] is a problem for the National Government and the States and local communities to work with together." One speaker from New York City attempted to animate the complexity of Americanizing the nation's growing legion of "others" through the schools and, in the process, illuminated the racialized undertones of school reform. Speaking on behalf of his colleagues, he explained, "We feel somewhat like the darky who was asked by his capitalistic friend if he would point him to the Fourth National Bank." Striving for humor, he continued, "The darky replied, 'Why, goodness me, I don't even know where the First is.'"[32]

Even as the conference's speakers outlined different Americanization endeavors, collectively they agreed on several points. First, they emphasized the importance of speaking and teaching correct English and cast Americanized English as fitting hand in glove with American ideals. "Without a knowledge of English," Claxton explained, "one can never begin to know the American people and American ideals."[33] Second, the presenters visualized the schools as the front line of defense, with one speaker from New York City offering, "The schools are in a position to become the first American institution to which the unstinted allegiance of the foreigners may be pledged."[34] Finally, and most importantly, the conference's speakers concurred that Americanization depended on the nation's public school teachers. "The raising up of a body of trained teacher-workers, who know these needs, know how to meet them in methods, technique, and measurable results," a presenter from Lowell, Massachusetts, emphasized, "is the supreme task of the field in which we are at work." Continuing, he offered, every "teacher must have 100 percent Americanism."[35] These Americanization conversations reflected contemporary ideologies about citizenship and power and in turn shaped local education policy.

Social commentators and education leaders, however, also identified teachers as the barrier to the important work of Americanization, attributing social problems ranging from rising illiteracy rates to disloyalty of public school teachers and, specifically, their lack of Americanism.[36] "The truth of the matter," Frank Wilsey, a member of New York City's Board of Education, explained to a local reporter in 1919, "is that the service is not attracting the teachers we need, both from the standpoint of number and mental caliber." At present, he continued, the schools claimed few of "the type of teachers needed if we are to solve the urgent problems of a democracy."[37] Likewise, John L. Tildsley, associate superintendent of New York City schools, attributed persistent problems to the fact that teachers "had been coming into the school system in recent years who had not had the benefit of American traditions and Anglo-Saxon ideals."[38]

Across the country, education leaders concurred that teaching was essential work poorly done. As William Ettinger explained, we "must raise teachers' profession to a dignity worthy of its mission."[39] However, as many commentators also agreed, the problems facing the teaching profession centered on teachers themselves. The "low regard of teachers by the public," William Maxwell, a New York City superintendent, explained, was a reflection of teachers' "low estimate of themselves and their calling."[40] Schoolteachers, John Gilmer Speed observed in 1895, were "looked down upon by nearly all classes, old and young, and generally thought to be unfortunates who have adopted teaching because there was no other way of livelihood open to them." Far from undeserved characterization, in Speed's estimation, neither teachers' "attainment nor their ideals entitle them to much higher regard."[41]

According to education reformers of national and local esteem like Rice, teachers' problems began and ended with their "professional incompetency."[42] Because of the growing demand for "successful teachers" and the perceived low supply of them, Rice and others called for reforms that would teacher-proof the schools. "As the number [of teachers] required preclude the possibility of limiting the selection to those who are born for the profession," Rice explained, "our only course lies in developing the requisite powers, as well as we can, where they are naturally weak."[43] Motivating this reform impulse was Rice's candid observation: "as a rule, our teachers are too weak to stand alone, and need consequently to be propped up by the supervisory staff."[44] In the name of teacher reform and professionalization, school leaders constructed the modern school bureaucracy, a reflection of the progressive faith in efficiency through organization. School leaders like Tildsley agreed it was necessary to "muzzle some" teachers and "bridle others" and that a carefully configured school system could do both.[45] Proceeding from a trust in expertise and aware of the supply issues confronting urban schools, education reformers argued that a properly executed "system" could trump "personality." Offering an example of two teachers, one with natural teaching ability and another less able but working in a highly supervised context, Rice asserted that the second teacher could be just as effective.[46] Through the "science of education," reformers confidently asserted that they could mitigate against the "ludicrous teaching" found in many schools.[47] Policymakers constructed the school bureaucracy and the "iron clad rules" that came along with it, as Andrew Draper observed, not with "the best" teachers in mind but instead "the worst." For Draper, a superintendent of public education in New York State who later served as the first commissioner of education in the state, in opting for bureaucracy school leaders were caught between Scylla and Charybdis. The new school bureaucracy with prescribed curricula, a regimented school day, standardized assessments, and hierarchized power structure was the cost of keeping "things in a passable condition." Surely, Draper conceded to readers of *The Forum* in 1899, some teachers would "lose their freedom, elasticity, and self-respect," but the new system would also "prevent positive disgrace."[48]

Over the course of the Progressive Era, the modern school organization emerged gradually. Like other progressive reformers, education leaders looked around and saw disarray, experiencing what historian Robert Weibe described as "dislocation and bewilderment."[49] As Joseph Rice described to his readers in 1892, "The characteristic feature of our school system may perhaps be best defined by the single word 'chaos.'"[50] Even as school leaders of the previous century attempted to create order where there was none, due to population growth, child labor and compulsory education laws, and increasing demands on the institution, by the early years of the twentieth century public schooling remained a loosely organized system susceptible to political pressures and individual desires. Education leaders agreed that the problems were many but disagreed about the underlying causes; for some, the troubles sprang from overly mechanized instructional techniques, whereas others highlighted organizational waste.[51] Regardless, reformers agreed that teachers could not be left to their own devices to make educational decisions. Drawing upon the progressive faith in rationality and expertise, school leaders and policymakers at the local and national levels called for the development of standards and structures that would regulate the quality of public education across the United States and decrease the reliance on teachers. The want of reliable standards, Rice argued, meant that "each individual teacher has, thus far, been a law unto himself; permitted to experiment on his pupils in accordance with his own individual educational notions, whether inherited from his grandmother or the result of study and reflection, entirely regardless of what was being done by others."[52] In his analysis, the gamut of educational problems beginning with low levels of student attainment and extending to organizational disarray traced to a reliance on teachers as decision makers.

Progressive education reformers, like progressive reformers writ large, did not speak with one voice; even as they agreed about the significance of public schooling and that it served a social role, they debated what that role was and how it could be fulfilled.[53] For some, like Teachers College professor and education psychologist Edward Thorndike, faith in scientific inquiry and measurement went arm in arm with the new bureaucratic organization. Drawing upon Fredrick Winslow Taylor's 1911 *Principles of Scientific Management*, one camp of progressive reforms identified the rationalization of institutions as the pathway to efficiency and social improvement. "Education," Thorndike wrote in 1912, "is just beginning to give promise of quantitative knowledge, of descriptions of facts as numerically defined amounts, and of relations or laws in terms of rigid, unambiguous equations."[54] For a growing legion of education scholars and reformers, teaching and learning were measurable. "Whatever exists at all exists in some amount," Thorndike famously wrote in 1918.[55] This essential premise and the research that stemmed from it gave way to textbooks, curriculum guides, and tests: in short, the widespread standardization and regulation of schooling.

Meanwhile, progressive reformers like philosopher and professor John Dewey argued that education was not merely about the production of future workers but that it was rooted in a deep moral imperative. Juxtaposed with standardization, Dewey called for experiential learning. "The only true education," he wrote in 1897 while still a professor at the University of Chicago, "comes through the stimulation of the child's powers by the demands of the social situations in which he finds himself."[56] The scholarship produced by both camps suffused schools of education, forming the bedrock of teachers' professional preparation. However, beginning in large urban centers like New York City and gradually spreading across school systems nationwide, progressive ideas rooted in objective measurement and rationality took root, prompting one historian to note that Thorndike won and Dewey lost.[57]

The first step in the construction of the modern school bureaucracy occurred in the late 1890s as New York City policymakers dismantled local control of schools in favor of a centralized system that consolidated a range of smaller school boards into one, unifying the boroughs of Manhattan, the Bronx, Brooklyn, Queens, and Richmond. However, even with the new organization and school construction projects, city leaders were unable to keep pace with the demand for public schooling. According to an article printed in *The Outlook* in 1898, approximately six thousand New York City students could not attend public school because of space constraints.[58] As both the number of students coming to the schools and the expectations placed upon public education mounted and as confidence in teachers continued to slide, education reformers and policymakers turned to the progressive mantra of efficiency through organization with even greater fervor. The product was a highly hierarchized bureaucracy with clearly demarcated channels of power and distributed and differentiated responsibilities.

According to a flow chart printed by the Department of Education in 1918 (figure 3), "the public" exerted its voice and expressed its desires at the ballot box by electing members of the Board of Education who would then appoint a superintendent. After that point, decision-making authority resided endogenously with all layers of authority pressing down upon teachers and pupils. The bureaucratization of the public schools gained considerable momentum during

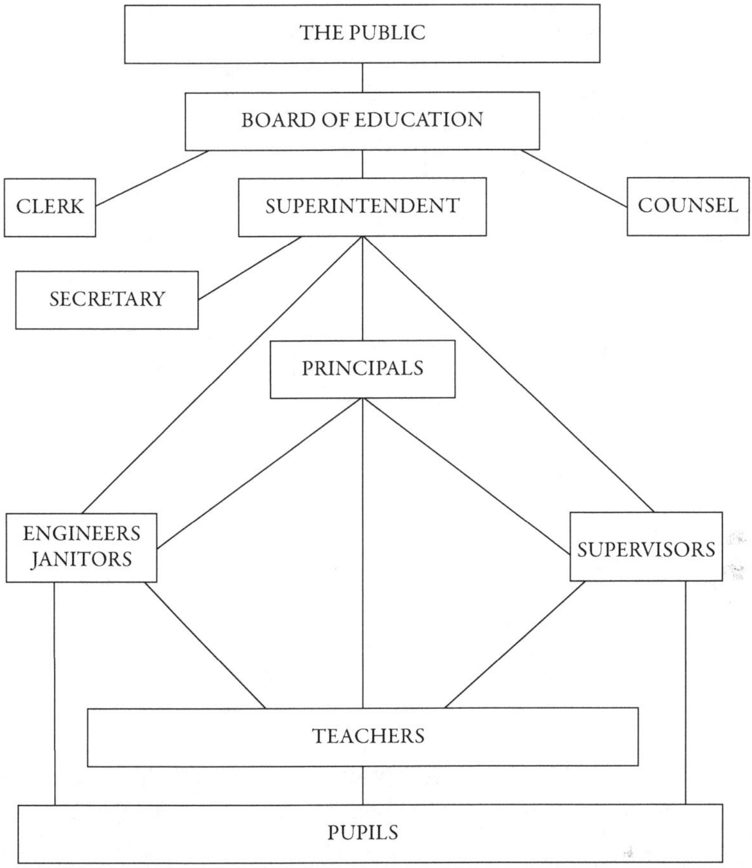

FIG. 3 Huron plan of school organization. (*Source*: U.S. Bureau of Education, *Biennial Survey of Education, 1916–18*, vol. 1 [Washington, DC: Government Printing Office, 1921], 130.)

the first decades of the twentieth century in spite of criticisms from teachers and visible public figures like Dewey, but even as the imperative to order and regulate the schools shaped reforms, education leaders of the day still debated who ought to exercise the controlling voice.[59] In 1899, Nicholas Murray Butler, a university scholar who would become president of Columbia University and receive the Nobel Peace Prize in 1931, chronicled recent achievements in the field of educational research. Examining the work of other university-based scholars, Butler noted the "striking additions to the literature" that distinguished the field from the earlier generation of "well-meant works" produced by practitioners in a "camp-meeting style" that ultimately "did no good." In his assessment, university-based research "opened a new era" for education reform.[60] Scholars like Butler emphasized that the root of expertise traced to the university and pointed to overreliance on school administrators and top-heavy school bureaucracy as emergent problems.[61] Local school leaders simultaneously developed an alternate definition of expertise that situated authority in their hands. As one administrator explained, Butler's criticisms provided more "evidence of the uncertainty in trusting theorists and amateur experts for any suggestion in which they have no responsibility."[62] Practical experience and managerial knowledge, school administrators argued, held far more value than the research produced by out-of-touch academics. Well aware of the tensions, Rice explained the dynamics to readers of *The Forum*: "Educators themselves cannot come to an agreement in regard to what changes, if any, are desirable or feasible. Many educators—men of learning and experience—do not appear to be in sympathy with the system of education advocated by reformers." Still others, he continued, "question the feasibility of carrying out its demands in the common schools." In spite of these disagreements, policymakers, reformers, and school leaders agreed on one salient point: control could not rest in the hands of "the great mass of our teachers."[63]

Regardless of who was in charge, with few worker protections in place, during the early years of the Progressive Era teachers found themselves fined and fired arbitrarily. In the name of increased efficiency and managerial control, in 1897, New York City's school committee on bylaws and legislation approved a measure that enabled school leaders to fine teachers or suspend their pay for charges of insubordination. During the same summer session, the committee also approved an amendment that called on principals to monitor and report incidents of teacher tardiness by the minute to superiors in the Board of Education and mandated that all records of lateness be a part of the teacher's permanent record used to determine "merit and fitness."[64] Through the early years of the twentieth century, teachers could be punished or dismissed altogether for getting married, having a child, moral infractions, and a host of other reasons. As one teacher anonymously explained, "A teacher who refuses to comply with the political demands has her place declared 'vacant' on any trumped-up charges. All the teachers, men and women, have just been assessed by the city machine."[65]

John Dewey, a critic of the growing school bureaucracy, wrote that "the situation would be ridiculous if it were not so serious." "There is not a single body of men and women in the world engaged in any occupation," he offered in 1913, whose "professional spirit" would not be hampered if "they realized that no matter how much experience they got, however much wisdom they acquired, whatever experiments they tried, whatever results they obtained, that experience was not to count beyond the limits of their own activity."[66] With few school recourses available to them, teachers aired their grievances to the public through newspapers. Teacher Alice Thompson wrote to a national audience in 1901 to describe the many ways "a superintendent would intentionally hinder any teacher." Recounting the "distressing and multifarious" supervision teachers faced daily, she categorized school leaders: there was the "superintendent with a hobby" who "must twist and turn every subject according to his whims and interests," the "fossil" who was willing to try nothing, and among several others, the "hindering superintendent" who simply "failed to grasp the real purpose of school organization."[67] In 1903, when eleven of the twenty teachers in a single school were "dropped" "without a word of warning," teachers looked to the public for answers. Perhaps one was "dropped because she was to be married in the fall," but what of the rest, the teacher-author wondered.[68]

In addition, city teachers across the country earned low and uneven remuneration. For much of the nineteenth century, school leaders paid the city's teachers according to a maximum salary schedule: members of the Board of Education established pay ceilings but local school administrators established specific rates. As discussed in the previous chapter, not only did most teachers' salaries fall well below the maximum rate, but teachers across the city earned vastly different amounts for completing the same work. Even as the discourse of professionalism surrounded public schools teachers from the start, teachers' pay paled in comparison to that earned by doctors, lawyers, and even other municipal workers of the day. According to an article published in *The Outlook* in 1897, "there are over 1,300 teachers in New York who receive less than $600 for their services; over 2,000 who receive less than the maximum paid the street-sweepers, $720; over 2,400 who receive less than the stablemen of the Health Department, $780."[69]

During the 1899 school year, New York City politician and state senator John F. Ahearn introduced a bill that would reverse teachers' salary schedules from a maximum to a minimum rate, ensuring that no regular teacher on an initial appointment would earn less than $600 per year. Under his proposed schedule, teachers with ten years of service would earn a minimum rate of $800 per year and teachers with fifteen or more years of service would earn a minimum of $1,200 per year.[70] The initiative, intended to decrease teacher turnover and increase the perceived stature of the work and, by extension, the quality of public school teacher workforce, earned the quick support of city teachers and local politicians. Local school leaders, however, opposed the measure from the start on a number of grounds. First, as city school superintendent Maxwell argued to local reporters, the increases "called for by the equalization of salaries" would cost "about $250,000"; such a measure would "impose a serious burden on the community."[71] Additionally, leaders like Maxwell maintained that the bill would be "detrimental to the best good of the schools." Paying teachers based solely on the length of service, they argued, would undermine most of the regulations and evaluations in place and, as such, would supersede if not entirely diminish school leaders' shared ability to control the teacher workforce.

The bill made its way through the state Senate but, responding to local criticisms, Governor Theodore Roosevelt threatened to veto the bill. Even though he expressed "himself in favor of an increase in the salaries of teachers," Roosevelt also held "that the increase should depend on 'merit'" and contended that "local authorities" ought to "have the power to increase teachers' salaries, and the passage of the bill would be a violation of home rule, which is Tammany's watchword."[72]

In the spring of 1899, Roosevelt called together Ahearn, Maxwell, and teacher representatives in an endeavor to find a suitable compromise. The result was an amendment "not wholly satisfactory to anyone": teachers would be entitled to a theoretical increase, but any actual raise would depend on the "approval of the Borough Board of Superintendents and the principal of the school where the teacher is employed."[73] With little motivation to increase salary, most teachers found their claims for raises denied. A sign of the growing distrust of school leaders, teachers took their cases to the courts. For instance, Anna I. Matthews and Catherine M. Forde, two city teachers, sued the schools for the amount "entitled to . . . under the provision of the Ahearn Law."[74] As public pressure mounted and the holiday season approached, school leaders reluctantly acquiesced, not wanting "to be held up to the public execration like another 'Scrooge,' at Christmas time, in the hundreds of thousands of homes in this great metropolis, where the influence of the teacher penetrates."[75] Even as teachers identified the minimum salary schedule as a victory that would elevate their pay and lessen the power of building leaders, the new measure also fit naturally into the new bureaucratic order as it made all teachers essentially alike and eroded their ability to differentiate themselves on the basis of expertise.

Furthermore, the uniform pay scales promised no equality: the remuneration of male and female teachers followed two separate schedules. In a report from 1900 on teacher salaries, William Torrey Harris, the commissioner of education, found that approximately 68 percent of the nation's public school teachers were women and, on average, they earned 10 percent less than their male counterparts.[76] Another study of teacher salaries, conducted by the National Education Association and focused on the nation's urban centers, revealed even wider pay gaps in 1905. In cities like New York and Chicago, women earned nearly half of male teachers' salaries and in some cases needed three times as many years in the system to reach the maximum pay rate established for their sex. For instance, female elementary school teachers in New York City began at a salary of $600 per year that would increase by $40 per year for sixteen years until finally reaching the maximum salary of $1,240 per year. In contrast, male elementary school teachers in the city began with a base pay of $900 per year that would increase at a rate of $105 per year for six years until finally reaching a ceiling of $2,400 per year.[77] In New York City and across much of the urban North, the pay debate centered on the gender divide, reflecting the nearly all-White composition of the school workforce there. In contrast, throughout the South from Baltimore to Texas, teachers and communities fought not only to raise the salary of female teachers but also to ensure that Black and White teachers earned equal compensation.[78]

"The Ordeal of Annual Election" and Early Tenure Policies

Teachers, many of them women working in elementary schools across the nation's urban centers, called for tenure as early as the late nineteenth century as an extension of a protofeminist logic that linked workers' rights with women's rights. In 1883, for instance, "an enthusiastic assemblage of several hundred" teachers gathered together in the hall of one New York City grammar school to advocate for tenure rights.[79] For these teachers, as for their peers around the country in Boston, Baltimore, and Los Angeles, tenure was an answer to the instable work environment they inhabited. In their workplace as in society, these women teachers had minimal voice and authority; tenure, in this earliest incarnation, was a matter of individual protection from arbitrary dismissals. In these first calls, tenure did not represent a lifelong job but instead defense against the personal and political whims of school leaders. As teachers in San Francisco argued in 1890, far from sinecure, tenure meant that "teachers cannot be removed at the pleasure of the appointing power [and] they can only be dismissed for violating the rules of the Board of Education, for incompetency, or for unprofessional or immoral conduct."[80]

Many local school leaders across the nation's urban centers stood in adamant opposition to teachers' first calls for job protection. Before local districts and states adopted tenure policies, teachers, not only subject to capricious dismissals, had to reapply for their positions each year. According to one superintendent from a Massachusetts school district, constant re-election was "a spur that helps to keep them [teachers] up with the times."[81] The insecurity teachers faced, he argued, was a potent tool for administrators. In 1883, school leaders in Baltimore identified tenure as a mechanism that could disrupt the most basic order of the schools. In calling for tenure, Baltimore's commissioner of education argued that teachers "were overstepping their ground." "The teachers tried to be smart," he explained to local reporters, "but were only foolish."[82]

In spite of this nearly uniform opposition, by the close of the nineteenth century, many local districts adopted tenure policies. Rather than a compromise or evidence of a teacher victory, school leaders came to support tenure on their own terms, defining it differently than did the female teachers who first brought the issue to the table. As crafted by school leaders, tenure reforms reinforced the burgeoning bureaucratic and national goals of public education. For instance, faced with calls for higher pay and budgetary shortfalls, New York

City policymakers wondered if tenure could be a convenient way to cut teacher salaries by 2 percent, a tradeoff of sorts.[83] More importantly, others offered, tenure could increase the efficiency of the entire organization of public schooling. "The ordeal of annual election," John Philbrick explained in his 1885 report, "is coeval with the modern organization and development of our common school system." In addition, he offered, tenure could help cultivate "the ideal teaching corps" by making positions appear more desirable; it would also "cost nothing to the public."[84]

School leaders agonized over the expenses associated with teacher turnover and time lost on constant rehiring; framed this way, tenure policies represented a cost-saving measure. "All who have had experience in the school-room," E. L. Cowdrick wrote to readers of *The North American Review*, "can testify that the greatest hindrance to successful work . . . is the fact that soon as the present term is done, in all probability a new teacher will be employed."[85] As concerns over teachers' lack of shared Americanism and calls for systematic organization spread, local urban school districts invested money and time in induction initiatives designed to fit teachers to the needs of the schools. The constant churn of the urban public school workforce inhibited efficiency and, by extension, student learning. "It takes at least two years to make a passable teacher out of a high-school graduate," one author explained to *Scribner's* readers, "and she will need another two years of experience before becoming acceptable for town or city schools, or really proficient in her calling."[86] The problem was amplified for local policymakers by the fact that once many individuals were made suitable for the system, they left. "Much actual damage," Cowdrick continued, "is done by delaying [pupils'] progress until the new teacher can classify the scholars, and much more time is lost while he is learning their individual dispositions."[87] The purpose of the new school bureaucracy was to create the professional teachers school leaders wanted, but high turnover rates consistently undermined that work.

Rather than granting teachers the sort of security they craved, early tenure practices combatted institutional instability and reinforced the quickly developing bureaucratic structure of municipal public schools systems. In Atlanta, for example, school leaders worried that the financial investment the district made in inculcating teachers was wasted for, "under present rules and regulations, no teacher in the Atlanta public school system is secure in her position for more than the current school year, regardless of her qualifications, her all-round efficiency or the character of her work."[88] Tenure, Chicago's school superintendent offered, would not make it more difficult to get rid of teachers but would "eliminate pull from the public school system."[89] Without tenure, teachers had been diminished to "itinerant laborers," and that reputation not only prevented more capable individuals from entering the field but impeded management, regulation, and standardization.[90] As city school systems faced supply problems that ranged from quality to quantity, teacher tenure represented a ready solution.

By the early 1900s, the local tenure practices that originated in urban localities gave way to statewide legislation. In 1909, officials in New Jersey, the first to pass such a measure, identified tenure policies as a way to both "stabilize the profession" and recruit others to work in the state.[91] Similarly motivated, in 1917, New York legislators approved their tenure bill, and by 1921 eleven other states had followed suit. Far from setting a new course in teacher reform, in implementing tenure policies, United States education leaders followed a precedent well established in Europe. By the time American tenure laws surfaced, Germany, Denmark, Switzerland, Netherlands, Finland, Norway, Sweden, Great Britain, and France all had existing tenure regulations.[92] Even as state laws varied in some details, across the board they shared several common features. First, according to one study of the policies published in 1925, "The general intent of all the laws seems to be to guarantee to teachers a security in their positions during good behavior and efficiency." So long as teachers adhered to school regulations, their positions would be safe. Second, all of the state laws required a probationary period that ranged from months to years. Before earning the rights associated with tenure, teachers would have to prove their fitness to school administrators. Third, all the legislation established that teachers could still be dismissed for an array of reasons including "manifest or proved physical disability," "proved lapse of moral character," "continued friction with co-workers," "lack of self-control," "habitual use of poor English," and general insubordination. Finally, and most importantly for teachers, tenure legislation extended varying degrees of due process. In some states, school leaders needed only to mail dismissed teachers a notification letter, whereas in others, like New York, teachers had the right to counsel and a hearing in front of the Board of Education.[93]

School leaders touted the systemwide benefits of teacher tenure but let out a collective groan over this last provision. As one New Jersey school leader explained, the problem centered on the potential "lodgment in office." Even as multiple pathways for firing teachers remained, school leaders worried they could face external scrutiny and embarrassment as dismissed teachers "engage[d] a lawyer" who would surely "put the superintendent on trial." The result, one author noted, was that school leaders could become more likely to "permit mediocre teachers" to remain in the schools.[94] Echoing those concerns, in 1917 William Wilcox explained to local reporters that the city's schools were "'burdened and clogged with many teachers who are unfit and unsatisfactory,' and whom it is practically impossible to remove because of their 'permanent tenure.'" Arguing that tenure laws forced school leaders to dismiss teachers "with all the technical and legal exactness required to convict them of a crime," Wilcox complained that the steps required to oust teachers were burdensome.[95] In spite of school leaders' concerns, teachers in New York City and across the nation continued to be dismissed for a host of reasons.

City Teachers and the Fight for Marital and Maternity Rights

Reformers and school leaders initially envisioned teaching as short-term work for young women living in the parental home awaiting marriage, but women increasingly turned to public schools for a career. By the early twentieth century, over 90 percent of teachers were single and, as a group, they ranked third on a list of female breadwinners.[96] More women teachers lived outside the family home than any group of women wage earners, and by 1900 teaching was "first in numerical importance among the professional occupations open to adult women and fifth among all occupations in which they enter."[97] In the nation's urban centers during these years, most women teachers were older than their nineteenth-century forerunners and traveled to the schools via institutions of higher learning ranging from normal schools to liberal arts colleges.[98] Belying school leaders' vision of women teachers as passive and docile, in urban centers across the nation, teachers fused their fight for equal rights outside the schools with their fight for better working conditions within the schools, advocating for a vision of the professional woman that stood at odds with how school leaders and reformers imagined teachers.[99]

It was from this activist orientation that fused workers' rights with women's rights that teachers advocated for tenure rights. However, even with those policies in place, female teachers lacked basic job security when it came to marriage and maternity. Rather than accept these circumstances, women teachers looked beyond the schools to fight for and win workplace protections that would change the course of women in the labor market. Across the nation, school districts maintained nineteenth-century regulations and routinely dismissed women teachers who married and became pregnant well into the 1920s. For education leaders and policymakers, the bans were part and parcel of the gendered nature of teachers' work and essential to upholding the field not only as a distinct woman's profession but also as a highly appropriate one that would not challenge or degrade traditional notions of domestic femininity. Concerned both about the preservation of the paternal home and the efficiency of the schools, education leaders in New York City and elsewhere held steadfast to their position that marriage and motherhood disqualified women from the schools throughout the early years of the twentieth century. According to school leaders in California, the compromise was clear and unacceptable: "If the married teacher attends to her school duties properly she must of necessity neglect her home duties, or if she does not neglect the home she must necessarily neglect the school work."[100] Annie Nathan Meyer shared similar concerns about mother-teachers with readers of the *New York Times* in 1913. "Since it has been proved that over three times as many hand-fed babies die as babies fed at the breast," she asserted, "it is clear that no woman can possibly remain efficient both as a mother and a teacher in the public schools."[101] As there could be "no home without a mother," a front-page article from the *New York Times* cautioned that the practice of allowing such teachers to remain in the schools would create "absentee mothers," a phenomenon with dire social consequences.[102] For many school leaders and social commentators, teaching was not for the benefit or fulfillment of the women who engaged in the work but instead for those they served. "It is far better for the children in the schools and far better for the youngsters in the homes," an article in the *Washington Post* explained in 1913, "that mothers should not be teachers."[103]

However, as suffragist activism spread among teachers and increasing numbers of women turned to the schools for permanent employ, women teachers of the Progressive Era challenged these conventions. Some teachers did so by remaining single and opting for spinsterhood. Even though single teachers were common during these early years, as historian Jackie Blount has detailed, some found the trend worrisome.[104] For instance, Kate Gannett Wells alerted her national readership that as women became more educated they also became less interested in marriage, liking "men unless they pose as their husbands." The distractions of "professional life," she continued, "preoccupied the minds of those who want to do something with themselves," leading "many" to "feel superior to a man." "In this way," Wells explained, "the tendency of the modern woman to a profession lessens her liability to marriage."[105]

Linking workplace policies and social policies, other women teachers argued that the right to marry, have children, and maintain employment in the schools was fundamental to their social authority.[106] As Beatrice Forbes-Robertson Hale, president of the League for the Civic Service of Women, explained to Mayor Mitchell of New York City in 1914, teaching "will always remain a woman's profession and women will always bear children. These two facts, which have been made mutually destructive by the present board, can readily be reconciled by the use of a little common sense." Continuing, she explained, "The present policy of the Board of Education creates a feeling of deep resentment among teachers and their friends, for it not only penalizes maternity and removes many of the finest teachers from the schools, but it seems to indicate an autocratic attempt to regulate the private lives of citizens by dictating to them the circumstances under which they shall work." How could the board of education, Hale and others wondered, grant leaves of absence for illness but not for childbirth? Such practices, she asserted, seem "not only a negation of humanitarianism, but a negation of democracy."[107]

Communities of single women teachers persisted well into the 1930s, at which point social critics began to target spinster teachers as threats and instead championed married women as appropriate school role models.[108] However, before school leaders called for marriage as proof of character, during the first decades of the twentieth century, teachers in the nation's urban centers understood marital and maternity rights through a suffragist lens. Some teachers, like those in Washington, DC, in 1915, argued publicly that marriage made women better teachers.[109] Many others, though, chose to protest dismissal policies individually and quietly by refusing to report marriages and hiding pregnancies, practices that enraged school board members. "Too many of the women teachers in the public schools contract secret marriages," one newspaper informed city readers in 1913. "Intentionally practice[ing] deceit," such teachers—women "living a lie"—were "not fit instructors for youth."[110] On a "hunt" for secretly wed or pregnant teachers, school leaders in New York City demanded that all teachers immediately disclose their status and encouraged the public to anonymously report teachers.[111] Part of a "movement to force the resignation of women teachers who marry, or are married," Board of Education members in New York City maintained that such teachers were guilty of "neglect of duty."[112] Falling beyond the purview of tenure protections, suspicions of changed marital or maternal statuses were cause for immediate dismissal. As school leaders in Indiana maintained in 1904, when a teacher married, there was no need for formal paperwork for she "married out of her position."[113]

By 1914, owing in large degree to legal intervention, many school boards shifted their stance on the marriage of women teachers. Reasoning that "the type of woman who looks forward to having a home of her own" is "above all the type desired as a teacher," local school districts amended marriage banns, but mandated that women teachers report matrimony.[114] However, even with the shifting legal landscape, one study published in 1927 revealed that teacher contracts in eighteen states still prohibited marriage for women teachers and in Rhode Island, married women did not earn statewide tenure protection until 1965.[115] In New York City, where married teachers could retain their positions, they still encountered restrictive policies. In 1915, local school leaders approved that "no married woman shall be appointed to any teaching or supervising position in the day schools unless her husband is incapacitated from physical or mental disease to earn a livelihood, or has continuously abandoned her," and further that "married women teachers could not be promoted in the system."[116] Effectively restraining married women on the lowest rungs of the school hierarchy, education leaders maintained that while in certain instances married women teachers could remain in the schools, they could not advance within them.

The struggles for teachers' marital and maternity rights were entangled but also fought for and won separately. Henrietta Rodman, a longtime New York City public school teacher and active participant in the local and national suffrage movement, emerged as a leading voice for mother-teachers. In a satirical letter printed by the *New York Tribune*, Rodman invited readers, "won't you come with me . . . to see a game of mother-baiting? The next one will be played at the Hall of the Board of Education, 500 Park Avenue, on Wednesday, at four o'clock." Highlighting the skewed and unfair power dynamics teachers faced, she continued, "The majority of the members of the Board of Education are expected to play on one side, and on the other, two women, each with a baby a few days old." "The object of the game" was simple, she continued: "kick the mothers out of their positions in the public schools. It will be played according to the rules of the Board of Education." Though a "rather rough" game, much like "wife-beating," in Rodman's assessment it was one school leaders played for the so-called "good of the women."[117] City and state leaders viewed Rodman's letter as an act of defiance and suspended her without pay for a full school year for insubordination in spite of widespread views that she had "excellent training" and was "one of the best teachers in the city of New York." According to State Commissioner of Education Finely, "the responsibilities" of teachers "involve no freedom in speech but they do carry an obligation of respect, fairness and scrupulous regard for the truth."[118]

Maternity rights remained beyond the bounds of the tenure protections school leaders created; teachers, unwilling to choose between career and family, turned to the legal system to contest their dismissals and fight for professional stature. The case of Bridget C. Peixotto played out across city and national newspapers and led to the resolution of the "teacher-mother question." Peixotto, who worked in the New York City school system for eighteen years, served as the teacher in charge at Public School 14 in the Bronx. On February 3, 1913, she requested a leave from her position and notified her superiors of her impending absence. Peixotto reported the cause of her time out as "some affection of her ears and nose" and submitted "a physician's certificate describing her condition"; the board granted her leave without question. However, as school leaders later learned, Peixotto secretly wed in February 1912 and when she took her leave, in addition to suffering from a sinus infection, she was also seven months pregnant. Even though the initial reason for leave that she put forth along with the doctor's note were "sufficient to justify her absence," when school leaders learned of her deception, she was suspended on the grounds of "neglect of duty." In a hearing before the full Board of Education on June 25, 1913, Peixotto was found guilty of all charges and dismissed.[119]

Peixotto, described by one author as a "handsome woman" who was "fond of outdoor sports," took her case to trial and on the way established the argument that became the legal basis for overturning maternity bans for women workers, writ large. "I will contest the issue to the end," she asserted. "The Board of Education, in permitting married women to teach while prohibiting them from carrying out the fundamental function of marriage—the bearing of children—is acting illegally. Its action is manifestly against public policy. It is positively immoral and will not be sustained by any court."[120] As boards of education around the United States held that teachers could be dismissed, even with tenure, for reasons ranging from "neglect of duty" to "immorality," justices nationwide concurred with Peixotto that marriage and childbirth constituted neither offense.[121] In sustaining Peixotto's appeal, Justice Seabury of the New York Supreme Court asserted that "the policy of our law favors marriage and the birth of children." Provisions that barred women teachers from engaging in these natural activities, he reasoned, were "repugnant to law and good morals."[122]

In spite of Seabury's 1913 decision, New York City school leaders upheld Peixotto's dismissal, maintaining that she acted deceptively. Not until 1915 did State Commissioner Finely overturn that decision and reinstate her position, conceding that the courts found that child bearing, as a natural outcome of marriage, was not a dismissible offense.[123] With their hands forced, local school leaders in New York City had no choice but to re-evaluate their policies on mother-teachers. Beginning in 1915, maternity, like marriage, was no longer cause for immediate dismissal. However, important conditions remained. For one, school rules mandated that women teachers report all changes in their personal status to the board. Further, education policymakers ordered that mother-teachers notify superiors immediately of pregnancies and take a mandatory two-year unpaid leave from the schools. Refusing to take the leave or report status changes constituted finable and even dismissible offenses. The basic protections earned represented a mixed victory for women teachers and came at a high cost: not only regulated and monitored, marital and maternity rights came at the expense of women teachers' advancement in the system.

Tenure and the Quest for Academic Freedom

As the Progressive Era pressed on, teacher unionization grew from a local endeavor to a national movement.[124] By 1916 and the rise of the American Federation of Teachers (AFT), the local activism that rooted teachers' rights within a broader framework for women's rights faded in part because questions of marital and maternity rights had been resolved and in part because of changes in union leadership. As male high school teachers replaced the women elementary school teachers who launched teacher unionization initiatives and tenure discussions, the focus shifted from workplace rights to a vision of professionalism that attempted to link teachers with higher-status fields.

Writing to a colleague in the spring of 1912, Henry Linville, a New York City high school teacher who would later become president of the city's Teachers Union, vented his frustration regarding fellow teachers. "The great majority of teachers," he explained, "regard with dumb or indifferent interest the rather new proposition that they might sometime take a hand in deciding out of the abundance of their experience what policies are best for making education effective." Concerned primarily with the day-to-day affairs of their isolated classrooms, from Linville's vantage point, the city's teachers remained contentedly removed from the larger questions of education reform. If only he could get these teachers to "think about their work," he wrote to his friend, "we shall see a more effective lot of teachers." Linville closed his letter with bated optimism; such a change could "be some inducement to able young men to come into [the] system. . . . As things are now, there is small chance for a man of ability and independence."[125] For Linville, the preponderance of female teachers and their perceived anti-intellectualism were barriers to the professionalization of the occupation.

This new generation of union leaders defined teacher professionalism through the lens of masculine authority, respect, and stature, even as the national population of teachers remained firmly female-dominated. In appealing to prospective members, union materials emphasized myriad ways in which the growing school bureaucracy and school leaders, in particular, emasculated teachers. "The disgrace of being a teacher lies not in the low compensation, not in the low esteem accorded by the Prominent Citizens, not in constant association with immature minds," one union member explained in *American Teacher*, the AFT's publication. "It lies," the author continued, "in the necessity of working always under the direction of superiors for whom you can have no respect."[126] Similarly, in an advertisement intended to spur membership, editors of *American Teacher* posed a number of queries to readers: "Do you seek greater recognition?" Do you feel "ineffectual for lack of adequate power?" Are you "sick and tired of your job because it is not suitably regarded?" "Do you feel humiliated by petty penalties and by trivial tyrannies imposed from above?" "If you do feel all these stirring dissatisfactions and are not wanting in courage," the brief union-made questionnaire closed, "join the Teachers Union."[127] The Teachers Union, leaders promised, would strive to flatten the growing hierarchy of the schools and put teachers on an equal footing with school leaders. As another pamphlet promised, the union "will work to develop standards for teachers and for teaching which have hitherto been handed down from above."[128]

Out of this new vision of the professional teacher came a new understanding of tenure policies that departed from both earlier teachers and school leaders. In 1915, the American Association of University Professors (AAUP) adopted their "Declarations of Principles," which linked tenure to academic freedom. Establishing university professors' authority and legitimacy as experts, the AAUP maintained that without tenure and academic freedom, professors could not "rightly render [their] distinctive and indispensable service to society." Further, without their academic freedom protected, the association maintained, professors would be unable to "maintain such standards of professional character, and of scientific integrity and competency."[129] Drawing upon the language of the AAUP and the prestige of that field, the new, largely male, leadership of the AFT and big-city locals extended the concept of academic freedom to public school teachers.

For this generation of union leaders, tenure was about much more than economic security or the "certainty of keeping a job." Instead, recasting teachers' responsibilities, the union maintained that "it is imperative that teachers be free if the schools are to meet the responsibility of the modern conditions of American life impose[d] upon the schools." Moreover, they argued that the "perfunctory kind of tenure which is more or less in existence which avoids the frequent turnover among teachers under ordinary circumstances" was a tool that benefitted school leaders but deprived teachers of respect.[130] In redefining the parameters of existing tenure policies, union leaders sought to elevate the stature and authority of the profession and its union. During the years of the Progressive Era, local and national union leaders entwined tenure with academic freedom and steadfastly devoted their time and limited budget to fighting for the reinstatement of teachers dismissed for reasons relating to academic freedom.

In the fall of 1917, the New York City Board of Education, led by its president, William Wilcox, dismissed three teachers. All employed at the De Witt Clinton High School, Samuel Schmalhausen, Thomas Mufson, and Henry Schneer were each charged with "holding views subversive of discipline in the school and which undermine good citizenship." As John L. Tildsley, the associate superintendent of the city schools, maintained, there was ample "evidence against the three men sufficient to warrant their dismissal."[131] Union leaders like Linville did not take issue with Tildsley's evidence, but even as all parties agreed on the basic details, school administrators and union leaders clashed over whether the events represented infractions worthy of dismissal or the incarnation of teachers' professional rights and authority.

On October 22, 1917, Schmalhausen assigned an in-class activity: write a letter to President Woodrow Wilson. One student, fourteen-year-old Hyman Herman, used his letter to vent his frustrations and hone his creative flourishes. Chastising Wilson for declaring war without "consult[ing] the people," Herman went on to write, "You are ready to slaughter us all in order that we may enjoy in death what we are now lacking in life."[132] For board members, the essential problem sprang not from Herman's words but from Schmalhausen's lack of admonishment. As Wilcox explained in a letter to the editor of the *Evening Post* later reprinted in *American Teacher*, Schmalhausen "evinced no reaction of patriotic indignation, and showed no appreciation of the need of vigorous effort on his part to correct such views in his pupil."[133] During his trial, Tildsley handed Schmalhausen another copy of Herman's assignment and asked him to correct it as he wished he had. Alongside a passage in which the student wrote that a time "will come when people [are] not so ignorant,"

Schmalhausen marked, "exaggerated, excessive, emotionalism." Beside Herman's statement "you are ready to slaughter us all," Schmalhausen asked, "Is there any sanity in this assertion?" In his summary notes to the student penned during the trial, the teacher offered, "For a thoughtful student this statement sounds irrational, sorry to find this unintelligent comment in your work, why did you write this?"[134] Though perhaps less colorful, the other two teachers allegedly committed similar infractions. Mufson, Wilcox charged, apparently thought "it was proper to be neutral in class while a discussion on the relative merits of anarchism and the present United States Government was going on." And Schneer, in addition to distributing a reading list with questionable titles, maintained that "patriotism should not be discussed in the school, [and] that persons wearing the soldier's uniform should not be allowed to speak to the boys in the school assembly."[135]

Even as the cases against the teachers were straightforward as far as members of the board were concerned, for union leaders in New York City they were about a much more important principle: teacher authority and union power. On December 11, 1917, the High School Committee of the Board of Education unanimously voted to dismiss the teachers and on December 20, 1917, after "four hours of debate" by union members, the board sustained the guilty verdict and dismissed all three.[136] The issue was far from settled: union leaders raised over $10,000 to support their fight and engaged in a protracted legal battle that ended a full year later when New York State's acting commissioner of education, Thomas E. Finegan, refused to overturn the board's decision.[137] Rather than deterring union leaders, the case of the DeWitt Clinton teachers became a symbol in a much larger fight that continued as the union disputed the dismissals of several other teachers, including Mary McDowell, a Quaker teacher; Gertrude Pignol, a U.S. citizen born in Germany who admitted that while she was opposed to that country's actions, she did not want to see it "crushed" in the war; and, perhaps most notably, Benjamin Glassberg, a history teacher fired in 1919 for reportedly suggesting in class that "there were two sides to the Russian question."[138] Sustaining the Glassberg fight for more than four years through various legal appeals, union leaders presented the struggle for the reinstatement of dismissed teachers in the name of professional authority and as a fundamental contest between union power and administrative power.[139]

New York City teachers, led by Linville, wanted control of their classrooms as educational experts, and they also wanted to stand equally with administrators and teacher educators. Offering fourteen points of change, the Union offered a vision of teacher autonomy that railed against the bureaucratic order of supervision and managerial control, the hallmark of Progressive Era school reform. Unionized teachers demanded "the cessation of all interference on the part of the principal or other school officials with the general rights which teachers possess in common with all other citizens, including the distribution of literature." In the union's vision, teachers and school leaders had separate responsibilities, but one was not superior to the other. Instead, they called for "the development of a friendly spirit of cooperation on the basis of complete understanding and mutual confidence between teachers, the Board of Education, the Board of Superintendents, and the Board of Examiners."[140]

To legitimize their new sought-after status, Linville reached out to various teacher educators, aligning his project with theirs. Linville imagined that teachers, under his tutelage, would be education reformers in their own right and professionals on par with school administrators. But the desire of Linville and organized teachers to be put on equal footing with administrators and teacher educators never came to fruition. In addition to fighting for the reinstatement of dismissed teachers, Linville spent the better part of 1920 petitioning the Board of Superintendents to grant him a year's leave with pay so he could conduct a scientific study of the schools. When they denied his request, Linville enlisted the support of labor leaders and educators from around the city in a letter-writing campaign. Despite the dozens of letters in his support, the board remained staunchly uninterested in his proposed inquiry.[141] Similarly, in 1924, the Union submitted yet another proposal to the Board of Education to establish an experimental school. Not only would teachers test the newest educational theories of the day, but they would do so without the restrictive oversight of a principal or superintendent. According to union leaders, the school would enable teachers to "see the new school movement in operation and feel themselves a part of it instead of a merely academic interest in a movement that is sweeping past them."[142] Implicit in these proposals was union leaders' convictions that first, teachers knew what constituted good education better than anyone else and second, the reason it had yet to take shape in the city's schools was because of the stifling administrative structure. Again, the board denied the request.

Despite Union leaders' persistent efforts to redefine teacher professionalism and flatten the school hierarchy, school leaders remained unconvinced. First and foremost, for the city's educational policymakers, the union's calls for academic freedom and defense of teachers charged with disloyal behavior seemed to be a symptom of the larger problem plaguing the nation's public schools. Whether teachers were simply exercising academic freedom or articulating seditious ideas, board members did not care: according to school leaders, teachers did not have the right to do either. During these years of conflict abroad and expanding diversity at home, social commentators agreed that public schools existed to stabilize and preserve broader national goals. As State Commissioner Finely noted in 1917, "each school should be a national centre for the teaching of patriotism and loyalty to the ideals for which this nation is fighting."[143] Agreeing, another social commentator proposed, "The whole social structure may be undermined by teaching what is fundamentally wrong."[144] "Knowledge of history and of civics is an important factor in the teaching of Americanism," one speaker at the Bureau of Education's 1919 conference on Americanization noted, "but the inculcation of an enthusiasm for Americanism is better." The core question was simple: "Do our teachers teach these things?" For the presenter as well as many onlookers the answer was disappointing: "hardly."[145] The crux of the issue for policymakers centered on the simple fact that teachers were neither uniformly teaching the ideas nor modeling the behaviors fundamental to patriotic Americanism, and, in their estimation, the clearest evidence of this deficit was the union's defense of dismissed teachers charged of disloyalty.

In response to union leaders who called for academic freedom, school leaders framed their own work as "an active campaign to eradicate disloyalty from the schools."[146] For Wilcox, the dismissed teachers, as well as those who defended them, "have a slight conception of loyalty to the National Government." "It is possible," he continued, "that this may be due to education under foreign Governments with different ideals." According to Wilcox and other officials in New York City, "any teacher who does not stand for America first, last, and all the time, and who cannot be trusted to inspire in the pupils love for the American flag and all it stands for" was a menace to the public school system and to the nation.[147] School leaders interpreted teachers' fight in the name of academic freedom as a sign of self-interest and insisted that given teachers' social responsibility "there [was] no room for jealous regard of individual rights and individual opinions."[148] In a speech to parents and teachers on the city's upper west side, Joseph Wade, another district superintendent, explained "there must not remain in our schools a single discontented teacher, for there is a spirit of restlessness that will grow up among our children unless those above them are absolutely loyal and continue teaching obedience to authority."[149]

New York City's school leaders did not stand alone in their position; policymakers and government officials from around the country supported their steadfastness. Lending his support to the board's dismissal of the three De Witt Clinton teachers, Theodore Roosevelt, by this point a colonel stationed at Sagamore Hill, wrote, "I heartily approve the effort to secure the dismissal of all teachers. . . . A public school teacher should stand in loyalty and Americanism precisely where we expect an officer of the army or navy to stand, and should be held to an equally rigid accountability for the slightest symptom of disloyalty, or of failure in thoroughgoing Americanism."[150] The presence of the teachers union complicated matters for school leaders. Dismissing teachers charged with insubordination was one matter. But likening un-American attitudes to a disease, they also feared that the persistence of the union would spread across the entire teacher corps, undermining the very goals of the new school bureaucracy. In response, school superintendent William Ettinger barred the union from holding meetings on school grounds.[151] As New Jersey officials noted,

"Every teacher and school official in times like these should give his whole heart and mind and devotion to the country's noble cause." Rather than hide behind the "cloak of so-called 'academic freedom,'" public school teachers must work "to make democracy safe for the world."[152] Tenure or not, those that could or would not conform to the ideals of Americanism in speech, thought, and action ought not to be in the schools at all, concurred policymakers in the city and around the nation.

The number of teachers dismissed for disloyalty combined with the union's rationale that, rather than reprehensible, such behaviors were the right of professional teachers led officials to seek out broader corrective measures. In the spring of 1920, Clayton R. Lusk, a republican senator in the New York State Legislature, introduced six bills intended to ensure loyalty among the state's public servants. Among other provisions, the Lusk Laws mandated that public school teachers demonstrate their loyalty by passing an examination and that "no certificate shall be given to a teacher who has advocated a form of government other than the Government now existing in the nation, or who has advocated a change in the Government by force, violence or other unlawful means." The bills were signed into law on May 9, 1921, and Governor Nathan Miller assured, "No one need fear the result of this measure, unless he wishes to teach criminal sedition or to practice fraud, and those who desire to do that seek license, not liberty."[153]

During the years of the Progressive Era, the discourse of blame that motivated education policy continued to land upon teachers. As generations of education reformers had and would, school leaders of the early twentieth century linked social problems to ineffective schools and identified teachers as the cause. But rather than employing a static language, education reformers of the day viewed school problems against the backdrop of immigration and World War I. Offered in the name of teacher professionalization but bound up in gendered and racialized ideas, education leaders highlighted bureaucratization as a way to teacher-proof the schools. As the "science of education" took root, teachers' work became standardized and regulated, something school leaders interpreted as a measure of increased efficiency. However, education reforms and the faith in expertise that brought new order and structure to the schools also isolated teachers to the lowest rungs of the school hierarchy with neither voice nor authority.

Though perhaps seemingly at odds with the reform impulses that generated the modern school bureaucracy, tenure policies arose from the same context and highlight the contradictory definitions of the professional teacher. For the policymakers who ultimately implemented tenure laws, the provisions were for the benefit of the system. A way to protect the investment local districts made in teacher induction, minimize the costs associated with teacher turnover, and ensure that sound Americans knowledgeable of school rules stood at the blackboard, in the hands of school leaders, tenure policies fortified institutional stability. For teachers, tenure represented something else entirely, but that vision changed over time. The women elementary school teachers who initiated tenure reform discussions envisioned the policy as a fundamental worker protection entwined with their broader fight for women's social, political, and economic rights. However, even with tenure rights, women teachers continued to be fired for getting married and having children. Realizing that tenure offered no protection, these women fought for marital and maternity rights on their own, outside of the schools, decades before school leaders argued that all teachers ought to be married, as discussed in chapter 3. These women teachers successfully compelled New York City school leaders to revise the grounds for dismissal, but the broader bureaucratic tendencies that placed teachers on the lowest levels of the school ladder and inhibited their professional advancement persisted.

The rise of the national teachers union in 1916 ushered in a new generation of teacher-leaders. Unlike those who initiated tenure talks, AFT local and national leaders, a largely male group comprised of high school teachers, understood tenure as a pathway to professional autonomy and respect. Linking tenure to academic freedom, they fought for the reinstatement of dismissed teachers and the flattening of the school hierarchy by leaning upon traditional, masculine notions of professional authority. However, these union leaders were no more successful than the teachers who preceded them in achieving their vision of tenure protection. School leaders remained unconvinced and pointed to the union's defense of teachers charged with disloyalty and insubordination as a signal of all that was wrong with the schools. In name, tenure offered teachers status and authority, even as teachers disagreed about the status and authority they sought. In practice, however, tenure policies were part of a much larger reform that identified teachers as the problem and teacher regulation as the solution, increasing the distance between teachers and professional stature.

3

Teacher Education and the "National Welfare"

Professional Preparation, Character, and Class during the Great Depression

During the Depression years, policymakers, reformers, and social commentators once again agreed that public education stood among the nation's most powerful social institutions and that it was falling short of its mission; once again, blame for the state of affairs landed squarely on teachers and their perceived lack of professionalism. As Dr. Clyde M. Hill, the chair of Yale University's education department, observed in 1937, the "general professional incompetency" of teachers was the fundamental barrier to school improvement.[1] A textbook designed to expose teachers in training to key educational issues asked, "Do you think teachers are biological failures? Would they starve to death if they lost their jobs and had to 'work'?"[2] According to leading figures around the country, both the cause of and solution to teachers' deficiencies hinged on their professional preparation. "The difficulty now is that too many teachers do their work no better than could be done by a layman who had no training," Daniel Cooke explained in his 1933 volume *Problems of the Teaching Personnel*.[3]

Evidence of the widespread concern, in 1933 the Department of Education commissioned a series of studies on the preparation of teachers. According to the first volume, "one of the largest and most important undertakings in the United States is education." The study's authors noted that public schools were significant for financial and ideological reasons, and that nationwide, spending on public schooling was second only to war and protection-related expenses. Further, they affirmed that public education was "fundamental to a democracy." Reiterating what by these years had become a well-worn trope but also identifying a new area of reform, the authors of the federally funded study declared, "The teacher is the most important single element in determining the success of our public-school systems. The preparation of teachers and provisions for their continued development while teaching are, therefore, of very great national concern."[4] Education leaders at the federal, state, and local level concurred that the nature of teacher preparation required considerable "upgrading" before teaching could attain "the status of a profession."[5] In their review of teacher education curricula, authors of another volume of that same federally funded study asserted in 1935 that teacher preparation affected "the national welfare," "immediately and in the future."[6] For these researchers and policymakers, the preparation of public school teachers affected directly the quality of the nation's public schools.[7] As New York State Governor Herbert Henry Lehman explained in a convocation address, "No State can afford to spend a third of a billion dollars on its public schools without being vitally concerned about the type of person admitted to the teaching profession."[8] This new policy focus and line of reform framed teacher education as a problem of national importance and had significant consequences for the nature of teacher preparation, as well as how teachers understood their professional identity and responsibilities.

This chapter explores a period of critical change. As the first section, "The 'Science of Education': University-Based Schools of Education before the Great Depression," chronicles, during the early years of the twentieth century, schools of education in New York City told a tale of extremes. At one pole was the city's Normal College, discussed in chapter 1, which provided young women with an education centered on the practical needs of local public schools. At the opposite pole stood schools of education in the city's elite universities: Teachers College at Columbia University and the School of Pedagogy at New York University. These private institutions situated the study of education within the liberal arts traditions of the university. Faculty leaders at Teachers College and the School of Pedagogy explicitly designed their programs in contrast to the normal school approach that was gaining visibility nationwide. To be sure, across the city, state, and nation other schools of education existed that were more similar than different.[9] This chapter tells the story of these extremes precisely because during the Depression years those differences melted away and the results had implications for the nature of teacher preparation nationwide.

In a gradual process that began in the 1920s and extended into the 1960s, normal colleges faded from the American higher education landscape. In what historian Christine Ogren characterized as "mission leap," by the onset of World War II, nearly all normal colleges had given way to teachers colleges and by the 1960s, they had become state colleges and universities.[10] The common trope surrounding the history of teacher preparation centers on what Christopher Jencks and David Riesman have called the "mimetic tendency of normal schools."[11] Jurgen Herbst offered the classic declension narrative: over time, normal schools became more like universities and, in doing so, abandoned teachers.[12] This history of transformation in New York City reveals another story, as discussed in the next section, "'An Old Order Is Passing': The Rise of Applied Learning in University-Based Schools of Education." Amid a confluence of three critical factors that sprang from ideologies of public schooling and the discourse of blame—exogenous local policies, market pressures, and gendered assumptions—during the years of the Great Depression, faculty leaders at these elite programs adopted the forms and practices of the normal colleges they had once derided, swapping the esoteric grounding that characterized their early histories for an applied orientation.[13] In making this curricular shift, education school faculty at once responded to the discourse of blame and institutional financial pressures and also differentiated the nature of teachers' professional preparation from that of doctors, lawyers, and others. Theorists have traced professional authority to the esoteric knowledge imparted in university-based programs; it is from this knowledge base that members of professional occupations gain status, authority, and respect. In turning away from those conventions, even as schools of education admitted more students and expedited their preparation, the shifting nature of teacher education denied teachers the most fundamental building block for professional credibility.

Without an academic grounding of the sort that legitimated other professional occupations, teachers looked elsewhere to define and rationalize their professional authority, as chronicled in the final section of this chapter, "'A Houseful of Good Company': Character, Class, Culture, and Teachers' Professional Identity." The turn toward practical learning hastened teachers' professional preparation and supported their calls for higher pay, but it also undercut their shared professional authority and differentiated them from aspirational fields like medicine and law. Increasingly, teachers viewed their professional preparation as a transactional arrangement that led to employment and salary increases but was otherwise irrelevant. In their professional writing and through their labor organizations, teachers articulated a professional persona divorced from higher learning and instead framed their professional stature and responsibility against the backdrop of the Great Depression and an idealized vision of the American family bound up in gendered and racialized norms. Character education sat as the crown jewel of Depression-era curricular reform and teachers argued that they were especially well suited to lead the charge in this endeavor not because of what they had learned but because of who they were. Without an academic foundation for their professional expertise, teachers rooted their professional authority in their cultural capital as guardians of an imagined and, during these years, fragile American middle-class home.

The "Science of Education": University-Based Schools of Education before the Great Depression

From the late nineteenth century through the first decades of the twentieth century, the majority of teachers traveled to the public schools by way of the city's normal college. In 1870, the Normal College of the City of New York opened in rented quarters. Founded to prepare women to teach in the city's public schools, the tuition-free, all-female college was "filled to overflowing" with about 1,100 enrolled students in just ten weeks.[14] Based upon a four-year high school course approved by the city's Board of Education, the "chief purpose" of the college was to "encourage young women . . . to engage in the work of teaching in elementary and secondary schools."[15] As James Kieran, president of the Normal College, explained in 1912, all courses for prospective teachers must be "concrete and more practical."[16] Even as the institution changed its name to Hunter College in 1914, fashioning itself after liberal arts colleges, it remained unwaveringly committed to the vocational goals of teacher preparation through World War II when the institution opened its doors to men and broadened its academic offerings. The name change, the college's president assured, "will enable us to render the City even better service than in the past."[17] Standing in contrast to the Normal College and, later, Hunter College, were its neighbors at the northern and southern ends of Manhattan.

Founded in 1890 and 1898, respectively, the School of Pedagogy, later named the School of Education, at New York University and Teachers College at Columbia University focused instead on the preparation of school leaders and the growing field of education research and situated their work within the academic traditions of the university.[18] According to a School of Pedagogy bulletin from 1912, faculty sought to "meet the needs of students of superior academic training and of teachers of experience who are prepared to study educational problems in their more scientific aspects and their broader relations."[19] Among the first university-based education schools in the nation, these two institutions framed their work through the classic rhetoric of the academy and, as a bulletin from the School of Pedagogy published in 1900 explained, focused on the "advanced study of the science of education and the art of teaching." In an endeavor "to furnish a thorough and complete professional training for teachers," faculty at these two programs offered "instruction in the history of education, in educational psychology and sociology."[20] The School of Pedagogy categorized its work as of "distinctively university grade."[21] Not alone in their focus, university-based education faculty around the nation framed their work through the rhetoric of the academy. For instance, in 1921, Dean Henry Holmes of Harvard's Graduate School of Education noted, "we are deeply concerned to develop research, for which there is even greater need in Education than in other subjects."[22] As Edward Shaw, the dean of the faculty of pedagogy at New York University, explained to a national audience, the new institutions would bring "together all that bears upon pedagogy" from "descriptive, experimental, and physiological psychology, from the domain of medicine, from ethics, from philosophy, from aesthetics, from sociology, from the principles and art of teaching, and from comparative studies of different national systems of education."[23]

In implicit and explicit ways, faculty members and school leaders at Teachers College and the education school at New York University defined their work against the city's Normal College. In the late 1880s, Grace Dodge, a prominent Teachers College patron and founder of the Kitchen Garden School, traveled to the state capitol to oppose a plan that would allow the city's Normal College to grant degrees.[24] Casting the normal school experience as educationally inferior, faculty leaders at New York University established that students with a degree from a normal institution could attend the School of Pedagogy as nonmatriculated students but could not earn a degree from the university.[25] Implementing a parallel policy, Teachers College allowed graduates of normal institutions to be admitted only as "unclassified students."[26] Whereas the Normal College sought "to encourage young women . . . to engage in the work of teaching in elementary and secondary schools," the elite university-based education programs in the city instead targeted experienced teachers seeking to leave the classroom and become administrators or university professors; the majority of these were men.[27] At Teachers College, faculty agreed that "the requirements for admission should emphasize maturity, experience in teaching, and academic scholarship."[28] Teachers College dean James Russell explained in 1919 that "it is not our policy to duplicate work . . . [and therefore] we do not offer instruction to young students who on their graduation would be expected to go directly into the elementary school system."[29] Associating practical training with the trades and differentiating their work from normal schools, in 1924, faculty at Teachers College argued that their academic curricula "raise[d] the level of service from that of the skilled artisan to that of the professional leader and educational statesman."[30] According to Teachers College professor Paul Monroe, the program of study stemmed from a "belief in the 'high calling' of a teachers profession."[31]

These three institutions not only prepared teachers in two contrasting ways during their early histories, but they educated them for different types of school settings. In 1915, the Board of Education reported the sources of License No. 1, the city's certificate for grade-school teachers. Hunter College was first on the list with 257 students successfully sitting for the exam. Teachers College presented just 7 students and the School of Pedagogy only 1.[32] In the spring of 1920, George Ryan, a member of the city's Board of Education and chairman of the committee on teacher shortages, inquired about this situation to Teachers College dean James Russell. "Although Teachers College is in this city," Ryan wrote, "there are few of its graduates or graduate students who enter the public school system. This leads me to the opinion that the college does not recommend to its students and graduates that they accept positions in New York City schools. Is this the fact?"[33] Russell responded to the inquiry within the week, explaining that "a large percentage of our students are candidates for administrative positions [in the city]." Russell concluded his correspondence by pointing out that "many of our best students can find positions in other parts of the country which are more congenial and which pay larger salaries than those in New York City."[34]

Because so few of their students became public school teachers in the city, school officials at Teachers College and the School of Pedagogy at New York University designed preparation programs separate from licensure dictates, unlike leaders at the Normal College and its progeny, Hunter, who explicitly crafted an education in concert with municipal school leaders that would prepare students to sit for and pass the local certification exam. Free from external regulation, from their founding through the first decades of the twentieth century the education programs at Teachers College and New York University adhered to the larger academic traditions of the university, focusing on global knowledge rather than local immediacies. In his *Confidential Report to the Trustees of Teachers College*, Dean Russell celebrated that "instead of a local institution, Teachers College has become national and international."[35] The curricular offerings mirrored this orientation. Undergraduate students entering with "two years of professional training in the state or city normal schools or teachers colleges approved by New York University, or two years of standard college education," took the following roster of courses to earn the Bachelor of Science or Bachelor of Arts degree (table 1).

The traditions of higher education that shaped these programs extended beyond their curricula. Even as women entered the academy as students in greater numbers than ever before, the university remained a male-dominated space.[36] Teachers College offers a prime case in point. Founded in 1880 as the Kitchen Garden Association, an independent training institute for young women, the school offered "vocational training, sufficiently thorough and dignified to check their [female's] aimless craving for a vacuous culture."[37] Once the school affiliated with Columbia University in 1898, that project immediately lost visibility as school officials touted advanced inquiries in the "science of education." Even as women comprised nearly 90 percent of the city's entire public school teaching population, they were eclipsed by men in number and

Table 1
Report to the Dean of the School of Education

Group I—General Subjects	Points
English	8
History	4
Psychology	4
Economics or Social Sciences	4
Government	4
Science	4
Mathematics	4
Group II—Professional Subjects	**Points**
Educational Psychology	4
Philosophy or Principles of Education	4
History of Education	4
Principles of Teaching	4
Educational Measurement	4
Observation and Practice Teaching	4
Educational Sociology	4
Special Methods	4
Group III—In the field of the student's special interest	**20**

SOURCE: *Report of the Dean of the School of Education for the Years 1920–1921 and 1921–1922*, in *NYU Report of Officers*, NYU Archives.

visibility at the highest levels of school leadership positions and in schools of education.[38]

Although founded in 1890, the School of Pedagogy did not include a female professor until 1908. In 1909, 22 full-time faculty members comprised New York University's School of Pedagogy; 4 of these professors were women and all of them taught in the domestic arts program.[39] Teachers College replicated similar patterns. In 1915, Teachers College's School of Education consisted of 36 full-time faculty members; 4 were women. The college's Faculty of Practical Arts consisted of 38 full-time faculty members; 11 were women and only 2 held terminal degrees.[40] The ratio of male to female students followed similar patterns. In the 1914–1915 academic year, Teachers College awarded 356 Bachelor of Science degrees, 90 percent of which were awarded to women; this group of graduates represented 75 percent of all degrees Teachers College awarded that year. Meanwhile, of the 67 students awarded Master of Arts degrees, 58 percent were men, and all of the 4 Doctor of Philosophy degrees granted went to men.[41] Such trends were hardly unique to New York City. During the 1920–1921 academic year, 70 percent of candidates for a degree in Harvard's Graduate School of Education were men, but 75 percent of special students were women. That year the school conferred five Doctor of Education degrees, all to men.[42] Teachers

College and the School of Pedagogy at New York University pointed to their graduate programs to gain stature across the university, where the ratio of male students and professors replicated similar patterns.

As tuition-reliant institutions with little financial support from their larger universities, these elite schools of education turned to their substantial population of female undergraduates for solvency. As Dean Russell of Teachers College noted in a confidential report from 1912, "the classes of lower rank are supporting the graduate courses."[43] Teachers College and the School of Pedagogy struggled with this reality as they balanced survival against status. Dean Thomas Balliet of New York University understood that an institution like the School of Pedagogy competed internally with other programs at the university and with neighboring institutions. Too much focus on the "academic" and not enough on the "practical," Balliet worried in 1919, may "ultimately demand that special teachers' colleges be established for the training of classroom teachers . . . in which the scope of university departments in education would be limited to research." At the same time, he also noted that professors in the education program and across the university were reluctant to allow coursework with a practical orientation to count toward higher degrees.[44] In 1921, the school sided in favor of the traditions of the larger university, changing its name to the School of Education and replacing the Doctor of Pedagogy degree with the Doctor of Philosophy degree; despite fears of pushing away students, the undergraduate curriculum remained academically oriented.[45] Faculty elsewhere identified a similar juxtaposition. "As against training, of whatever sort, stands research," Dean Holmes of Harvard noted in his 1923 report. "The two are of course neither incompatible nor unrelated, although they are at times in conflict."[46] Teachers College walked the same tightrope as faculty members attempted to balance "quality education" with the growing student body.[47] As was the case at New York University's education programs, officials at Teachers College sided with the traditions of the larger university during this early history, pushing practical learning to the periphery and offering a generation of future educators an experience rooted in the traditions of the academy. Faculty members at both institutions noted the value of practical experience but maintained that all such training occurred outside of the curriculum. For instance, in 1916 Teachers College leadership encouraged qualified students to enroll as substitutes and others to volunteer their time in the schools, but none of this work carried any credit and all of it was separate from students' course of study.[48]

"An Old Order Is Passing": The Rise of Applied Learning in University-Based Schools of Education

By the early 1930s, the effects of the Depression spread to all corners of the nation. As unemployment levels surged in nearly every occupation, in relative terms, teachers, particularly in New York City, remained safe. While Chicago teachers went months without a payday, Los Angeles teachers saw promised pay hikes rescinded, and Atlanta teachers faced salary cuts, New York City teachers earned their regular salary schedule and annual increments.[49] Because teaching represented stable work, more and more individuals knocked on the school's doors, causing supply lists to swell. For members of New York City's Board of Education, "the oversupply of teacher eligibles" represented an "opportunity" and "need" "for higher requirements for admission" in teacher training programs.[50] Educators nationwide expressed similar sentiments. In 1935, the federal Office of Education reported, "Teacher selection is a difficult task, both because of the large number of applicants and because of our present inability to measure objectively the factors correlating highly with teaching success."[51] As federal policymakers asserted in 1935, the "conditions are propitious for the elevation of standards for teachers."[52] Local school leaders looked to relationships established in the city decades earlier, turning to institutions of teacher preparation as partners in this project. In this formulation, policymakers envisioned schools of education as a powerful filter. However, more than simply desiring teachers to have more training, education leaders demanded a more uniform and practical preparation. A core problem, according to the authors of the *National Survey of Teacher Education*, was the "wide variety of practices in the education of teachers." Even as the research team noted that the variety of preparation models was a long-standing issue, they argued that developments ranging from "growth of secondary education" to the "increasing costs of education" necessitated standardization.[53]

New York City's Board of Education "encouraged teachers to take professional courses at local colleges or at teacher-training schools" as early as 1900, but local school leaders felt the recommendation had little effect, as "there was no compulsion attached to this suggestion."[54] In 1931, New York City's Board of Education created a new policy that officially linked teacher education to salary increases by requiring all teachers on permanent license "to offer an approved thirty-hour course as a pre-requisite for obtaining the salary increment."[55] This salary-for-education policy constituted a powerful market intervention in that it changed who went to schools of education and why, and brought a new brand of preparation to the city: in-service teacher education.

Education leaders looked to the professional preparation of other professional fields to affirm teachers' collective professional deficiencies. "Teachers," the authors of the second volume of the *National Survey of the Education of Teachers* offered, "are expected to be as well educated as members of the professions of law, medicine and the ministry." However, they continued, "it is clear that the educational level of the preparation of American public-school teachers is much below that of other professions."[56] Even as the traditional professional fields remained aspirational models at a rhetorical level, the nature of teacher education reforms during the Depression years only further differentiated teachers from other professional groups.

Policymakers' vision for the professional preparation of teachers solidified its vocational orientation at a time when the rest of the university witnessed a resurgence of the liberal arts and classic courses of study.[57] Capitalizing on similar oversupply issues, medicine and law, for instance, also witnessed increased regulation. However, unlike the 1931 policy that came from the district and was imposed on teachers and schools of education, in the fields of medicine and law policies came from within and were supported by the state.[58] Guided by legal and medical professional associations, across the country university-based professional preparation in these fields opted for greater selectivity and exclusivity over expansion.[59] As historians have documented, professional associations like the American Association of Collegiate Schools of Business worked in concert with university programs to set standards.[60] Exogenously imposed, the new standards for teachers created greater uniformity at a time when other professions moved toward greater specialization.[61] During the 1930s, for instance, legal and medical professional education programs continued their moves away from clinical- and practitioner-based practices in favor of curricula that yielded scientifically-informed "intellectual boundaries."[62] Professional authority and respect grew from these university-made boundaries. Education school leaders made curricular changes to the nature of teachers' professional preparation guided by the discourse of blame, financial pressure, and disparaging gendered assumptions. Shifting curricular priorities differentiated teachers from other professional occupations while aligning them more closely with the vocationalized trades, even as they were offered in the name of professionalization, highlighting that teacher professionalization was similar to other fields in name only. These changes occurred most visibly in New York City; because of its size and significance, the area housed competing models of preparation but went on to shape the nature of teacher preparation nationally.

In the preceding decades, faculty leaders at Teachers College and the School of Education at New York University declined invitations for municipal partnership, but the economic realities of the Depression changed their response. The early years of the Great Depression rattled Teachers College and New York University's School of Education. With small endowments and minimal support from their larger universities, these institutions relied on tuition for survival. During the first years of the 1930s, the schools witnessed an exodus of students. In 1932, Teachers College lost nearly 12 percent of its student body from the previous year when over 800 students left.[63] The School of Education lost nearly 15 percent of its student body over two years when over 1,200 students failed to return in 1933.[64] Meanwhile, the student population at Hunter College exploded; in 1929, the college counted a total enrollment of over 22,000 as it welcomed students looking for lucrative work as well as those who could no longer afford to continue their training at private institutions.[65] Teachers College and the School of Education saw their rosters plummet as students refused to expend their limited resources at the same time Hunter opened a second campus in the Bronx to keep pace with growing demand. The economic context of the period shaped school leaders' appetite for the 1931 policy. According to one school official, "in a university such as New York University, nine-tenths of whose income is derived solely from student fees, it is obvious that its policies must be determined by this financial consideration."[66]

In one regard, calls for partnerships between universities and public schools were alluring to leaders at university-based schools of education because they represented financial security. However, in another regard, these relationships and the sort of practical, job-ready skills policymakers demanded represented a departure from the previous trajectory of elite university-based schools of education. Officials at Teachers College and New York University's School of Education realized that the reforms of the period would not only expand but also change the market for their services. By 1930 there were over forty-seven thousand teachers in New York City, and 80 percent of them were women.[67] By comparison, in 1930, women comprised 3 percent of all of the city's lawyers, justices, and judges and 5 percent of the physicians and surgeons in the city.[68] As faculty members at university-based schools of education braced for the Depression, female students represented both a lifeline and a new challenge. During the Depression years, faculty leaders at Teachers College and New York University retooled their programs, identifying curricula rooted in applied learning and practical knowledge as both suitable for their new students and financially expedient. In an endeavor to compete for these new students, faculty leaders at Teachers College and New York University retooled their institutional image, approach, and offerings, replacing the earlier academic orientation of teacher preparation for the practical learning they had once derided.

The 1931 salary-for-education policy in New York City applied to teachers already in the public schools. As a result, one of the first and simplest steps these institutions took in appealing to future students came in the form of scheduling. Though Teachers College and the School of Education had offered part-time and summer programs of study during the preceding decades, these programs exploded during the 1930s as more working teachers populated their programs than ever before. As the director of the Bureau of Educational Services reported to the dean, because of more flexible schedules, "a greater number of students are afforded opportunity during these difficult days to earn money while attending Teachers College."[69] By the 1935 academic year at Teachers College, more students enrolled in the summer session than in the traditional program.[70] From 1931 to 1936 the number of students carrying four points or less increased by 40 percent.[71]

New York University's School of Education summer program also grew popular during these years due to recruitment strategies. Making an active appeal to students, the school mailed materials to prospective students with titles like "Summer in New York." "Classes at New York University are informal," prospective students read. "Men and women dress for the weather. After class hours there are many favorite retreats: on the roof tops there is usually a breeze even on the warmest days, and iced punch is served every afternoon to all who stop at the Students Building. During the week ends and many other times . . . students go out to the parks and beaches easily reached by subway or boat or bus or auto."[72] Beneath the text was a cartoon of two people sitting by a pool (figure 4). Officials at the school attempted to entice teachers to spend their limited resources by highlighting amenities, services, and lifestyles but said nothing of the actual learning that might take place. By 1939, New York University's *Summer Bulletin* informed prospective students that "the summer session and intersession . . . are in reality an extension of the academic year of the School of Education."[73]

Beyond a limited recruitment initiative isolated to the city's elite programs, the expansion of already popular summer sessions in teacher education took hold in universities across the nation during the Depression years. According to the authors of the third volume of the *National Survey of Teacher Education*, "the summer session is tending very rapidly to become another term or quarter in the regular year's work of the various institutions of higher education." Lauded by education leaders, the study's authors recommended that "summer sessions should continue to be organized."[74] The School of Pedagogy's 1900 *Bulletin* explained that "the plan of the institution places it upon the same basis as that of the best schools of law, medicine and theology."[75] By the Depression years, a student of education could satisfy all degree requirements during nontraditional hours, but students in "law, medicine, dentistry and engineering" could not.[76] The convenience of this course of study differentiated it from other professions and marked a distinct break from past forms in these two university-based schools of education.

Even as social events and extracurricular activities became a fixture in higher education across the nation, the liberal arts curriculum remained intact across the university.[77] Such was not the case, however, in programs of teacher education. In their most direct, successful, and lasting attempt to entice students, school officials at Teachers College and the School of Education at New York University transformed the teacher preparation curriculum. By the 1930s, the "science of education" had fallen out of favor and replacing it was a "professional school where everyone interested in any phase of education may gain inspiration, added power and renewed faith."[78] University-based education professors across the city extolled the virtues of useful and readily applicable information and distanced themselves from the

New York City is not a summer resort, but thousands of persons come to New York to study during the summer. They come from almost every State in the Union, from climates more temperate and climates more torrid than that of New York.

Classes at New York University are informal. Men and women dress for the weather. After class hours there are many favorite retreats: on the roof tops there is usually a breeze even on the warmest days, and iced punch is served every afternoon to all who stop at the Students Building.

During week ends and many other times when good planning makes free time available, the students go out to the parks and the beaches easily reached by subway or boat or bus or auto. Jones Beach State Park is unmatched—it has games of all kinds, pools for swimming and diving, and white-sand beaches miles long where the whole Atlantic Ocean offers escape from the warmest weather.

New York City is warm in July, but tourists come here from every part of this hemisphere and enjoy it. There are flower gardens on the sun decks of skyscrapers and miracles in blossoms surround the fountains in Rockefeller Plaza. Most of the theaters and many of the restaurants are now air conditioned throughout the summer. These modern conveniences are welcome, of course, but for people who live in the City, and visitors too, the maximum thrills are the ride (for a dime) on an open-top bus up Riverside Drive and the sail (for five cents) on the ferryboat down New York harbor, past the Statue of Liberty, to Staten Island.

FIG. 4 "Summer in New York." (*Source*: Papers of Chancellor Harry Woodburn Chase, box 38, folder 2, New York University Archives. New York University Special Collections, Records of the Office of the President of New York University [Harry Woodburn Chase].)

academic formalism that previously shaped their work. In an endeavor to recruit students, a professor in New York University's Department of Secondary Education publicized that faculty members were "less concerned about 'scholarship' than about the knowledge and techniques of effective social engineering."[79] Continuing, Forrest Long explained, "we do not pretend to know all the answers. . . . [We] are not 'fusty pedants.'" Instead, "education 'clicks' in a friendly person to person relationship."[80]

Practical learning has become synonymous with teacher training, but the curricular intervention was motivated by several ancillary factors. First, the new curriculum represented a way to get students and their tuition dollars in and through programs quickly. The expediency of the course of study proved to be one of the major recruitment tools employed by these institutions. The "chief" factor in course offerings, Clarence Linton observed in his study of Teachers College students, must be "the financial limitations of students and the dependence of the College on student fees."[81] In 1938, William F. Russell, dean of Teachers College and son of the prior dean, reported that the school's curricula would now prepare students "for professional service with maximum effectiveness in a minimum time."[82] Second, the move toward practical learning represented a way to manage growing student populations. Institutions like Teachers College and the School of Education at New York University worked out of the same physical plants in which they were founded. Not willing to turn students away but limited by space, school officials identified practical field-based learning as a way to solve their facility dilemmas. In his 1932 report, Russell explained, "although the number of students has increased, there has been no addition to accommodations." He identified "new types of teaching" and "the use of practical situations and field problems" as ways to relieve the pressure.[83] Third, the move toward applied learning was a response to perceptions of the new students these institutions hoped to attract. In 1930, 80 percent of all of the teachers in New York City were women; as these institutions attempted to capitalize on the 1931 salary-for-education regulation, this population became their new target audience.[84]

Higher education continued to constitute a masculine space during the 1930s even as women represented more than 40 percent of all students enrolled in higher education institutions.[85] Rational and objective inquiry, the cornerstones of the academy, seemed a poor if not dangerous match to women's "inherent" natures. According to George Schuster, president of Hunter College, the goal of education for women must be "sound intellectual training guaranteed not to lead those who receive it too far from active pursuits." "While busy with books," Schuster warned his audience of female teachers-in-training and their professors, students must "blend social welfare with hymns, nursing with oratory, philosophy with the rearing of children." In Shuster's assessments, appropriate "active pursuits" for this cohort of women students centered on traditional notions of feminine capacities. In his closing remarks, he counseled, "We need to think above all in terms of womanhood and its special problems. I have been a great admirer of what has been done at several colleges . . . to prepare young women for family life, home-making and the care of children. And, I shall hope that we may be able to do something similar."[86] Echoing this view and revealing the growing connections between university faculty and local school districts, in 1935, Clyde Miller, a Teachers College professor and the director of teacher assignments for the city's Board of Education, explained to *Newsweek* readers that rather than academics, teachers needed "a pretty face, a ready smile, a well-shaped body attractively clothed."[87]

Drawing upon early articulations of the female schoolteacher as nurturing, pious, and maternal, the married teacher represented normalcy and stability in this period of economic instability and political turmoil.[88] Traditional notions of the mother-teacher informed how school leaders and teacher educators viewed female teachers. Affirming their support for the married teacher and the gendered assumptions that suffused that identity, Teachers College's committee on teacher training turned to Walter Terpenning's essay "The Educational Veil." "A much more intelligent policy," the committee members quoted in their final report, "would be to require for each applicant, in addition to a good scholastic record, a pleasing personality, good character, a marriage certificate and possibly a couple of well-disciplined off-spring, or at least evidence of a reasonable probability that the applicant can and will secure a husband and lead a normal family life. This provision would . . . raise the standards of the teaching profession."[89] The female teacher, city educators concurred, was effective and valued because of her femininity. The turn toward applied learning sprang, at least in part, from these enduring perceptions of the female intellect as it ensured that this largely female student body would focus on appropriate "active pursuits" for women.

By the Depression years, the number of prospective students seeking teacher preparation at the undergraduate level ballooned alongside the population of working teachers seeking advanced coursework. Unwilling to turn their backs on this prospective student body, school leaders at Teachers College opened New College in 1932. According to its announcement, the college would focus on the preparation of "teachers for nursery schools, kindergartens, elementary and secondary schools." Defining New College as an "affiliated school," prospective students would benefit from the faculty and facilities of Teachers College proper but would also remain separate.[90] Describing New College's curriculum, faculty members explained that "there is evidence at hand that an old order is passing." In form and function, the curriculum there juxtaposed the academic with the practical, blazing a new tradition that distinguished the education of teachers from the work of the rest of the university at similar elite institutions. "Vigorous activity," faculty members explained, would stand "in place of academic neutrality."[91] "Experience from books alone is not sufficient"; instead, students must demonstrate the ability to "utilize" all knowledge.[92] In this framework, learning without clear and immediate application was a waste of the future teacher's time.

During the Depression years, the mantra of applicability suffused the entire enterprise of university-based education programs. In 1934, both Teachers College and the School of Education began to offer a new degree: the Doctor of Education. During the first decades of the twentieth century, the School of Pedagogy railed against this degree identifying the similar Doctor of Pedagogy degree as subordinating. By the Depression years this new course of study attracted more students, nearly doubling the number of students enrolled in doctoral study.[93] According to school officials at New York University, a dissertation for the Doctor of Education degree must offer "an immediately useful contribution to educational practice."[94] Paul Mort, director of the Advanced School at Teachers College, warned "every step should be taken to prevent [education] from becoming academically minded."[95] While students enrolled in the Doctor of Philosophy programs interacted with faculty and students from across New York and Columbia universities, students in the Doctor of Education track remained firmly within the walls of the respective education programs. Institutions like the School of Education and Teachers College cast the Doctor of Education degree as emblematic of the highest level of work offered in education. In creating such boundaries, however, these programs distanced themselves and, more importantly, the work of educating teachers from the rest of the university.

This is not to say, of course, that earlier forms of academic learning disappeared from university-based schools of education entirely. Institutions like Teachers College and the School of Education at New York University continued to award advanced degrees in the history, sociology, philosophy, psychology, and economics of education. These courses of study, however, remained distant and discrete from the teacher education program. At Teachers College, for instance, only candidates for higher degrees could major in educational foundations. In his 1936 report, Dean Russell characterized the history of education as too "academic and out of touch with current problems" and "educational psychology as of relatively little use" to future teachers.[96] Adopting a new divisional structure, during the Depression years these institutions separated the work of educating teachers from the classic scholarship of the university.[97]

In the preceding decades, education faculty understood themselves as a part of their larger universities, often resisting curricular changes on the grounds that they would distinguish their work from that of their peers across the academy. By the Depression years, however, the education faculty at Teachers College and New York University adopted a different understanding of their place in the university. In the early years of the twentieth century, education students at New York University took courses across the university. At the same time, students examined the fundamental questions of education outside of the School of Pedagogy, writing dissertations on education-related topics in non-education departments. By the Depression years, the School of Education sought to end these practices and school officials offered a two-pronged argument. First, this sort of diffusion hurt the School of Education financially. Any student studying education, school officials quipped, ought to be registered for courses in the School of Education. Second, by the Depression years, faculty members began to argue that education programs offered a discrete way of studying education that could not be replicated elsewhere.

This new standpoint created friction on university campuses between faculty housed in schools of education and those in other units. In 1936, for instance, W. A. Hannig of the New York City Board of Examiners argued, "Education is comparable as a profession with law, medicine or the ministry" and, as such, "teachers should be trained for their work just as must lawyers, physicians and ministers." For Hannig and other policymakers, however, raising standards meant requiring teachers to take more education courses focused on technical skills and practical knowledge. Virginia Gildersleeve, dean of Barnard College at Columbia University, emerged as a key dissenting voice. The new requirements, she blasted, would serve only to "discourage educated persons from teaching." Finding a sympathetic compatriot at Teachers College, Dr. Ben Wood concurred and noted that an emphasis on "professional courses" would only lower the caliber of students in schools of education, "at least 60 per cent" of whom were "below the present average of liberal arts freshmen," and further "alienate many excellent students."[98] For Gildersleeve, not only did the curricula at Teachers College and other schools of education have little to do with "good teaching ability" but, she argued, "there is no certainty that courses in education warrant the time given to them."[99] Meanwhile, as Gildersleeve maintained that teachers ought to be recruited from the liberal arts colleges, Dean Russell contended, "teacher education cannot become a 'mere byproduct' of a course in general culture." Instead, for him, the elevation of "teaching standards" required "a special institution for teacher training."[100] Three years later, the same debate continued, extending from Barnard College to Columbia College when Dean Herbert E. Hawkes "warned against overspecialization in professional courses" by teachers. "Evidence from many parts of the country," he explained in his annual report, "indicates that our teachers in the public schools too often lack adequate background in knowledge, both of their subject matter and of human nature." For Hawkes, "many [teachers] possess neither the social nor the scholarly competency which teachers of our youth should have" and this was a direct function of the nature of their preparation.[101]

Similarly, by the 1930s students enrolled in New York University's School of Education programs students took all of their courses within the parameters of the school. At the same time, school officials fiercely guarded the right of the School of Education to stand as the only pathway into teaching. Faculty of education debated with their peers across the university about who could become a teacher and how. In 1935, Dean Baer of New York University's College of Arts and Pure Sciences explained to F. C. Borgeson, the coordinator of teacher training in the School of Education, that several students would like to become teachers and were interested in earning a license but also that they had no intention of transferring programs. Pointing to coursework in applied learning, Borgeson refused to allow any compromise: these students failed to meet the School of Education requirements.[102] The training offered in the city's schools of education, faculty members increasingly argued, was fundamentally different than and separate from the work of the rest of the university.

Following an early dip in student enrollment, during the Depression era university-based schools of education experienced significant growth. In 1938, the School of Education at New York University counted over 12,000 students in their undergraduate and graduate divisions, an increase of 70 percent over 1930 levels.[103] In that same year, Teachers College's registrar counted 7,948 students in the college's undergraduate and graduate programs and an additional 8,410 students matriculated in the summer session, a 30 percent increase over enrollment numbers from 1930.[104] Though school leaders feared for their institution's survival in the early years of the Depression, the turn toward applied learning represented a quick and sustainable pathway to solvency by expanding admission to a broader array of students and expediting the pathway to completion.

This growth, however, was surrounded by an aura of ambivalence. Schools of education around the nation secured their place in the university, valued for the tuition dollars they generated. At the same time, schools of education found themselves on the periphery of the university's larger academic endeavors, isolated figuratively and geographically from other departments and units of study. Moreover, even as university-based teacher education programs decisively shifted curricula in a new direction, faculty remained caught between the pull of earlier traditions and the push of the policy context. In 1936, Dean Russell convened a committee on teacher education. "Our most embarrassing moments were experienced," the committee reported, "when members of the Board of Regents of New York State accused us at Teachers College of fostering and defending the present required 'points' in history of education, educational psychology, etc."[105]

Exogenous policy pressures prompted growth but at a cost that concerned some faculty. Faculty members at these institutions struggled with what the Dean Russell characterized as "conflicting ideals."[106] Though faculty members succeeded in increasing the quantity of students, they bemoaned their students' quality. Teachers College's committee on teacher education called for renewed "interest in weeding out poor material." Reporting that too many students entered academically unprepared, the committee echoed faculty frustrations that "it is practically impossible, in student years, to improve some aspects of intellectual capacity."[107] Faculty members celebrated the growth of their programs—a direct consequence of externally dictated teacher policies—but agonized over the consequences. "We have encouraged greater participation of students . . . by late-afternoon and early evening offerings," a Teachers College committee report noted. However, the report continued, "this may be an appropriate time to consider whether we may have gone too far in this direction."[108]

Further, even as faculty at Teachers College and New York University retooled their curricula to offer a practical training in response to local and national policymakers' calls, those same school leaders also felt that university-based schools of education were failing to hold up their end of the bargain. In 1938, in their annual report, New York City's thirty-three assistant superintendents called attention to the twin factors shaping the day's educational landscape: teacher preparation and character education. "Relatively few teachers," they announced with dismay, "are ready at this time to take up the Activity Program," one of the district's primary curricular experiments. Instead, teachers "have been trained in techniques of formal recitation" and have to "depend very largely on the training they received in their own schools."[109] Observing that "teaching still falls somewhat short of equaling the time given to professional preparation" for other fields and sensing that university-based programs were not offering the sort of instruction they desired, during the 1930s local school leaders offered a range of free, district-sponsored in-service education courses that competed directly with offerings from neighboring universities.[110] In an endeavor to move teachers away from the "rigid and rather impersonal disciplinary school tone," New York City school leaders offered a range of classes. In the 1936 academic year, of 644 public schools surveyed within city limits, 10,047 teachers took 14,073 courses at local universities and through the district. Teachers enrolled in "professional" courses like Mental Hygiene and Methods as well as an array of "nonprofessional" courses including Astronomy, China Decoration, and Swimming. All in-service courses offered through the district centered on "professional study of certain more immediate larger problems of our school system," and board-appointed instructors, many of whom were administrators, were careful to avoid content that was "too theoretical to result in any practical help to one teacher."[111]

Even as school leaders reasoned that all education was of value to teachers, they expressed concerns about allowing teachers to select coursework on their own. For instance, one teacher opted to enroll in a course on interior decorating for in-service credits. In a survey, she rated that course as "valuable" and when asked how, she explained that "she had been recently married and had been decorating a new home." In another example, a teacher chose to enroll in a foreign language course but her principal felt she was "weak in methodology" and that a "wiser selection could have been made." Examples such as these prompted school leaders to wonder who ought to benefit from the course: the teacher, as an individual, or her students. Only a question at the rhetorical level, for city school leaders the answer was clear and they called for a "more systematic organization of courses" and "supervisory advice" in selecting classes. Additionally, they advocated for coursework of immediate value and readily translated into the classroom such as The Problem Child, Remedial Techniques, and Testing and Measurement.[112] Teachers' professional preparation has historically existed in a complex environment at the nexus of competing forces. During these Depression years, teacher educators in New York City made curricular modifications as they shouldered the blame for the quality of the nation's teachers and responded to institutional financial pressures and calls for municipal partnerships. The product—applied learning and applicable knowledge—would become the gold standard in teacher education. It would also set teachers apart from the forms of preparation that granted other fields professional legitimacy.

"A Houseful of Good Company": Character, Class, Culture, and Teachers' Professional Identity

Graduates of university-based schools of education articulated critical ambivalence about the nature of their professional preparation alongside faculty and school leaders. In one regard, teachers pointed to their education as a marker of their professionalism, using it to legitimate calls for higher pay and increased prestige. In a debate sponsored by the Women's City Club in 1936, Abraham Lefkowitz of the New York City Teachers Guild argued that new requirements and standards would "involve great expense to the teaching profession," but Lefkowitz and other city teachers also recognized advantages in the new regulations.[113] An informal survey of Guild members found that through the Depression years, 47 percent of teachers were employed in some sort of after-school work and 39 percent were in debt.[114] New York City, like other school systems, turned to Works Progress Administration (WPA) and substitute teachers to help meet the needs of the growing student body. By 1938, over one thousand WPA teachers filled the city's schools.[115] Such practices, the Guild argued, undermined teacher professionalism.[116] "The longer we permit nearly twenty percent of our high school staff to consist of substitutes," Guild leaders reasoned in 1935, "the more difficult it will become to maintain our present standards and to achieve higher standards."[117] The extended education requirements served a critical role in organized teachers' calls for greater respect and higher pay. In a Guild-sponsored radio address, one teacher explained to the public, "Our training is as detailed and as expensive and as painstaking as the training of any doctor or dentist or lawyer or accountant . . . [but] the average teacher takes home a monthly check in the neighborhood of $200. What doctor or dentist or lawyer or accountant, after years of service would be satisfied with an income of $50 a week? Judged by any standards, he would be considered a failure."[118]

At the same time, though, teachers also derided their education school training, arguing that even if that preparation bolstered calls for higher pay, it was largely irrelevant to their work lives. At one Teachers Guild sing-along, members mocked schools of education. To the tune of "Battle Hymn of the Republic" they crooned, "We must throw out the window all the training that we had / We'll find that boys are maladjusted, but they're never bad . . . / Our schools are marching on."[119] Poking fun at passing pedagogical fads, teachers described their professional education as a necessary but superfluous part of their careers. To little avail, organized teachers fought for control over their professional preparation during these years. In February 1931, members of the Teachers Union called for "a complete reconstruction of the course of study for the training schools."[120] Rather than passively accept education, unionized teachers demanded "professional standards of our own choosing."[121] As practical knowledge and applied learning permeated schools of education, teachers argued that they learned those very lessons more clearly and powerfully on the job and therefore on their own.

A complex set of entwined circumstances including the Great Depression's economic and social milieu and the politics of teacher unionization framed city teachers' vision of professionalism as they sought to build an identity deprived of the esoteric knowledge that lent credibility to other professions. By the Depression years, teachers, particularly married women teachers, like women workers across the labor market, found themselves and their union constrained.[122] In one regard, working women meant unemployed men. In another, amidst growing clamor over the state of the American household during the economic collapse, working wives and mothers only contributed to the perceived degradation of the home. Finally, against the backdrop of the Red Scare, teachers who advocated for themselves too forcefully seemed not only greedy but politically dangerous. While protofeminist teachers of the Progressive Era fought for workplace protections, historian Lois Scharf noted that the Depression had a "deleterious effect on . . . feminist consciousness."[123] Rather than abandon their fight for authority and respect, teachers in New York City and elsewhere redefined the terms of the conversation, casting their professional expertise within the context of the domestic ideal of the middle-class home. As historian Marjorie Murphy observed, "conditions in the schools brought on by the Depression greatly transformed teaching as a job."[124]

The Teachers Union, Local 2 of the American Federation of Teachers (AFT), had been a mainstay in the unionization movement since its formation in 1916. However, during the interwar years, a growing faction of young radical members created internal tensions and garnered the attention of watchdog groups. Union president Henry Linville wrote to AFT leadership to inform them of the situation and explained, "Briefly, the situation is one in which political groups, mainly communist factions, growing up in the trade union field in New York City, have slowly but steadily penetrated our Teachers Union. Sometimes these groups force their inter-factional quarrels into the meeting of the Union. . . . If nothing is done, the immediate future holds out the prospect of irreparable damage to the Union and to the entire effort to organize teachers of New York City and elsewhere."[125] For Linville and many of the older members of the Union, these new unionists, seemingly growing in number with each meeting, not only threatened much of what they had worked for over the past decades but their very identity as professionals. In the estimation of many long-standing members, these new teachers were uncontrollable, forceful, and dangerous: while they were all members of the same profession, these new unionists were somehow different.

Just months after Linville wrote to the delegates of the AFT's nineteenth annual convention, much of the Union's leadership, led by Linville, along with many long-standing members, decided that the situation had become unworkable and left to form their own association, the Teachers Guild. Over the next decade, the Guild and the Union remained bitter rivals as they fought for the membership of New York City's public school teachers.[126] By 1941, because of a feared Communist threat, the AFT revoked the Union's charter, and by 1950 the city's Board of Education refused to negotiate with and recognize the Union as a reputable organization, barring members from the schools. In contrast, the Guild spurned radical politics and militant action, casting itself as a "mainstream" organization comprised of "ladies and gentlemen" as it created ties with educators across the school landscape.[127] In response to school leaders' visions of the professional teacher and the incendiary local and national economic and political contexts, teachers in New York City and members of the Guild located their professional identity in an idealized notion of family life that was suffused with gendered and racialized overtones.

During another sing-along sponsored by the New York City Teachers Guild, teachers cheerfully crooned to the tune of "Paris in the Springtime," "I need money for a new dress / I need money for a new suit / I need money for the butcher, when he hollers / I need money for some shirts, with white collars."[128] The "preoccupation with class divisions" emblematic of this era infused how teachers understood their work: the vision of middle-class professionalism they offered was above all a domestic vision.[129] Whereas women of the early years of the Progressive Era situated their calls for professional authority within the suffragist movement, many women teachers of the Depression years retreated from that formula.[130] In a reflection of the political and economic context, female teachers of the Guild argued that the money they earned through their work in the schools, rather than liberating them from or redefining their domestic responsibilities, only made them better able to complete their household tasks. This rhetoric of domesticity sustained male teachers' professional persona, too. In casting themselves as the masculinized head of household and extending this image into the classrooms, male teachers softened the stigma of working in a feminized field: just as there was an important and powerful place for men in the home, so too was there in the schools. For instance, at another popular community sing-along sponsored by the Guild, to the tune of "Hernando's Hideaway," teachers sang, "I must rely upon the Guild / A happy future it will build!"[131] For these male teachers of the Guild, cast as heads of the household and sole breadwinners, teachers' low pay threatened their middle-class strivings. Male and female teachers of the Depression years functioned in the public world, but notions of private spaces inextricably informed their work identities.

Even as teaching remained a female-dominated enterprise, school leaders continued to specifically recruit male teachers, identifying their presence in the schools as inherently professionalizing, and because of the economic collapse, more men entered the teaching profession during the Depression years than had since the rise of the common school in the mid-nineteenth century.[132] Teaching represented stable work and most of the new male entrants gravitated to the high schools, an expanding space perceived to be more prestigious than the female-dominated lower grades where school leaders agreed that "a distinctly lower standard for elementary teachers was very generally accepted."[133] Organized teachers and social commentators argued that not only was teaching an appropriate space for men to inhabit but that there were elements of the work that they were particularly well-suited to perform.[134] In his essay "The 'Bad Boy' and His Teacher," printed in *High Points*, the teacher periodical sponsored by the New York City Department of Education, A. H. Lass suggested that men could deal with many of the behavioral problems marring the schools in ways that female teachers could not. In a similar vein, in 1938, Phi Delta Kappa, the professional education fraternity, published *Teaching as a Man's Job* and distributed it to high school seniors. The book, dedicated to "young men interested in education," warned readers to "make no mistake about it, teaching is a man-sized job."[135]

Local and national reformers coveted male teachers, arguing that just as there was an important place in the home for men, so too was there in the schools, and this same domestic vision framed policies around female teachers.

Due in large degree to the workplace activism of suffragist teachers during early years of the twentieth century, New York City abolished marriage banns by 1915, even as city officials required female teachers to report all personal status changes. In spite of that policy change, over the next decade, critics of the married female teacher argued that she represented a financial drain on the system: each time she gave birth or cared for her own sick child, she forced the city to hire a substitute. Nationwide, these points of opposition accelerated during the Depression as social commentators blamed working women for unemployed men. Some critics pointed to the mother-teacher's "divided allegiance." Could she adequately manage her domestic duties and her duties in the school? The city's Board of Education, however, rebuffed such claims. "The subject of employment of married teachers is no longer debatable," one board member noted in 1938, but his reasoning bore little resemblance to the protofeminist logic that initiated marital rights for teachers. "If there is anything that is debatable," he continued, "it is whether we should have unmarried teachers."[136] School reformers, like teacher educators, correlated traditional feminine gender roles with teaching credibility and maintained that married women represented better, more stable role models for children in this time of social and economic upheaval.[137]

Race, too, informed this vision of teacher professionalism, albeit implicitly. African Americans bore the brunt of the Depression years. Racial violence in the form of lynchings tore across the South and, in the North, Black adults faced an unemployment rate three times higher than their White counterparts.[138] By 1934, there were approximately 350,000 Black people living in the city, representing approximately 5 percent of the total city population. That year, Black teachers represented just 0.6 percent of teachers in the New York City schools.[139] As in other workplaces during the Depression years, available jobs went first to White applicants. Compounding this issue, local school boards in the North continued to debate the propriety of hiring Black teachers, particularly when that meant they might teach White students. Even as teachers of color attended the city's institutions of teacher preparation, they had significant difficulty finding employment in area schools. In Mount Vernon, a community about thirty minutes from New York City, Frank J. Nardozzi, president of the local board of education, agreed with the Dr. William H. Holmes, the local superintendent, that "Negro teachers should not be employed in the local schools except for classes in which Negro children are the majority." Citing a "storm of protests for parents when once we assigned a Negro substitute teacher," Holmes and Nardozzi asked, "are we to consider first the plight of the two or three unemployed Negro teachers?"[140] After a protracted battle to hire a teacher of color in New Rochelle, another community outside of New York City, the local school board appointed Miss Ethel O. Harris to work in a school that was approximately 90 percent Black. Dr. Leon R. Scott of the local National

Association for the Advancement of Colored People characterized her hiring as "one of the most outstanding events that has occurred in race relations in New Rochelle." Continuing, he explained, "It will give Negro Children a new hope and a greater ambition. It will make white people realize better that Negroes can, with distinction, perform the most important tasks of life." Harris, who held teaching degrees at the undergraduate level from New York University and at the graduate level from Teachers College, hoped that her good work "may be a means of opening up other positions in the school system of other New York cities for members of the Negro race."[141] In spite of Harris's aspirations, employment opportunities for teachers of color remained exceptionally low as hiring practices and perceptions converged to present Whiteness and teaching as analogous.

In an offshoot of Progressive education ideologies and a reflection of the class anxieties at the heart of the Great Depression, city school leaders argued in 1938 that "the development of our boys and girls into wholesome and well integrated personalities should be the ever present and predominating aim of all school routines, practices, organizations, and curriculum." According to the assistant superintendent of the city schools, "so many of our youth are anti-social in behavior." Character education would act like a social balm, easing the devastation wrought by the Depression, but school leaders also warned that the "effectiveness" of the entire program rested on "teacher personality." Rather than content knowledge or theories, in the estimation of school leaders, teachers needed enthusiasm, sympathy, friendliness, and optimism. In addition, teachers needed to be able to help their students navigate an increasingly complex world. "The movies, the radio, the automobile, the airplane, are centers of interest" that captivate children, the assistant superintendent noticed in 1938. More powerful than any social change, the most pressing problems children faced were in their own homes: "the observant teacher knows only too well the disastrous effect of child life of widespread economic insecurity among parents."[142]

Beyond book learning, school leaders reasoned that professional teachers needed impeccable character traits that pupils could emulate and the skill and tact to encourage students in the right way. School leaders framed their vision of the professional teacher through the philosophies of Dewey and Thorndike, placing teachers at the intersection of competing ideologies. As Dewey wrote in 1938, teachers were uniquely suited to improve "society through improving the individuals who compose it."[143] However, drawing on Thorndike's fundamental theories of quantifiability, school leaders asserted that improvement must be measured. The lived experiences of teachers positioned them to guide students on character education and life adjustment, policymakers allowed, but the desired outcomes would be regularly assessed through a range of exams beginning with the "McCall Brightness test to establish as a base for comparison" and extending to the Wrightstone tests on facts, social beliefs, and personality traits.[144]

Character education formed the centerpiece of teachers' professional identity during the Depression years. Teachers argued that their expertise in this area was separate from any university-based preparation and instead traced to their domestic credibility, calling upon idealized notions of the American family home in this time of distress. In their professional publications, teachers wrote about the changing world and the problems facing the schools. Elsa Becker explained to her colleagues that teachers "have seen some drastic changes in the functions of the schools."[145] City teacher Alfred Vogel concurred, noting in an essay that "education has once more reached a turning point."[146] The effects of the Depression spilled out across the city's public schools as more poverty-stricken students than ever before filled the schools. According to these teacher-authors, the problem was personal as the economic downturn rattled students' home lives. "In the troubled faces of their parents [students] see only confusion," Vogel observed. "If their homes are ravaged by unemployment and want, they suffer inwardly with the acute sensitiveness of the young."[147] Pointing to their cultural capital as professionals rather than to their university learning, teachers argued that they were uniquely suited to help their students, imbuing their professional responsibility with a social mission.

In the assessments of these teacher-authors, it was neither unemployment nor lack of adequate housing nor general want that created problems for students. Instead, the root cause traced to pupils' family lives. "How many of our behavior problems are due to the fact that parents are inadequately prepared for the profession of parenthood?" New York City teacher Daniel Krane posed.[148] Helen Fried, another city public school teacher, concurred and suggested that the current problems that ensnared students and embroiled teachers would simply not exist "if each child came to [the schools] with a good inheritance, intelligent parents, and appropriate environmental influences." "Unfortunately," she bleakly observed in 1933, "this situation does not obtain."[149] Guild leaders offered similar sentiments in their *Report on Working Conditions and Teacher Morale*. According to the Educational Policies Committee, "the problem child . . . [is] largely a manifestation of the existence of 'problem parents.'"[150] Adding to this perspective, New York City teacher Andre Fontaine wrote, "Too many times in my years of work in the high schools I have been struck by the indifference of American parents who so often seem to feel that when they feed, clothe, and shelter their children properly and then send them to school, their responsibilities end. Equally, I have been struck by the erroneous idea of many foreign born parents that the sole purpose of sending their children to school is that they may get book learning."[151] Though they brought different misconceptions to the schools, both American and foreign parents needed, in Krane's words, "re-educating." In a call to arms, he implored fellow teachers: "We must teach the parents how to train the children. . . . Let us drive ignorance and misunderstanding out of our midst."[152] The policy story that had emerged in the mid-nineteenth century with the rise of municipally supported public education systems that envisioned schools as safeguards against deficit homes echoed into the Depression era, informing how teachers understood their students and framed their professional responsibility.

Teachers traced students' behavioral, physical, emotional, moral, and intellectual problems to the dilapidation of the American home. "The trend of social and economic progress has been to dislocate the home, unfitting it as a school for 'character' and 'personality,'" wrote H. G. Shapiro, another teacher. "Changing times," he continued, "have unfitted the home as a guide for the maturing youth and placed the burden on the school." For Shapiro and others, parents were simply not able to maintain the essential orders of their homes, "let alone the old-fashioned home ideals."[153] Becker articulated a common sentiment: "Teachers have always known that the youngsters they teach bring into the classroom the habits of conduct practiced at home and the attitudes learned there—along with their homework and luncheon."[154] In her opinion, "failure in school work has . . . its roots in upsetting home conditions."[155] "Progress," Shapiro explained, "has taken from the home and handed to the school an important social function—that of training the young in habits of personal development, giving them a standard code of 'good' conduct, and, possibly, suggesting to them as basis of a sex morality."[156] According to Fried, "the school must face the situation that character training is one of its most important problems today."[157] After all, Shapiro and others concurred, "the normalcy of the community depends on the training of its young in 'correct' social attitudes."[158] "In our hands," Vogel underscored, "more than in those of any other professional group, lies the duty of building the next generation of intelligent men and women."[159] Compensating for perceived parental neglect and imparting the morals of the stable home complimented and solidified the professional persona teachers imagined, even as it pertained little to the professional preparation they received or the constructions of professional authority that delineated other groups.

According to these teacher-authors, the inadequacy of students' homes was especially hazardous given the increased dangers and temptations of the outside world. Krane explained that teachers must "neutraliz[e] those factors in our contemporary life, such as dance halls, pool rooms, movies, 'art' magazines, slide shows and tabloid dailies, that tend to destroy the ideals and standards of socially commendable behavior."[160] Teachers like Krane lamented that for their students, "that old American home has passed out of existence." More than a physical structure, though, this place housed a particular set of cultural values rooted in economic security and normative gender roles. "Time drags heavily on the hands of our young lads and lassies," Krane explained, "and it is little wonder that they often hit upon the wrong pastimes."[161] Drawing on the language of culture and class, teacher Mary Denson called on her colleagues to "elevate [students'] tastes and build up their ideals of conduct, and stir their souls with beauty." In all things teachers do, Denson continued, "we are developing fine habits of work and important standards of achievement, decent ideals of person and conduct [and] aesthetic tastes for leisure time."[162] Amy Gardin, another city teacher, agreed as she beckoned her colleagues to "awaken [students] to brighter, nobler things."[163]

This vision of middle-class professionalism not only informed teachers' interactions with their students but also how they reconciled their place in a labor union. If doctors and other white-collar professionals did not have unions, why should teachers? Even more problematically, when would the demure female homemaker find herself in a union hall? However, even as unionization and associations with other workers challenged the markers of middle-class professionalism, as these teachers imagined it, so too did the low pay teachers received. One Guild pamphlet from the early 1940s titled *Are We Orchids or Vegetables?* described the dilemma.

> It's no wonder we thought we were hot-house orchids. We were tops in our classes at school. The Board of Examiners said our range of knowledge was remarkable. Our IQ's were high. Our "t's" and "d's" and "ng's" were things of beauty. . . . Common workers might have their unions—we had special tenure and seniority. Unions are fine for the vegetables of the species, for workers. But for fine flowers like the teacher, a highly trained and cultured professional group . . . well, what have we in common with plumbers, steamfitters, bricklayers, clothing cutters, machine operators, salesmen?

As this pamphlet presented them, workers and teachers were separate entities. It was for this very reason, Gguild leaders argued, that teachers needed unions. "Can we afford to be snobs?" Guild leaders posed to prospective members. "Whether we look at it from the point of view of profession or job," they answered, "we still belong with organized labor. We cannot afford to be blinded by our own brilliance."[164]

During these years, the Guild produced a number of pamphlets that carried the dual purpose of reconciling unionization and professionalism and attracting new members. One such pamphlet, "Public Opinion Is in Overalls," stated, "Labor is on our side. It has consistently supported the schools and the teachers . . . it prevented a salary cut for us . . . it was a major factor in preventing dismissals . . . it was in Albany fighting for increased appropriations of education and salary adjustments for teachers."[165] In this formulation, not only would the union protect teachers, but it would protect the children they taught. According to another Guild pamphlet, "Teachers cannot afford to stay aloof from the rest of the working force. . . . We owe it to these working people to join with them to see that their children get the best education possible."[166] Guild leaders emphasized that even if teachers joined the union, as they believed they must, prominent and essential differences persisted between teachers and other laborers. In another pamphlet, "There's No Madness in Our Methods," leaders explained, "We believe in the right to strike, but not for ourselves. . . . We live in Rome but we don't always do as the Romans do."[167] In celebration of the organization's first anniversary, *The Guild Teacher* ran the slogan "One Year Old! Alive (And How!) But *NOT* Kicking . . . And why should we be kicking?"[168]

The Guild of the Depression years eschewed militant action both as a bolster to their professional-domestic identity and as a way to differentiate themselves from the radicalized Teachers Union. In 1942, the Guild's Social Committee produced a flyer to invite current and prospective members to the "Guild Tea Dansant." The flyer promised that at the event, teachers would "Have a barrel of fun / a cup of coffee or tea / a plate of goodies and meet / a houseful of good company.[169] At the bottom of the flyer was a hand-drawn image of a man and woman dancing. Likewise, in the late 1930s, prospective members received an invitation on heavy stock stationary for "an hour of music at a membership tea . . . at the home of Mrs. Henry Morgenthau." In addition to refined company, guests would have the pleasure of listening to Yella Pessl on the harpsichord and Frances Blaisdell on the flute.[170] Another invitation to a union-sponsored tea party during the war years pictured a woman wearing a fur stole (figure 5).[171] Removed from the realities of the Depression and separate from their university-based preparation, these events bolstered teachers' claims of middle-class professionalism.

The curricular transformations that unfolded in New York City's two elite university-based schools of education during the Depression isolated teacher education from the rest of the university and differentiated the university-based education of teachers from other professional occupations. As the professional education of doctors and lawyers during the Depression became more specialized, the training of teachers generalized, even as policymakers explicitly looked to those fields as aspirational models. The education of doctors and lawyers cultivated a "regime of expertise" as the education of teachers emphasized the creation of practitioners.[172] During the early years of the twentieth century while in a state of relative financial security, these elite institutions declined invitations for municipal partnership, opting instead for the academic traditions of the university. By the Depression years, the discourse of teacher blame brought renewed attention to teacher education and the tuition dollars new policies like the 1931 salary-for-education incentive promised proved irresistible. The confluence of market pressures, exogenous policies, and gendered

YOU ARE CORDIALLY INVITED

to a

REPRESENTATIVE TEA PARTY

to be held at the

Guild Offices, 2 East 23 Street
New York City

on

Tuesday, February 17th, 1942,

at 4:00 p. m.

* * * * * *

Come and get a cookie in return for a suggestion.

How active on activity program for reps?—is the question.

New York Teachers Guild, #2, A.F.T., 2 E. 23 St., N. Y. C.

FIG. 5 Teachers Guild Social Committee, Invitation, February 1942. (*Source*: United Federation of Teachers Records, WAG 022, box 9, folder 29, the Tamiment Library/ Robert F. Wagner Labor Archives, New York University.)

perceptions placed the training of teachers on a separate trajectory in these two institutions and ushered in the rise of applied learning. Practical knowledge had long been the province of normal school preparation. This history reveals that those institutions disappeared in name only from the higher education landscape: the forms that characterized their approach infused university-based teacher preparation nationwide, and even at elite institutions that explicitly distained that project.

The nature of teachers' university-based preparation set them apart from other professional occupations but it did not stall their claims of profession. Instead, organized teachers and school leaders framed a vision of teacher professionalism that was detached from the university and grounded in gendered and, less visibly, racialized ideas about the American middle-class home. Character education, a centerpiece of Depression-era curricular reform, supported teachers' vision of domestic-professionalism informing how they understood their students and their place in organized labor. This framing extended the policy story that envisioned public schools as safeguards against deficient homes and teachers as mothers well into the twentieth century, but it also added a new component to that historical trope. Male teachers' professional identity was domesticated, too, as they rationalized their presence in the schools and labor organizations, as well as demands for higher pay by highlighting their domestic responsibilities as fathers, husbands, and breadwinners. In the face of persistent blame, teachers pressed on during the Depression years, redefining the terms of professionalism. However, deprived of a shared academic footing, teachers had only to point to their imagined cultural capital for stature and standing, defining themselves against the students they served and hardening divisions between local public schools and communities.

4

"The Enlistment of Better People"

Responses to the Teacher Shortages of the Post–World War II Years

In his annual report on the state of the schools in 1949, Earl James McGrath wrote, "American education is now in the most critical period of its history." "As commissioner of education," he continued, "I feel that I should be remiss in my duty if I did not vigorously draw the attention of the American public to the present inadequacies in our educational system."[1] Coupled with the images of euphoric servicemen and civilians celebrating victory in streets across the nation was the sense that public schools, "the bulwark of the democratic way of life," had deteriorated "to an alarming extent."[2] Commentators agreed that the problems were many and ranged from crumbling infrastructure to inadequate funding but also that one issue rose high above all the rest: the teacher shortage. To many observers, the sheer scope of the problem was both "surprising and unprecedented."[3]

In 1945, Benjamin Fine, the *New York Times* editorialist and education reporter, alerted readers that New York City alone faced a shortfall of thirty thousand teachers.[4] The following year, Ernest Melby, the outspoken dean of the New York University School of Education, wrote that the shortage had reached "crisis proportions."[5] In spite of various interventions including salary hikes and emergency licensure, teacher shortages persisted nationally; starting in elementary schools during the immediate postwar years, staffing shortfalls reverberated across the school levels over the next decades. Reporting on the issue again in 1954, Fine wrote, "A record of more than 35,000,000 pupils, an increase of 1,600,000 over last year, will crowd the schoolhouses of the land this fall." "Nor is the end in sight," he warned somberly. "The schools can expect an increase of 1,000,000 or more annually for the rest of this decade."[6] "Is it any wonder that here and there 'recruiting' has actually taken on hysterical aspects?" one commentator posed in 1948.[7]

During these years in American history, the connection between failing schools and teachers was the most tangible it had ever been, and the discourse of blame reached a fever pitch. School leaders, teacher educators, and organized teachers concurred in their calls for merit and quality in the development of the teacher workforce and warned against mediocrity. However, they defined the underlying causes of the shortage in competing terms and offered contrary policy solutions. Once again, teacher professionalization emerged as a panacea that could simultaneously attend to persistent concerns regarding the quality of the nation's public school teachers as well as emergent quantity issues. However, answers to questions surrounding what teacher professionalization meant and how it might be measured were up for grabs and hardly unanimous. The entwined concepts of merit and quality motivating contemporary education policy suggested objectivity and thus color blindness, but each was fundamentally racialized and bound up in racist assumptions, practices, and polices that upheld Whiteness as success and Blackness as failure.

This chapter begins with "'The Tidal Wave of Students' and Teacher Shortages: Demographic Shifts and Frets over Teacher Quality and Quantity," which explores the impact of population transformations like suburbanization on urban public schools. These shifts accelerated and complicated the shortages and informed the solutions policymakers generated. The next section, "The 'Big Business of Teacher Selection': Emergency Certification and Teacher Examinations," chronicles one way school leaders in New York City and around the nation sought to mitigate the shortages. Relaxing the barriers to entry meant more adults in the schools, but even as increasing numbers of critics blasted exams as biased, organized teachers rebuffed the idea arguing that certification exams were a critical measure of teachers' professional credibility. An array of competing teacher organizations continued to exist in New York City, but during these years, the Teachers Guild, led by Rebecca Simonson and Charles Cogen, rose to prominence, speaking for more teachers than any other organization and carving out space for the rise of the United Federation of Teachers (UFT), discussed in the next chapter. Policymakers and reformers across New York State also proposed other measures, and the next section, "Fighting against 'Educational Mediocrity': Salary and Merit Pay," explores two more initiatives.

Still other reformers and critics looked beyond the public schools and tied the cause of the teacher quantity and quality problems to schools of education. The final section, "'The Pedagogical Locusts Have Devoured the Harvest': Criticism of Teacher Preparation," examines how widespread critiques changed the landscape of teacher education, ushering in regulation and accreditation.

Shortage debates echoed nationwide, as were discussions of merit and teacher education. During these years, the distance between New York City and the rest of the nation began to close with the city standing less as an exceptional example or trailblazer and more as a heightened case of trends and debates unfolding elsewhere. The discourse of teacher blame carved out space for three different policy initiatives during the post–World War II years: emergency licensure and certification, salary and merit pay, and revisions to teacher education. Each set of reforms stemmed from ideologies about the role of public schools in urban settings and yielded tangible structures that shaped teachers' work lives, together only hardening the unspoken assumption that teaching was White woman's work.

"The Tidal Wave of Students" and Teacher Shortages: Demographic Shifts and Frets over Teacher Quality and Quantity

Population growth, diversification, and redistribution propelled and complicated teacher shortages nationwide. The so-called baby crop of the war and postwar years brought a "tidal wave" of students to neighborhood schools as births immediately following the war passed the three million mark.[8] In addition to growth, and against the backdrop of the simmering Cold War, during the postwar years the racial composition of the nation's northern urban centers began to shift.[9] A front-page story printed in the *Wall Street Journal* informed readers nationwide that African Americans were "lured" North "by hopes of" betters jobs and schools and "escaping the South's present racial tensions," and also that "the shift of Negroes from the rural South to the urban North marks one of the biggest population movements in U.S. history."[10] In addition, the advent of commercial air travel brought tens of thousands of Puerto Ricans to the mainland and, in particular, to places like New York City that had airports as well as the allure of diverse communities, jobs, and housing.[11] As Black individuals and families from the South and Puerto Ricans migrated North in search of opportunity and access, the face of poverty shifted and cities became increasingly segregated.

Concurrently, as families expanded and cities diversified, suburban communities emerged. Armed with GI Bill dollars and propelled by the burgeoning American middle class dream of home ownership and domestic life, increasing numbers of White families left cities for nearby planned communities.[12]

According to Nathan Glazer and Daniel Patrick Moynihan in their 1963 study of the changing demographic landscape, *Beyond the Melting Pot*, in 1950 alone the White population in New York City dropped by nearly half a million.[13] The images of picket fences and children riding bikes in cul-de-sacs that epitomized the ideal of suburban life were inextricably entwined with racialized fears. The rise of the suburbs was not simply a turn toward better options, but it was also an explicit turn *away* from the problems of urban life, many of which contemporaries associated with the shifting racial composition of the population. The *Wall Street Journal* article warned, for instance, that "school problems have also moved North with migrating Negroes." Similarly, in 1954, Fine reported, "the Puerto Rican migration to this country has created a huge educational problem for New York school officials."[14]

The planned Levittown communities epitomized the interconnection between the rise of the suburbs and racial animosity and how both informed public education. In August 1957, William and Daisy Myers purchased a three-bedroom house in Levittown, Pennsylvania. They were parents to three small children and both college educated; William served in the Army during the war and worked as a lab technician while also studying for a degree in electrical engineering. In a documentary titled "Crisis in Levittown, PA," Professor Dan Dodson, the director of New York University's Center for Human Relations and Community Studies, narrated, "they are close to the Levittown norm except in one regard: William Myers, Jr. and his family are Negros in an all-white community." Upon their arrival, violence erupted across the community garnering national and international attention. When asked by Dodson why she and her family moved to the area, one White woman explained, "We liked the advantages that Levittown seemed to offer in comparison to other cities and we understood that it was going to be all White." Speaking from her front lawn and flanked by two young children, she continued, "evidently, he [Myers] felt that they will be accepted socially and I don't feel that they ever will be." "The whole trouble with this integration business," she explained, "is that in the end it will probably end with mixing socially . . . and I think their aim is mixed marriages and becoming equal with the Whites. But the only way they're gonna do that is by education and bettering themselves, not by pushing in the way they have here." Before closing their conversation, Dodson asked, "Do you think Myers will be able to live here comfortably?," to which the unnamed women answered, "Comfortably? No!"[15]

The geopolitical ideological context of the postwar years compounded these demographic shifts and lent a renewed sense of urgency to public education. With the close of World War II and the dawn of the Space Race and the Cold War, Americans identified international competition, national security, and domestic welfare as critical aspects of the schools' social responsibilities. "The strength of this nation is composed of many ingredients, but the most important is the quality of its citizenry," Commissioner Earl James McGrath wrote in the 1952 annual report of the Office of Education. "Recognizing this fact," he continued, "we become increasingly conscious of the decisive role of the school in shaping our nation's future."[16] Offering a similarly broad view of the social function of schooling, teacher and union leader Abraham Lefkowitz explained to the delegate assembly of the New York Teachers Guild, "Civilization can still be saved by education," and he encouraged curricula oriented around "international economic and political problems from the viewpoint of world citizenship."[17] For some, schools were essential to innovation and the nation's ability to compete on an international stage, and for others, the most pressing duties were eminently local. In 1957, the research division of the National Education Association reported, "The American public is steadily delegating to the public school systems larger responsibility for the education and welfare of each child."[18] As one pamphlet created by the Board of Education of the City of New York informed teachers, "A schoolroom today is not what it used to be." Beyond the "3R's and keeping her class in order," a teacher must focus on the "welfare of our children."[19] The perceived threats to the child's welfare during these years were diverse, ranging from nuclear warfare to poverty, but in each case Americans looked to schools and teachers, specifically, to function as a first line of defense.[20] In 1948, the American Federation of Teachers sponsored a study titled *Goals for American Education* and dedicated the report to "the classroom teachers of the world, upon whose shoulders rests much responsibility for a better tomorrow."[21]

Social commentators and policymakers agreed on two key points during the postwar years as they had before: public schools were fundamental social institutions with far-reaching goals but their success depended on teachers. As education professor Willard Elsbree warned, "If some other country of comparable size and resources entrusts the education of its youth to a more competent and a more dynamic teaching corps than ours, we will slide into second or third place as a world power despite the size of our army and navy."[22] Offering a related point, Dorothea Blyler explained, "The public schools of America are the backbone of democracy." However, she cautioned, "the schools are only as strong as the teachers who direct them."[23] Established in 1951 by the Ford Foundation, the Fund for the Advancement of Education explicitly linked teacher quality to school success and in its widely distributed report, *Teachers for Tomorrow*, wrote, "more than anything else—far more than anything else—the quality of teachers and of teaching will determine the quality of education in the years ahead."[24] Echoing as both a promise and a threat, attention once again centered on concerns about the quality of the teacher corps. In 1946, Dean Melby of New York University's School of Education wrote in the *New York Times*, "Even more disturbing than the shortage of teachers is the fact that the intellectual and personal quality of those entering the profession appears to be dropping from year to year."[25] The next month, the *Times* ran an article by Fine with a similar punchline: "Those who are interested in teaching are in the lower 50 per cent of their classes scholastically, socially and physically." According to Dr. A. C. Flora, superintendent of schools in Columbia, South Carolina, "so many school children [are] taught by thousands of incompetent and untrained teachers."[26] "The teaching profession," Fine alerted readers around the country the following year in a front-page article, "no longer attracts the top young men and women of the community."[27]

Complicating these well-worn but amorphous fears of teacher quality were tangible quantity issues. In the years following the close of World War II, various national commissions forecasted a need for more than 1.2 million teachers over the following decade.[28] Without enough adults, qualified or not, to staff public schools, class sizes soared. According to Commissioner of Education McGrath, "in many communities the shortage of teachers has resulted in classes of more than 50 children. In others education has been curtailed by dividing the school day into two sessions."[29] For Paul Woodring, director of the Ford Foundation's Fund for the Advancement of Education, and members of the research arm of the philanthropy, "no question is more earnestly discussed these days among people interested in the future of American education than the prospect and consequences of what has been called 'the tidal wave' of students which will flood our schools." "Overshadowing" all other problems, they noted in *Teachers for Tomorrow*, "is the problem of securing enough really able teachers."[30] "The heart of the problem," Hollis Caswell, dean of Teachers College, concurred, "is recruitment."[31]

The solution to the shortages was clear and largely agreed upon: hire more teachers. But local school leaders around the nation found the reality of staffing schools to be quite complex. "'What is 'recruiting' for teachers?" asked one article in *School Life*, the official journal of the Office of Education. "Is it going out into the highways and byways and flagging passersby—suitable or not—to come take classroom jobs? . . . Or does 'recruiting' mean developing in young people an informed and emotional attitude that favors teaching as a career?" Far from "an easy job," one author forewarned in 1948, finding the "right kind of new teachers" "will be an uphill climb every inch of the way."[32] In spite of the challenges, commentators agreed that the situation was urgent. "Quality, not quantity, is the essence of the teacher shortage problem," the Ford Foundation explained. If not attended to, the philanthropists maintained, "the immediate losers" of the staffing shortfall "would be the children of a whole generation, and the ultimate loser all society," explicitly connecting local schools to national outcomes.[33]

For policymakers like Commissioner of Education McGrath, the key barrier to addressing the shortage was adequate information. "We need more reliable evidence than we now have as to why some young people are attracted to teaching while others are driven from it," he explained in his annual report. Perhaps even more importantly, he continued, "we do not know what makes some highly successful as teachers and others dismal failures."[34] In addition to definitive evidence, what was also lacking was any sort of consensus as to the root cause of the problem.

Sufficient numbers of individuals deemed to be qualified were not coming to the schools; that much was clear. Not only were local school leaders unable to find teachers to meet the growing population, but they were unable to keep up with normal teacher attrition. According to a report by the U.S. Office of Education in 1949, the total number of teachers decreased across all schools over the war years; policymakers expected as much and anticipated numbers to rebound following the war. That they did not caused confusion and concern.[35] "Teaching demands the best educated and best quality of your young people," the education fund explained in *Teachers for Tomorrow*, "but so do business, government and other important fields." "Teaching," they surmised, "is not as attractive as various alternative careers."[36] A National Education Association report from 1957 noted that "expanding employment opportunities for educated women have struck a severe blow to teacher supply."[37] Labor market competition and better options elsewhere contributed to the shortage but, as many observers noted, these were not entirely new factors: why were they causing such problems now? Answers to that question oscillated. In the estimation of some observers, the core problem was salary. As Dorothea Blyler noted, "attractive wages paid by industries . . . drew teachers away from their positions and students away from college."[38] McGrath concurred, writing, "One of the most important factors in the present short supply of teachers is the relatively low salary they receive in many communities."[39] But as many were quick to observe, even with salary hikes, shortages persisted.

Teachers argued that low pay was an important issue but just one of many that contributed to the shortage. As New York City union leader Charles Cogen noted, teaching was "arduous" work made only more complex by the sociopolitical context. Writing as the acting chairman of the Teachers Guild's Education Policies Committee, Cogen explained, "To put the current situation mildly, teacher morale is in the doldrums; inertia, indifference, apathy are the prevailing symptoms of this professional malaise. More bluntly, one is struck by the tone of discontent and bitterness that sounds forth wherever teachers freely express themselves. It is a feeling obviously born of fear and insecurity, and culminating in hostility and distrust of authority, and resistance to innovations."[40] As the urban North diversified, its public schools segregated. In 1961, an article in the *New York Times* explained that the "steady increase in the number of Negro and Puerto Rican pupils is making school integration here difficult."[41] Not only had many White families left for the suburbs, but tracking policies combined with zoning regulations concentrated Black and Brown children together in certain schools and programs. "Today," one Board of Education pamphlet noted of teaching in the city, "it seems . . . an almost overwhelming job." "There are so many kinds of children to try to understand," the pamphlet posed rhetorically, "how can I understand them all?" Continuing, again in the voice of teachers, "What can I do to help children who come from bad home situations? Is there any use in even trying?" The pamphlet encouraged teachers to be sensitive and warned them that cultural and physical "deficiencies" may cause children to be "irritable in school or cross or sullen."[42]

Public schools in places like New York City offer a heightened example of the tensions playing out across the urban landscape. Even as schools and communities diversified, teaching remained a White-dominated profession. According to the U.S. Census, by 1950, fewer than 3 percent of the teachers in New York City were classified as non-White (either "Negro" or "Other Races").[43] And the historic *Brown v. Board of Education* decision only amplified the problem. Even as Black teachers were a rarity in northern public schools and had been unable to make inroads into New York City's public schools, they were a mainstay in the segregated schools of the South. Doubly taxed, Black families pooled resources to build schools and hire Black teachers.[44] The *Brown* decision ushered in the discourse of integration and equality and also the mass firings of Black teachers.[45]

Meanwhile, as increasing numbers of White teachers moved out of the urban communities in which they taught to the suburbs, New York City school leaders worried they were unable to compete with suburban school districts. According to a study sponsored by the New York City Board of Education, "for 5 years of preparation almost 30 percent of the suburban school systems pay on the average an excess of $150 over the New York City scale while for six years of preparation more than 50 percent pay an average excess that approaches $500," all in spite of years of pay hikes in the city.[46] With new school facilities, homogenous student populations, and the ability to avoid increasingly cumbersome "transportation difficulties," teaching in the suburbs emerged as distinctly easier, if not better, work, and these sentiments were inseparable from racialized perceptions of the urban landscape. It was "no wonder," the board's report concluded, "that teachers in New York City sometimes feel as if they are the proverbial 'second cousins' and envy the 'flight to the suburbs' of the novitiates into the profession."[47]

For others, the most unattractive aspects of teaching centered on poor relationships with supervisors. As one teacher anonymously wrote in the American Federation of Teachers (AFT) publication *American Teacher*, in response to claims that low salary caused the teacher shortages, "it would take a long letter to enumerate all the abuses in the school system today." "Many, many superintendents and principals," the author, writing under the penname "An Experienced Teacher," explained, "rather than exercise even a modicum of reason, merely domineer until the teacher is afraid to call her life her own."[48] Similarly, as Cogen cautioned in 1945, "emphasis on the 'professional status' of the teacher is calculated to shame him into an avoidance of the bread-and-butter aspects of the job and into a 'voluntary' taking-on of burdens that to a mere 'worker' would be intolerable." For Cogen and others, it was the conditions under which teachers worked that isolated them to classrooms and deprived them of voice that made teaching "less and less attractive."[49]

Offering yet another explanation of the teacher shortage and one starkly opposed to how unionized teachers understood the issue, for some critics and school leaders, the problem transcended salary and working conditions and centered instead on current teachers, turning to a well-worn process of problem definition grounded in blaming teachers. Even as teachers increasingly argued that the *actual* conditions of their work lives impeded recruitment and retention, policymakers in New York City and around the nation argued that teachers would be more satisfied if they had a better "self-image." Too many teachers, according to one document prepared by New York City's Board of Education in 1961, suffered from "self-pity," a malady that was "contagious in nature."[50] New York University's Dean Melby, before a crowd of five hundred prospective teachers, explained that he had grown "disturbed" by teachers' tendency to "feel sorry for themselves" and dismissed low pay as a cause of the shortage, arguing, "Money gets less important as you get older."[51] Instead, for these critics the problem centered on the "spiritual poverty of many teachers" and the simple fact that they did not adequately understand the importance of their work in the nation's schools. Of course, some critics allowed, certain teachers left because of low pay, but according to John White, "many more leave teaching because of their inability to appreciate the grander purposes and more awesome challenges of the life of the teacher-scholar."[52] Increasingly, observers argued that teachers themselves had poisoned the well. "Teachers," Elsbree explained, "have produced in the minds of those whom they taught a distinct negative attitude toward education." "It is certainly true," he continued, "that too many drab, unimaginative men and women have been admitted to the teaching profession as well as many lazy ones who chose teaching because they prized the long summer vacations and the five-day week rather than because of any real qualifications for the job."[53] According to one teacher education textbook, "it may be confidently anticipated that respect for teachers will improve as more adequately prepared people enter the profession."[54]

For others still the cause of the teacher shortage rested somewhere else entirely: the nature of teacher preparation. During the postwar years, a sea of criticism engulfed schools of education. Following the wave of curricular changes during the Depression years, critics lampooned teachers' preparation as time-wasting, anti-intellectual, and ineffective and argued that schools of education sat at the nexus of the quantity and quality problems plaguing public schools. Synthesizing the milieu, Fine wrote, "American's vast system of teacher training is in need of drastic revision. The preparation that many teachers receive today is entirely inadequate."[55] Paul Woodring of the Fund for the Advancement of Education emerged as a leading voice and argued that "teacher education and teacher recruitment are closely related problems, for it seems obvious that better teacher education will attract more and better people into the profession." "As in every field," he noted, "advancement in education comes through the enlistment of better people."[56] Critics like Woodring and Arthur Bestor, a history professor at the University of Illinois, contended that the focus on education courses, pedagogical theory, and practical training in schools of education repelled strong students and sent weak ones to the public schools unprepared. According to a survey conducted by the *New York Times*, "many educators" regarded teachers colleges as the "'weak sisters' of the nation's educational system."[57]

Out of these various definitions of the problem arose an array of competing policy solutions and three broad reform discussions intended to solve the teacher shortage: emergency licensure and certification, salary and merit pay, and revision to teacher preparation. Bound up in each discussion was the discourse of merit and its counterpoint, mediocrity, and embedded within them were competing ideas about who the professional teacher was, how that person might be recruited and retained, and if those measures failed, how the professional could be created from scratch. According to Blyler, "the future of our country depends, in large measure, on the type of people admitted to the teaching profession."[58] However, as Daniel Davies, a professor at Teacher College, warned, "The professionalization of teaching cannot be achieved harmoniously by mere adjustment of breakdowns here and there under crisis conditions. More is needed than a few patches on the pants."[59] The shared discourses of professionalization, merit, and blame during the postwar years suggested consensus, but beneath the façade of common vocabulary was discord and debate over the terms of teacher professionalism, the very concept of merit, and the root cause of teachers' shared shortcomings.[60]

The "Big Business of Teacher Selection": Emergency Certification and Teacher Examinations

In 1947, "to get a first-hand picture of conditions," Benjamin Fine "made a nation-wide tour that covered the principle cities of the land from New York to San Francisco." Reporting his findings to readers of the *New York Times*, he wrote, "Everywhere the story was the same."[61] In the face of shortages, local school districts waived licensure requirements and granted emergency certificates or hired substitutes in an endeavor to bring adults to the schools. An attempt "to stem the trek away from teaching," emergency licensure initiatives brought hundreds of thousands of teachers to the schools by circumventing existing requirements including degrees, coursework, and examinations, but in many regards this strand of reform was fraught with problems and only served to amplify the discourse of teacher blame. Even as emergency license programs in Chicago, New York, Boston, and elsewhere proved to be effective stopgaps and allowed schools to remain open, they earned quick rebuke from across the educational landscape. As one author noted, children, parents, and communities would pay the price for substandard teachers brought to the schools through emergency pathways. In addition, Edgar Dale wrote, "let's also feel sorry for communities doomed in the future to the bungling and inept leadership which will come from the kinds of schools taught by unskilled and undertrained teachers."[62]

For Arthur Levitt, the president of New York City's Board of Education, teacher examinations were the "bulwark of the merit system."[63] School leaders in Florida concurred with their northern colleagues and argued that examination and certification practices ensured that "each child's education is directed by professionally prepared and capable teachers." Those standards, Florida educators maintained, represented a key line of defense against the misuse of public funds and wasting money "on incompetent teaching service."[64] Blyler concurred, noting that certification is "a merit system for teachers" that both "protects good teachers from the competition of poorly qualified teachers" and "guarantees the public the most for its money."[65] Policymakers agreed that even as lowering or "liberalizing" certification requirements was "the easiest method available to State boards and departments of education to increase the supply of legally qualified teachers," it was also "one of the most dangerous."[66]

In the face of attempts to loosen standards, some countered with calls for even greater uniformity. During the postwar years, teachers' pathways into the schools varied, sometimes widely, state by state, with requirements ranging from six hours of professional education to forty-four. Some states offered different classes and levels of certification, whereas others, like New York, offered one lifetime certificate.[67] The certificate, rather than a mere hoop, one member of California's State Department of Education suggested, "should be the badge of membership in the profession" and allow for advancement within the teaching field.[68] By 1950, policymakers in New York State and elsewhere identified uniformity, not simply within states but across them, as a key mechanism to confront both quantity and quality problems. In creating interstate reciprocal arrangements, policymakers broadened their applicant pools.[69] However, even as policymakers pointed to uniform standards as a beacon of teacher professionalism, the nature of those regulations set teachers apart from other male-dominated professional occupations in which endogenous associations created and regulated standards for entry.

In spite of the fact that teachers had little voice in the creation or maintenance of entry requirements and standards for their profession, they nevertheless emerged as among the most vocal critics of emergency licensure initiatives. In a letter to Max Rubin, the president of the city's Board of Education, Cogen explained that "the merit system of recruitment," which examinations embodied, and "high standards of professionalism" were indistinguishable.[70] "It was a matter of deep pride," Cogen offered in a press release, that the city's teachers "had been chosen solely on the basis of demonstrated ability in an examination where all candidates faced the same problems and were measured by uniformly designed standards."[71] For organized teachers, standardized certification and licensure requirements, regardless of the content, embodied the ideals of color-blind meritocracy even as other teachers and activists actively challenged that framing as a fallacy.

Additionally, organized teachers recognized the union-busting potential of emergency licensure initiatives. According to a 1945 article from *American Teacher*, too many districts avoided making permanent assignments and instead opted to employ "'permanent' substitutes" as cost-saving measures. In Chicago, for example, elementary school substitutes earned seven dollars a day; substitutes who worked more than twenty consecutive days in Toledo could earn a dollar more. "In Los Angeles and New York City," the AFT maintained, "it has been the practice to continue employing so-called permanent substitutes for as long as eight or ten years, thus saving money."[72] This was not merely an injustice to substitute teachers: for AFT officials, the presence of uncertified school workers "was a flagrant violation of the basic democratic, trade union principle of equal pay for equal work, and a threat to standards for regular teachers."[73] The erosion of uniform entry standards undermined the union's notion of professionalism, something that was increasingly bound up in labor representation and the mantra of collectivity.

Following the war and the rise of emergency licenses in New York City, members of the Teachers Guild mounted a defense of the exams, characterizing them as essential, albeit imperfect. The culmination of this work was their 1945 report, titled *For a Better Teacher Examination*, a revision and update of their similarly titled 1939 report. For Guild members, the move to weaken or sidestep certification and licensure practices was nothing short of an attack "upon the very foundations of the merit system," and the goal in updating their recommendations was to "revive a dying confidence in the soundness of the examination systems." Guild members' critiques of examinations centered on lack of fairness and transparency. "The feeling is widespread," committee members offered, "that 'the board is out to fail candidates' rather than to select as many competent teachers and supervisors as possible." For instance, Guild members claimed that the Board of Examiners unfairly strung along too many prospective teachers. "Instead of being used to disqualify candidates after they have passed other parts of the examination, passing the Oral English test should be a qualification for taking examinations." Proper, "cultured speech," free of accents, dialects, and regionalisms, was a fundamental qualification of the professional teacher, Guild members reasoned, and the exam ought to weed out candidates with "insufficiently meritorious speech" right away. In addition, the Guild committee called for the Board of Examiners to shorten tests, make results accessible, and treat candidates without "sarcasm, indifference and seeming hostility."[74]

Meanwhile, as organized teachers and many policymakers defended certification and licensure requirements and identified standardization as fundamental to professionalization, a growing chorus of critics questioned the objectivity of the exam. In 1958, Dr. Harry B. Gilbert, director of New York City's Board of Examiners, discussed a paper on the ability to measure and predict teacher effectiveness at a conference sponsored by the Educational Testing Services. "We in the New York City school system," he explained to the audience, "are in big business in teacher selection." Even as he and others were "somewhat uneasily aware of the tremendous complexity of devising prediction instruments," as a community, evaluators placed their faith in examinations. The results of the study in question revealed critical difficulties in attempts to assess and categorize teachers through exams and, Gilbert explained, "give us much cause for concern." "Yet," he continued, "we go right on making tests designed to predict overall teaching success." "If there is one conclusion we can draw from the studies under discussion," Gilbert reflected, "it is that the plain facts indicate that we cannot select such 'superior merit teachers' with any degree of confidence."[75]

Approaching problems with the test from a different perspective, others also criticized the purported objectivity and color-blind nature of the exams. As student populations in urban areas across the country diversified, the demographic composition of the teaching population remained largely unchanged even as policymakers actively sought candidates from non-White backgrounds. In New York City, for instance, school leaders appealed for candidates who spoke Spanish to assist with and support the growing numbers of Puerto Rican children entering the schools. In 1951, the *New York Times* reported that the schools had an "urgent need" for at least "1,000 Spanish-speaking teachers to cope with the influence of Puerto Rican children." According to one study, there were "only 233 instructors" in the schools who understood the "language of 25,000 children."[76] Three years later, Fine reported little progress as "many teachers" remained "unable to cope with the new conditions as they cannot speak Spanish."[77] Motivated by the growing postwar racial politics, advocates also called for more representation of Black teachers in the schools but experienced a similar lack of traction. In 1947, one local private school wrote to Hunter College, the city's municipally supported teacher preparation program, in search of a "Negro kindergarten teacher." Because of the Ives-Quinn antidiscrimination law, graduating students did not note their racial background on registration forms for the school's career services department. Prompted by the request, faculty members considered allowing students to identify their racial background according to a code—"100-white student; 200-negro student; 300-oriental student"—on various forms, including admissions, but "after thoughtful debate . . . the department voted against any code whatsoever." Regardless of their discussion of the merits and pitfalls of allowing students to identify their racial backgrounds, faculty members at Hunter could think of no teacher to recommend for the position.[78]

For critics, biased certification exams represented one key barrier to the diversification of the teacher corps. The Guild's committee on the teacher examination estimated a failure rate of 90 percent, and a mayoral report from the early 1950s lambasted the exam as "so stereotyped and routinized that only 'insiders' who understand the examination set-up are likely to pass."[79] In the early 1960s, the Board of Education commissioned a study on teacher mobility and the extent to which teachers felt promotional opportunities were open to all and fair. According to the interviews conducted by New York University's Center for School Services and Off-Campus Courses, while nearly 74 percent of the 829 White teachers questioned felt that access to opportunities was open and fair, only 58 percent of the 90 "negro" teachers agreed with that sentiment. Researchers could identify just two Puerto Rican teachers to interview and they were spilt in their responses, leading the team to report that 50 percent of these teachers agreed that "promotional opportunities are open to all."[80]

Claims of bias and discrimination clashed with the Guild's rhetoric of colorblind meritocracy and also with their broader social justice political orientation.[81] In an endeavor to reconcile these tensions, in the mid-1950s members of the Guild participated in a drive to bring southern Black teachers dismissed in the wake of the *Brown* ruling to the city's schools through a program called "Operation Reclaim." However, the Guild's participation in the experiment was short-lived. According to the city's director of teacher personnel, "negro teachers in the South who desire to become teachers in New York City frequently have speech patterns which would make it difficult for them to meet the Board of Examiners' standards."[82] Reflecting on the Guild's retreat from the program within the first year, union leader David Selden turned to the color-blind rhetoric of merit: since these individuals could not pass this fundamental aspect of the examination, there was no point in recruiting them. For Guild leaders like Selden, the problem was with the candidates rather than the exam.[83]

Meanwhile, during these same years, the Guild also sponsored an array of programs, some in the spirit of joviality and some more serious, designed to help members pass promotional exams and in contradiction to their stance on Operation Reclaim. In the Guild's 1954 Spring Conference booklet, Max Kline contributed a poem titled "Preparing for an Oral?": "I hear a moron say 'mis**chie**vous' / As though he thinks it rhymes with 'grievous.'"[84]

At a basic level, the poem brought humor and levity to the Guild's conference. However, it also served a preparatory function as it supported teachers in the pronunciation of difficult words often on the examinations. As Kline noted in the final lines of his poem, the exam and allure of merit it offered had social implications. In this incarnation, teacher professionalism, earned and exclusive, implied stature beyond the schools: in Kline's words, it positioned teachers to "leap the social barriers." In the early 1960s, the UFT issued another preparatory series of documents but without the humor. This time, the Federation commissioned Dr. George Friedlander, a speech pathologist, to organize a lecture-demonstration and series of worksheets as practice for the oral interview. Together, members preparing for promotional tests practiced enunciating groups of words. "Hanging from the swinging branches of the trees were the ripening fruits of the orchard, swaying and reddening in the sun," New York City's organized teachers recited together.[85] Fraught with contradictions, unionized teachers' defense of certification exams reflected the broader politics of race during the post–World War II years. When it came to teachers of color, the exam was an accurate and definitive measure of worth. When it came to their own White members seeking advancement in the schools, the exams transformed into a necessary hurdle replete with tricks and pitfalls that, if warned of in advance, candidates could avoid.

Fighting against "Educational Mediocrity": Salary and Merit Pay

Not long after local policymakers in large cities like New York, Chicago, and Boston offered emergency pathways into the schools did they realize that those initiatives were fraught with problems. In addition to sparking quick rebuke, emergency pathways were not wholly successful in filling classrooms with able adults, their primary objective. The postwar years changed the milieu for teacher hiring in dramatic ways. Prior to World War II, teaching in large cities represented coveted work that offered salary and a degree of status to the largely female corps. As a result, lists of eligible teachers who passed examination and certification requirements but could not obtain placements remained long. As principals needed to fill positions, they simply turned to the lists for a seemingly endless supply of vetted candidates. Following the war, principals in New York City once again turned to the list to appoint 905 teachers but to their great shock, more than half of those offered positions declined, an outcome one administrator characterized as an "unheard of condition." The majority of individuals on the list "have scorned these jobs, which in former years were considerably prized," the *New York Times* reported in 1945.[86] The problem, it seemed, was not that there were not enough prospective teachers but that there were not enough prospective teachers who, when faced with other options, wanted to work in the public schools. Shouldering concerns of teacher quantity and quality, city school leaders quickly realized that emergency pathways and similar stopgap measures alone would not be enough to confront the staffing problems of the postwar years; instead, they would have to do something they had not done before: actively recruit teachers.

During the war years, New York City school leaders made a first foray into widespread recruitment and the centerpiece of this largely unsuccessful and highly contentious line of reform was financial remuneration and reward. "Just to show that it is not provincial," Fine reported, "the New York City school system has issued an invitation to outstanding educators, regardless of where they reside, to apply for teaching and administrative positions here." For policymakers, the recruitment endeavor was part of a larger campaign to "bring 'new blood' into the city, thus avoiding the dangers of excessive inbreeding."[87] Following the war, Chicago school leaders similarly opened their "ranks to outsiders" and "for the first time in more than a quarter of a century" devised recruitment programs in colleges statewide.[88] By the late 1950s, motivated by the National Defense Education Act and Cold War concerns of national security and international competition, school leaders across the nation launched national recruitment drives. For instance, New York City's Office of Informational Services prepared an advertisement that appeared in newspapers nationwide. "Our country's security demands that we train sufficient numbers of skilled mathematicians," the announcement read. "New York City's Board of Education may have the job just for you—if you are a college graduate or a senior with a background in mathematics."[89] Recognizing the array of factors that impeded prospective teachers from coming to the city, including the allure of suburban schools and living, New York City's Board of Education created a collection of recruitment materials that touted the benefits of urban life. "Teach in New York City," a flyer sent to colleges across the country beckoned, the "cultural center of the world." Actively writing against the *Blackboard Jungle* portrayal in which city schools were dangerous places, the pamphlet publicized the "advantages of living and teaching in a city that has everything from the Met and Lincoln Center to world-famous museums and libraries."[90]

Policymakers across New York also understood that tangible considerations like remuneration figured heavily in their ability to attract top talent and fill the state's public schools. By 1947, teachers from San Francisco to Buffalo to St. Paul to Jersey City and elsewhere walked out of the schools on strike demanding higher pay. Even as many teachers won salary increases, states like New York mounted muscular defenses in an attempt to prevent similar future action. In the wake of the Buffalo strike, in which teachers won a $625 annual salary increase, the New York State Legislature passed the Condon-Waldin Act mandating a series of penalties for striking teachers and public servants including a five-year probationary status and forfeiture of seniority rights as well as any salary increases for a period of three years.[91] Even as the Condon-Waldin Act prohibited teachers from striking, it remained an open question whether local school leaders would have the political will to enforce the act's harshest provisions, and even as the act prohibited strikes, postwar militancy empowered teachers who realized they still had a range of labor disruptions in their arsenal short of a full strike.

The postwar years, however, were an enormously complex time in school politics: as teachers struck and tested their collective voices in new, more assertive ways, the brewing red scare served as a powerful counterbalance, tamping down dissent. New York State's Feinberg Law, colloquially named after the authoring state senator, sat at the nexus of fears of subversion in the schools, teacher shortages, and the rising tide of teacher militancy. At once, the law's various provisions carved out space for red baiting and the Communist purges of the 1950s and attempted to both minimize teacher discord in the state by creating a single salary system and entice more and better teachers to the schools through salary increases and a merit pay plan.[92] The Teachers Union, which had its AFT charter revoked in 1940 because of ties to the Communist party, and the teachers affiliated with that organization, bore the brunt of the Feinberg Law's provisions around subversive behavior. Cogen and other Teachers Guild leaders opposed the investigations that the Feinberg Law spawned in the name of academic freedom but also remained largely unscathed as investigators viewed Guild membership as a signal that one was not a Communist.[93] Instead, the Guild reserved most of its energy for engaging the single salary and merit pay provision of the law, each of which sparked debate.

For state lawmakers, sections 5 and 6 of the Feinberg Law that established the single salary schedule and merit pay plans represented a package of reforms intended to confront the quality and quantity problems generated by the teacher shortages. Before the Feinberg Law, school districts in New York, as did those around the country, paid elementary, junior high, and high school teachers according to separate salary schedules, creating a career ladder of sorts that cast high school teaching as the most prestigious and involved work and elementary teaching as entry level. During the first years following the war, shortages around the country were most acute in elementary schools, where the first wave of baby boom children entered kindergarten. Salary equalization, state policymakers argued, could help bring teachers to the places of greatest need: elementary schools. Elementary school teachers celebrated this provision as a victory. However, even as the salary equalization cost high school teachers nothing, they opposed the plan, arguing that it devalued their work, bringing to the surface long-standing tensions within the teaching profession animated by gender divides.

The merit pay provision brought organized teachers together in the way the single salary schedule drew them apart: on this matter, they were opposed. The allure of meritocracy, a term coined by British sociologist Michael Young in 1958, spread internationally and in spite of Young's satirical framing, as the concept reflected the prevalent mood and suggested an objective way to measure success and influence.[94] According to the law, following six years of service teachers could earn pay increases only through promotional increments. Rather than receiving the annual step increments, teachers would need to offer evidence of exceptional service and only teachers of "superior merit" would earn a salary increase. For state policymakers, the merit provision would spark competition and innovation and allow school districts to pay teachers their actual worth. Drawing on free-market theories, proponents argued that remuneration of this ilk would both recruit a new brand of person to the field who was eager for competition and higher pay and encourage others to do better. Merit pay, in this formulation, would function as a reward and an incentive. In appraising the law, Abraham Lefkowitz, the Guild's legislative representative, noted "we regret that we cannot claim 100% victory." While the organization lauded the single salary schedule and the guarantees of increases for at least the first five years of the teacher's career, "the outstanding weakness," Lefkowitz wrote, "is the superior merit provision," and he called on teachers not to rest until it was eliminated.[95]

The Single Salary Provision

Single salary schedules, first codified in New York but then adopted in cities and states across the nation, represented a victory for both elementary school teachers and teacher organizations for related but also distinct reasons. At a first level, the schedule promised equity across school divisions. Though women had dominated the teaching profession since the earliest days of the common schools, they were concentrated in the elementary schools, whereas male teachers often made their way to the high schools. By 1950, for instance, of the 43,587 public school teachers in the New York metropolitan area, 73 percent were women. The GI Bill brought unprecedented numbers of men to the public schools and most of them found positions in the public high schools, where the gender breakdown was nearly fifty-fifty. Meanwhile, the elementary schools, which housed the greatest number of teachers, remained staffed by nearly 90 percent women.[96]

According to Guild president and former elementary school teacher Rebecca Simonson, "single salary policy means that all teachers, regardless of grade level or subject they teach, receive the same salary if they have the same educational qualifications and years of experience." For Simonson, the Teachers Guild, and teacher organizations nationwide, teacher qualifications—the embodiment of their merit—could only be objectively accessed in three areas: certification examinations, degrees and credit hours earned, and years of service. Continuing, Simonson explained, "This policy is equitable and just. It closes the door to possible discrimination against individuals and groups." For champions of the schedule, not only would a single salary induce more teachers to come to the elementary schools but it would right the misperception that high school teaching represented more important or more difficult work. "An elementary school child deserves as good a teacher as a high school child," Simonson noted. And further, "all children must attend elementary school . . . but only slightly more than half of children who enter high school ever graduate. It might be argued that the elementary school positions should be staffed by the best qualified teachers," she suggested in 1957. As very few teachers could "afford the luxury of teaching in lower paid positions," in Simonson's estimation, the single salary schedule would allow teachers to work in the spaces where they felt "they are most able."[97] In a speech delivered at a meeting of the League for Industrial Democracy, during the war years, Simonson highlighted the strained position of elementary school teachers, noting that it was not until the high schools that teaching "begins to take on dignity."[98]

For labor leaders, more broadly, the single salary schedule marked a key step in the development of the union mantra of collectivity for teachers. In the summer of 1956, Chicago teacher and labor leader Carl Megel spoke at the American Federation of Labor and Congress of Industrial Organizations convention in Pittsburg and called for single salary plans to be adopted nationally. Compensation of this type, he argued, would eliminate favoritism and "educational mediocrity." For Megel and the AFT, after certification, the only way to measure a teacher's merit was through training and experience. Megel's speech and, in particular, his cautions about mediocrity were captured in an article by the Associated Press; the following morning, people across the nation read of the connections between low salary, differentiation, and educational mediocrity.[99] For national labor leaders, the single salary schedule was less about elementary school teachers than it was a cornerstone in the developing mantra of union solidarity.

In spite of this support from union leadership, the single salary schedule amplified long-standing tensions within the teacher corps. From the start, high school teachers opposed the plan, maintaining that it devalued and deprofessionalized their work. As baby boomers made their way to high school in the 1950s, so too did the teacher shortages, which only served to intensify high school teachers' opposition to uniform pay plans. According to a pamphlet titled *Crisis in New York City Public High Schools* by the High School Teachers Association (HSTA), "once the preeminent in the nation," New York City high schools "are in a crisis stage." Causing this problem? According to the

HSTA, "the continued underpayment of the high school staff has contributed materially to aggravate the situation which is undermining the foundations of the secondary school system." In contrast to elementary school teachers, union leaders, and policymakers who argued that teaching, regardless of level, was a singular job, high school teachers maintained that teaching at the secondary level constituted different and more difficult work and likened high school teaching to obtaining a professional promotion.[100] Prior to the single salary schedule, elementary school teachers could earn a maximum pay of $3,390 in thirteen steps, junior high school teachers could earn a maximum pay of $3,830 in twelve steps, and high school teachers could earn a maximum pay of $4,500 in fifteen steps.[101] The single salary schedule erased the disparities across levels and, by 1956, all city teachers could earn a maximum of $7,600. The HSTA argued that equalized pay not only hurt the morale of high school teachers and degraded their professional stature but also treated them unfairly. In terms of percent increase over prewar levels, high school teachers' salaries increased by approximately 68 percent, while elementary school teachers enjoyed a raise of more than 124 percent. "Because of the imposition of the so-called single salary method of payment," the HSTA complained, "New York City high school teachers have suffered unfair economic treatment since 1947." For members of the HSTA, a male-dominated group, pay was important but so too was the psychic value of differentiation. Without that, they argued, "qualified personnel who might otherwise enter the teaching field are turning to more lucrative endeavors."[102]

Boston was one of the few cities that did not have a single salary plan by the mid-1950s and the opposition of high school teachers played a key role in maintaining salary differentials. "In Boston," an article in the *Christian Science Monitor* explained, "teachers automatically receive a few hundred dollars more because they teach at the high-school level. The trend in more large cities has been to do away with this—giving all teachers at all levels equal pay for equal experience in training." In spring 1956, three hundred elementary and junior high school teachers squeezed into a committee hearing room to call for salary equalization and three hundred more, "kept from the hearing room by fire laws, listened from the halls." Despite their strong showing and the national precedent, the city's four hundred high school teachers mounted a powerful opposition. Joseph Lee, the chairman of the committee, explained that "we should concentrate on aiding the high school teachers first in order to encourage more professionals to fill the growing need."[103]

At its base, the opposition from high school teachers struck a historic chord. For school leaders around the nation, male teachers represented a coveted yet elusive breed and with the close of World War II, school leaders made their most direct and successful plea for male teachers. "How to reorganize . . . to suit the needs of the returning veteran," one Guild report explained, warranted "immediate concern."[104] In the winter of 1946, Guild President Simonson wrote to the Board of Education regarding returning teacher-veterans. "What is to be done for the veteran who indicated his desire to return to the school system?" What would the board do, she inquired, "to render his return and adjustment to the school system as simple and effective as possible?"[105] Writing on behalf of the Board of Education, Associate Superintendent Jacob Greenberg explained that administrators would ease veterans' return to the schools. "If the veteran is interested in being transferred to another school, a complete list of school teaching vacancies is placed at his disposal," he wrote. And further, the board agreed to waive "existing sabbatical leave regulations . . . in order to grant sabbatical leaves to veterans who are interested in studying under the GI Bill of Rights."[106] In 1946, *American Teacher* ran an advertisement for Encyclopedia Britannica Films. Encouraging schools to buy this media, a young veteran dressed in a suit and tie stood before a chart measuring flame speed. The caption above him advertised, "He made men out of boys! He's out of uniform now—back in the schoolroom where he taught before Uncle Sam called him to duty. . . . He'll be eager to take the lead in using films as a dynamic instruction tool in his own school."[107] The following month, Irvin Kuenzli wrote that "the Veterans of World War II should constitute a splendid source for securing teachers for the schools in the postwar society." However, he cautioned, "we cannot hope to attract this splendid group . . . when the rates of pay are so disgracefully low."[108] The presence of men in the schools, many contemporaries argued, could professionalize teaching.

Following the war, Phi Delta Kappa launched a recruitment program designed to bring men to the schools and in 1948, Louis Kaplan, the head of the department of education and psychology at Oregon College of Education, contributed an article in the association's publication explaining why male teachers were needed. Enumerating six points, Kaplan argued that men "are usually more stable and better adjusted than women teachers" and that male teachers' presence in the schools would teach the female student "how men behave and how she should behave toward them."[109] In another article printed in *Phi Delta Kappan*, Francis Horn got straight to the point: "We all know that it is low salaries which keep men out of teaching or which makes so many men who stay in teaching frustrated and harassed individuals." According to Horn, the single salary, even as it "greatly arouses our female colleagues," was the fundamental barrier to the recruitment of male teachers. Harkening back to the family wage argument, Horn and other advocates of pay differentials argued that male teachers required more money as heads of households. Men, Horn argued, "must use the advantages we have, control of school boards and administrative positions, to put through a sound family allotment plan," for "it is imperative that we have more men in the schools." Pay differentials, for Horn and many high school teachers, were not only critical to luring men to the schools, they were professionalizing. Either teachers "are professional people" or "they are simply employed men and women—laborers, if you will," Horn posed. "I am convinced," he closed his article, "that the rise of unions in the teaching profession has been undesirable."[110]

Merit Pay

Whereas the adoption of the single salary schedule revealed tension and discord within the teacher corps, calls for merit pay unified classroom teachers. Merit pay plans first surfaced in Gary, Indiana, St. Paul, and Minneapolis during the early 1920s and fizzled out of existence during the Depression years. Following the war, calls for merit pay surfaced again, first in Pennsylvania in 1945 and then in New York with the Feinberg Law in 1947. Under the New York State plan, optional for local districts to implement, teachers would earn step increments on a single salary schedule for the first six years of service. Following that point, teachers in districts with the plan could earn promotional increments by submitting "objective evidence" of a range of "special contributions" including "exceptional service to pupils" and "exceptional service to the community through non-school activities." Under the New York plan, after the first several years of service, increased salary would come only from "demonstrated merit."[111] For many observes, the Feinberg Law presented an exciting moment. "Never before in the history of public education," one newspaper article noted, "has an attempt been made to obtain from a body of more than 30,000 teachers and supervisors their ideas concerning what constitutes good teaching."[112] According to Dr. J. Cayce Morrison, assistant state commissioner of education in New York in 1948, calling on teachers to "demonstrate professional progress to be entitled to salary increments" represented "the greatest experiment in improving the teaching service of the public schools that the country has witnessed since Horace Mann founded the first normal school."[113]

Following the enactment of the law and its adoption in localities throughout the state, with the exception of New York City where leaders opted out due to fierce opposition from organized teachers, Governor Dewey and Dr. Francis T. Spaulding, the state commissioner of education, assembled a special committee of assistant superintendents charged with defining teacher merit. All agreed that teachers should "possess those characteristics that make for a wholesome personality in a democratic society." The committee also agreed that "love and friendliness to youngsters" as well "sympathy" and "sound judgement" were critical factors in teacher success and professionalism.[114] Even as advocates noted opponents' "phobia" of merit, they argued that the pay plan would help to professionalize teachers and improve the public schools.[115] For A. S. Barr, all of the confusion and antagonism centered on "the naiveté in the application of evaluation techniques." "The evaluation of human efficiency is an exceedingly complex and difficult matter," but one grounded in science, he assured.[116] The "lock-step fashion" in which teachers had been paid, proponents of the plan offered, was not only deprofessionalizing but also undemocratic.[117] "In a democratic society," Wendall Wilson wrote in 1960, "reward should be based on the quantity and quality of the contribution made by the individual."[118]

The merit pay provision promised at least three gains for public schools. First, it would be a cost-saving measure. Too many districts, Terrel Bell explained in his book on recognizing and rewarding competence, increased "the salaries of some of the poorest teachers to the level of the best in order to pay the best on a scale commensurate with contribution."[119] Second, competitive remuneration would enable schools districts to lure better people to come to the schools and to reward them with competitive salaries. Third, like boats rising with the tide, merit pay plans would entice mediocre teachers to do more. "Merit pay is not only an equitable way of recognizing superior quality of service," one supporter summarized, "it is also a means of encouraging improvement in the teaching process."[120]

For organized teachers, there was no middle ground on the issue; instead, offering an array of opposing points, unionized teachers in New York and around the country enumerated the dangers of merit pay plans. For leaders and rank-and-file members of the AFT, merit rating was "a dangerous mirage," a phrase coined in 1957 by Mary Herrick of the Chicago Teachers Union and a leader in the national organization.[121] Policymakers promised professionalization and higher pay, but organized teachers saw partiality, disempowerment, and the erosion of the union. For Herrick and others, merit evaluations were nothing more than a "last ditch salary system based on subjective ratings."[122] Unionized teachers, like policymakers, agreed that teachers were important and that good teaching mattered for student success. But what was good teaching? In Herrick's pamphlet *Merit Rating: Dangerous Mirage or Master Plan*, produced for the AFT, she observed "there is no agreement upon what constitutes 'goodness' in teaching." Many, including Wisconsin professor A. S. Barr, generated lists of characteristics of effectiveness that included attributes like intelligence, emotional stability, buoyancy, attractiveness, and refinement. For some, Herrick noted, "the teacher is to be creative and adventurous, talkative, vivacious and witty, and at the same time sober, reserved, and modest." In other evaluation plans, teachers should be "self-confident, forceful, courageous, independent, insensitive to social approval, self-sufficient and self-assertive, and at the same time, an 'easy going realist facing life, not excitable, polite, tolerant, flexible, trustful and charitable."[123] The only way to avoid subjectivity "and protect the superior teacher from unfair, inadequate, inept, or vindictive rating," Carl Megel explained to listeners in 1955 on the Christopher King Sounding Board, a national radio program, "is a salary based on training and experience."[124] Merit ratings in these schemes, union leaders argued, would judge teachers' professional worth and offer reward based on "mere vague impressions." And further, exactly what, they asked, would be the tangible difference between "a teaching performance which should be rated 'Superior' and one which should be rated 'Excellent'?"[125]

Bringing to the surface long-simmering trust issues, teachers expressed little faith that building leaders could evaluate them fairly and argued that subjecting teachers to high stakes evaluation by administrators was degrading. The AFL resolved in October 1947 that basing teachers' salaries "on rating schemes . . . would place in the hands of school politicians a powerful weapon by which the freedom and initiative of the classroom teachers would be seriously curtailed and political bootlicking, rather than professional efficiency in the classroom, would be encouraged."[126] Promotion would be based on merit in name only, cautioned John Eklund, the president of the Denver Federation of Teachers, but it would really be a consequence of the teacher's "subservience" to the principal and the "building of patronage."[127] "Demoralization" would be inevitable, Simonson offered. The merit evaluation plan would cause administrators "to play one [teacher] against the other"; "it would breed suspicion and rivalry." Perhaps most important of all, Simonson and others asked what problem this intervention solved. "What is wrong with our profession?" she posed. Offering her own answers, she listed "lack of preparation and equipment and thousands of sub-standard teachers on emergency licensure." The merit system, she concluded, would intensify "old-fashioned supervision, a system of rewards and punishments," but leave the underlying problems intact.[128] Finally, even if principals found an objective method of evaluation, how, union leaders asked, could they feasibly evaluate all teachers?

In teachers' collective estimation, regardless of school level, the proposed arrangements were destined to fail and teachers would be the casualties. In June 1950, *High Points* published a parody sung at the twentieth anniversary of the Abraham Lincoln High School. To the tune of the popular Eileen Barton song released that year, "If I Knew You Were Comin' I'd've Baked a Cake," teachers sang, "If I Knew You Were Coming I'd a Made a Plan": "Knock knock knock . . . well, well, my chairman's here! I haven't seen you in over a year! / Chairman: 'I know it's eighth period. I know it's Friday. I know it's June 16th. But you don't mind if I come in to observe you this period, do you?'"[129] For union leaders, the writing was on the wall: under merit plans, teachers who wished to advance and earn more money would have no choice but to conform to the whims of building leaders, sacrificing their professional credibility and authority for financial gain.

Teachers were not the only ones to oppose merit evaluation plans on these grounds. Prominent education leaders like Professor Willard Elsbree of Teachers College and Dr. John Studebaker, the U.S. commissioner of education, expressed strong doubts as well. For Elsbree, merit rating plans would further drive apart teachers and administrators. "Instead of feeling free to discuss her difficulties and problems with the supervisor and asking for help," he forecasted, "the teacher tries to hide her weaknesses, minimize her faults, and cover up her failure. This not only renders rating more difficult, but tends to defeat the primary purpose of supervision." Offering a different line of criticism, Studebaker noted that perhaps certain teachers were better than others but, calling attention to the fickleness of evaluation plans, he asked, by how many dollars and cents?[130]

"Teaching is a complex art in which no single method has been demonstrated to be right or best," Herrick noted, contributing a sentiment shared widely among teachers and across universities. Moreover, as school leaders in places like New York City and elsewhere knew all too well, the context of the individual child and the circumstances of the community and school environment were significant factors that contributed to teachers' willingness to work in particular areas. Merit evaluation plans seemed to turn a blind eye to these issues, in the estimation of organized teachers. "Teachers with inadequate equipment, in poorly cared for buildings under double-shift conditions, will not show as tangible accomplishments with perhaps much greater personal effort as if their work were being done in more favorable surroundings," Herrick offered.[131] "Merit rating," Megel told listeners of the King radio show, "disregards the type of environment in which teaching takes place."[132]

Another key critique leveraged by teachers, organized or not, against merit evaluation was the fact that policymakers were misguidedly applying business models to the education sector. Writing under the pseudonym of Jay Belmock, one teacher characterized merit plans as the product of "the conservative industrialist and the businessman": "Businessmen claim that teachers have become bogged down in the stalemate of security. Pointing to their own success in paying salaried personnel on the basis of what they feel each contributes to the smooth functioning of the total organization, they claim that fresh, dynamic ideas are the product of a merit pay plan. Competition is once again the magic ingredient that will cure all ills. This is hogwash." Continuing, Belmock offered, plans like the ones proposed in the Feinberg Law "might well destroy our educational structure by replacing the cement of patience, understanding and quiet competent skill with the dog-eat-dog mixture of competitive striving to gain a few more dollars than your colleagues are receiving."[133] "We realize that, to the general public, merit-rating sounds sensible," wrote Margaret Walsh and Harriet Pease, leaders of the Empire State Federation of Teachers, in *American Teacher*. Responding to the common refrain "It is used in industry, why not the schools?" Walsh and Pease offered that the nature of teachers' work and of the schools, generally, were not comparable to business conditions. For one, many of the "most important and far-reaching" consequences of good teaching "lie in the field of intangibles, among those things which can not be measured, often times not even observed."[134] Concurring, members of the Schenectady Federation of Teachers offered in opposition to merit plans the fact that "the lasting effects of a teacher's work, unknown even to himself, may appear in a pupil's life many years later. Who is qualified to set monetary value on one teacher as opposed to another?"[135]

Finally and perhaps most importantly among all the critiques, for union leaders, merit pay plans were seen as unambiguously anti-union and designed to corrode teacher organizations. Merit pay, Belmock noted, would "destroy the unity" of teachers.[136] David Tiedman, a Harvard professor and advocate of merit evaluation plans, explained in a speech delivered to the New England Association of School Superintendents, "The issue is professionalization or unionization."[137] Union leaders were caught in a difficult spot, at once agreeing and disagreeing with Tiedman's claim. During these years and over the history of teacher unions, labor leaders strenuously denied that profession and union existed in contradiction. However, they also agreed that the version of professionalization policymakers offered through merit pay plans was dangerous. In many regards, Tiedman's remark encapsulated the entire debate where, at the base, organized teachers and policymakers defined teacher professionalism and merit in competing terms. For organized teachers, merit was a badge the professional teacher owned; unchanging and static, merit could only be assessed in three spaces: certification, degrees earned and credit hours completed, and years of teaching experience. At its core, organized teachers' definition of profession echoed fundamental labor principles of standardization and collectivity. For policymakers, merit was flexible and fluid, both earned and demonstrated over a career. Organized teachers allowed that even as the notion was enticing superficially, it was simply untenable in public schools where "teachers work in a mass occupation under conditions over which as individuals they have little control."[138]

In 1951, the merit pay situation exploded in Schenectady, New York. Unlike New York City, which had opted out of the merit pay experiment, many cities upstate opted in, and even as organized teachers there offered the same points of contention as their peers downstate and around the nation, evaluation initiatives proceeded. In many regards, the situation was both a realization of organized teachers' worst fears, the embodiment of all that could go wrong with merit rating schemes, and a true gift as it provided tangible evidence of their criticisms. The 1950–1951 school year was the first time merit rating had been applied to classroom teachers in the city. In the fall, officials from the central board of education notified 188 teachers that they would be evaluated if they wished to obtain the promotional increment; 12 declined to participate, most because of retirement. It was not until the following August that teachers learned the outcome of their evaluation: 149 had been promoted and 27 had been declined promotion.[139] Upon hearing the news, the Schenectady Federation of Teachers prepared a flyer that read, "VERY IMPORTANT: Please circulate this bulletin *immediately* among all the teachers in your building." "We have been told that 27 teachers did not receive merit rating promotions this year. We do not know who these teachers are." Offering assistance and support, the flyer closed, "in union there is strength."[140] By the fall of 1951, the Schenectady Federation of Teachers had identified the twenty-seven teachers and the AFT promised financial support to defray legal expenses.[141] For local union leaders, the cases provided clear evidence of discrimination against teachers: some teachers claimed that derogatory statements in their files were false or misleading, others claimed principals never actually observed their teaching, and still others "stated that their activity in the Schenectady Federation of Teachers has apparently been an important factor toward unfavorable rating."[142] Considered in sum, for teachers in Schenectady and around the nation, the case plainly demonstrated that systems of merit pay "have never successfully worked out in practice."[143]

William Schoomaker, the teachers' lawyer, constructed a six-point defense. First, under the Feinberg Law, teacher evaluations were to be a continuous process in which principals and teachers met regularly for observation and to discuss feedback. In the case of the twenty-seven teachers denied promotion, Schoomaker argued, "Teachers being evaluated received no 'appraisals,' 'conferences' or 'discussions.'" Instead, "there was only a 'spring check-up.'" For Schoomaker and members of the Schenectady Teachers Federation, "the practice was an outright negation of the accepted principles that evaluation should be a continuing process." Second, even as commissioner regulations required that "each teacher's confidential record shall be available to that teacher," the teachers were unable to access their materials until the board announced their decision. Third, the feedback offered by evaluating supervisors was "extraneous and irrelevant."[144] In Schenectady, principals rated teachers according to a guidebook in which they evaluated teachers on personal and professional qualifications including grooming and sense of humor, measures of teaching effectiveness including "pupils show interest and enthusiasm," and relations with colleagues and the public including "meets parents easily and graciously" and "makes friends for the school system."[145] The twenty-seven teachers denied promotion received feedback such as "I believe she spends her time outside of school with her sick husband" and "he needs to develop a sense of humor."[146] In Schoomaker's remaining points, he argued "there was no uniformity in correlation between services and numerical rankings," rankings were subjective and "irregularly obtained," and "there was not sufficient observation of appellants to permit a valid evaluation."[147] In February 1952, before Schoomaker had finished presenting his case in court, the Schenectady Board of Education voted to eliminate merit rating and revert to a single salary schedule that included regular annual increments.[148]

Even as the merit provisions of the Feinberg Law never took root in New York City, organized teachers remained on high alert and deeply wary of any mention of merit evaluation. A brief skirmish during the fall of 1958 between then–Guild president Charles Cogen and city school superintendent John Theobald highlights the incendiary nature of the topic and the growing power of the teachers union. In the first weeks of October, local newspapers quoted Theobald as expressing interest in the idea of bringing a merit pay plan to the city. When Cogen wrote for clarification, Theobald responded, "I believe the Guild has misunderstood my stand with regard to teachers' salaries." However, while he noted that "our salary schedules are in need of revision upward," he also wrote, "I feel very strongly . . . that teachers should not automatically go to the maximum of the schedule, regardless of the manner in which they perform their duties." Continuing, Theobald explained that even as "a system of merit increases" would "require some very careful study," ultimately he thought "that it can be done."[149]

Six days later, Cogen sent a telegram to Theobald expressing teachers' alarm at his "repeated public references to merit rating" and requested a meeting "to discuss salary increases on an acceptable basis for all teachers."[150] Not willing to waste any time, the next day the Guild issued a press release. "There is a real school crisis in New York City," the release began. "We deplore the injection of the Superintendent of the controversial question of merit rating of teachers into this serious situation. We have sent him a telegram to this effect. Whatever merit rating has been attempted, it has been destructive of teacher morale. Furthermore, discussion of this tangential issue diverts attention from the seriousness of the present issue. The school crisis cannot be solved by press releases or gimmicks."[151] Having not heard back from Theobald, the next day, October 22, 1958, Cogen sent a letter to the editor of the *New York Times* that the paper printed on October 27 after first running another article that contextualized the core tensions for readers. According to Cogen, "Superintendent of Schools Theobald has thrown a bombshell in the form of a so-called 'merit rating' salary program, into an already demoralized school system." Offering five points of well-worn criticism on the topic of merit pay plans, Cogen characterized merit evaluations as the "ultimate in the mechanization of the man of conformity" and a "cutthroat pecuniary appraisal of a teacher's subtle influence upon the minds of our children." For Cogen, "New York City teacher salaries are lower than those paid in surrounding areas. Teaching conditions are worse. Morale is poorer." From the vantage point of Guild members, Theobald's insertion of merit rating into the conversation was "an evasion, not a solution."[152]

In addition to writing the letter to the *Times*, Cogen turned to other labor leaders to mobilize support. Writing to Harry Van Arsdale Jr., president of the Central Trades and Labor Council, Cogen explained, "So-called merit rating schemes violate fundamental union principles. Under merit rating, instead of the pay going with the job, salaries are determined by the opinions of one's supervisors. . . . 'Merit rating' is destructive of union solidarity, since it pits teacher against teacher in the competition for the limited quota of premium pay jobs." Not only was the plan potentially union busting but, in a great affront to Cogen, "Instead of calling teacher representatives in and talking the matter over, the Superintendent tossed his merit rating bombshell publicly at press conference where there was no opportunity for contrary opinion to make itself known."[153]

After seeing Cogen's letter to the editor, Superintendent Theobald wrote back to him on the same day. "Dear Charles," he began, "Your recent letter to the *New York Times* on the question of merit raises amazed me. I had not thought of you as one who would jump so readily to conclusions which do not exist." In an attempt to moderate the rising temperature, Theobald backed away from a merit pay plan and suggested that "the time has come for us to do some thinking about a constructive program to build the kind of system that you and I believe in."[154] Cogen responded on November 11, 1958, not yet willing to back down. "You were quoted that you unequivocally favor merit rating," Cogen explained. "This has a traditional meaning in the profession, and I believe we were warranted in thus interpreting it." Continuing, Cogen cautioned Theobald against using such an "emotion-laden term with all its unsavory connotations." Cogen's objective in the correspondence was not merely to squash the discussion of merit pay but also to attend to the broader issue of neither being included nor informed of Theobald's thinking on educational policy matters before the public. "Would it not have been better to sound out teacher opinion before a pronouncement on the subject which you well knew carried the potential of disquieting the overwhelming majority of the staff," he asked. Cogen closed his note by looking forward to their in-person meeting on November 21, 1958.[155] Days later, Theobald responded with a brief and friendly note. "Dear Charlie," the correspondence began, revealing a collegiality and cooling of temperatures between the two men. Theobald acknowledged that "I might have avoided some misunderstandings if I had followed somewhat different procedures in announcing that I favored a merit rating plan." "As time goes on," Theobald offered, "I think you and members of the supervising and teaching staff will come to realize that there will always be consultation on all matters as a professional policy. I trust that we can establish relationships that will enable us to exchange ideas on a professional basis to our mutual advantage."[156] With that, the two men reached a détente, establishing the terms for which topics were simply not permissible and who must always have a seat at the table.

"The Pedagogical Locusts Have Devoured the Harvest": Criticism of Teacher Preparation

The postwar years marked the emergence of widespread criticism of teacher preparation, in which teacher educators were simultaneously blamed alongside classroom teachers and also engaged in the blaming. This circular rhetoric of blame gave way to the modern standards and accreditation movement, which contributed to the further regulation and rationalization of teachers' work lives. Tracing the quality and quantity problems beleaguering the teacher corps and the general haze of mediocrity engulfing public schools directly to schools of education, critics sought to dislodge teacher training from their historic moorings and called for an education rooted in the liberal arts. Meanwhile, education faculty, occupying a complex space on their respective university campuses and struggling for their survival, continued the retreat toward vocationalized education set in motion during the Depression years. Arthur Bestor, a history professor at the University of Illinois, and the Fund for the Advancement of Education, led by Paul Woodring and supported by the Ford Foundation, represented the leading voices of criticism. For them, the public school's core problems—including shortages—traced back to an unprofessional workforce. A reoriented teacher preparation curriculum, they argued, would not simply send better-prepared teachers to the schools but would also entice better people to consider teaching as a profession.

"Teaching, we will all agree," Bestor wrote, "ought to be considered a profession and not a mere trade or vocation." Even as teachers received more university preparation, in his estimation, it was the wrong kind of education. "Though longer years of training are now required," Bestor explained, "the pedagogical locusts have devoured the harvest." Instead, in his estimation, what prospective teachers needed more than anything was "a thorough education in the liberal arts and sciences, undistorted by vocational considerations and pressures." Schools of education "robbed" teachers of the ability to study the liberal arts "by the multiplication of artificial requirements in mere pedagogy." Shifting the preparation of teachers away from schools of education to the rest of the university "will do more to advance the teaching profession in public esteem than any other step that can well be taken," Bestor argued, for "it will make public-school teaching an attractive career once more to young men and women of serious intellectual capacity."[157]

Striking a similar chord, the Fund for the Advancement of Education supported experiments in teacher preparation through their "breakthrough programs" "designed to attract able men and women into the teaching profession" and "to make careers in teaching more attractive" by breaking "through the barriers of tradition that have made it difficult for colleges to prepare teachers."[158] For Woodring and the rest of the education fund, schools of education represented the "traditions" that teacher preparation needed to escape. Reflecting on the purpose of education in the postwar era, in 1957, Woodring wrote, "In a free society, all individuals . . . must make important decisions for themselves. If they are unable to do so, if their lives must be planned for them, the society is no longer free, however benevolent the controls may be." For Woodring, a liberal education was the cornerstone of an educated citizenry, and "it seems that the great majority of our citizens, including many of our teachers, have need of better liberal education than they now receive, or have ever had." Rather than specialization in pedagogy, Woodring and the experiments the education fund sponsored pushed teachers to consider the broad implications of their work.[159]

In this endeavor, faculty at schools of education found themselves increasingly spurned by the philanthropic organization as many grants went to liberal arts programs and those creating strong connections with local school districts. According to Woodring, "within the fund there is a growing conviction that the public schools should play a larger part than they have in the preparation of teachers. They are closer to the problem than are schools of education." For example, faculty at Barnard College received a $67,500 grant in May 1956 to support the creation of a "colloquium in education which brings students preparing for teaching careers into contact with distinguished men and women." Of particular note is the fact that Teachers College, Columbia University's education school, did not receive funding and that one of the "distinguished men and women" the Barnard Colloquium featured was Teachers College professor William Heard Kilpatrick. Among one of the largest grant recipients was Yeshiva University, under the leadership of Myron Lieberman. Awarded $525,000, the sponsored program was geared toward graduates of liberal arts programs who would receive $2,000 teaching fellowships to carry a three-quarters load in a local public school where they would be "fully responsible for some classes and observe and teach others under supervision." Four evenings a week, students would meet at the university for seminars where they would discuss and reflect on their work in the schools.[160]

Meanwhile, faculty members at schools of education were constrained, at least in part, by the institutional norms and arrangements of their universities. Considered the "step-children of the alma mater," with small endowments and minimal university support, schools of education relied entirely on tuition dollars. Columbia University and other similar institutions spent 100 times as much on the education of medical students as it did on that of teachers. One article in the *New York Times* called attention to this "tragic paradox": even as teaching was considered by many to be the "most important profession in a democracy, the education of teachers was the poorest and most neglected."[161] During the postwar years amid the teacher shortages and rising tide of criticism aimed at teacher preparation programs, education faculty navigated the tightrope between their place in the university and functioning as a self-sustaining institution. In his inaugural address as president of Teachers College, Hollis Leland Caswell opened his remarks by stating, "We value highly our place in the university," but in the next sentence offered, "it is my deepest desire that Teachers College shall render distinctive service."[162] At New York University, education professor Alonzo Myers wrote, "It is quite probable that New York University's School of Education is now in one of the most critical periods in its existence. Decisions made at this time and in the near future will to a large degree determine the prestige and influence of the School of Education for the next fifteen or twenty years." Speaking on behalf of his colleagues and writing to University Chancellor Chase, Myers explained that many education faculty felt a need to "justify [the school's] existence." "Teacher education, at New York University, as in many other institutions," he continued, "has become 'cheap' education." Hamstrung by financial constraints, Myers cited rising concerns about "the quality of the educational services rendered by the School of Education." Myers understood that the School of Education was an integral part of the larger university and agreed that it "can and should continue to make its proper contribution to university overhead costs." However, for Myers, it was equally important that the School of Education "no longer be treated primarily as a 'moneymaker' which is expected to support desirable but deficit-producing university activities." "There are some high and tight walls," Myers warned "that must be broken down before we shall be able to serve as well as we should our graduate students looking toward education as a career."[163]

The financial constraints under which schools of education operated, and which informed and constrained their response to criticism, were not simply a function of long-standing university funding structures. Even as critics attributed staffing shortages to schools of education that were neither preparing enough nor the right sort of teachers, education professors argued that the shortage tied their hands as well. Not only were fewer students coming to schools of education, faculty members argued, but given the great need of local public schools, they could not afford to be so choosy when making admissions decisions. "We happen to be living in a period when the quality of this army we replenish each September is under scrutiny," wrote Van Cleve Morris, education professor at Rutgers University, "and we are often accused of professional negligence by our critics who contend we are responsible for the poor showing many of our products make in our schools." Even as Morris and his colleagues objected "strenuously to the popular belief that 'anybody can teach school,'" because of the persistent teacher shortage, faculty at training institutions also realized they could not expect "the finest and best of their students."[164] In his 1947 report, Dean Russell of Teachers College understood the bind in a slightly different way. Should the college admit only those students of "tested ability," letting go of faculty members and renting out unused space, or admit the students who actually applied?[165] For school leaders around the country, the choice was obvious. New York University's Dean Melby explained that "each year thousands of men and women are certified to teach, who by no stretch of the imagination can be considered qualified for their task. They are accepted chiefly because no better applicants can be secured."[166] The supply problems that constrained the public schools constrained schools of education, as well, argued Melby and others as a partial defense.

For other faculty members, however, the forms of teacher preparation that characterized schools of education were not a function of constraints and limitations but instead a reasoned approach grounded in research. As critics called for teacher preparation to broaden and center on the liberal arts, some education faculty around the country instead made the case for a narrowing of the curriculum and retreated further into the vocationalized preparation that emerged during the Depression years. Drawing on the traditions of the university, these scholars termed themselves "educationists" and made the case that the study of education represented its own field replete with its own distinct traditions and norms. "The objective has been to arrive at a discipline of education," wrote Merle Borrowman, another Teachers College professor, "which will make more widely available both the broad integrated knowledge and the technical skill of the exceptional teacher."[167] According to Karl Bigelow, also a professor at Teachers College, critics like Bestor fundamentally misunderstood and underestimated the teacher's work. Not merely intellectuals standing in front of the nation's classrooms, effective teachers required, in Bigelow's estimation, "special knowledge and skill."[168] Concurring, Caswell offered, "some people believe that a liberal education provides all the competencies needed for educational work. This view fails to recognize the complexity of education and the specialized competence required by educational work."[169] In 1954, the faculty at Hunter college conducted a study on the "attitudes, values and traits desired of graduates of the Hunter Teacher Education Program," claiming that the results offered "a composite picture of the kind of person they think the teacher in our society should be or become." According to the study, Hunter faculty assigned "less importance to the possession of superior intelligence as an important trait of elementary and secondary school teachers to all traits but one—that of 'physical attractiveness.'" Instead, for faculty members there, the most important attributes for future teachers included "emotional stability and flexibility," "a sense of humor," and knowledge of "curriculum methods and materials."[170] Even as some faculty members such as Myers of New York University warned that many students traveling through schools of education "tend to be over-professionalized," many others like Bigelow maintained that the purpose of the school of education was to expose students to the "vocational implications of their subjects."[171]

In part alienated by their universities' funding structures and the prioritizing of the liberal arts, and in part choosing to walk away in a new direction, faculty members at schools of education across the city and nation forged strong connections with local school districts in the midst of criticisms during the postwar years. When looking at their graduates, faculty members at schools of education realized they were not preparing teachers in a generic sense but instead teachers for a specific place. "It is well known that the bulk of the New York City teaching force comes from the public and private universities of the city," a recruitment document produced by the Board of Education in 1959 offered. "It is important," the report continued, "that the lines of communication with the officials of these institutions be constantly strengthened."[172] According to one document by the New York City Board of Education, faculty at schools of education and in particular those supervising student teaching assignments served "in the capacity of a middleman with very definite functions to perform," including securing placements and procuring "professional materials."[173] Increasingly standing as partners in the same projects, faculty members at schools of education turned to local school boards to learn about the specific teachers they needed in terms of subject and level as well as the attributes and qualities administrators desired. In 1957, Marjorie Smiley and Arthur Sprague, faculty members at Hunter, conducted a study sponsored by the college's Office of Institutional Research asking principals in the city and surrounding suburbs about the areas in which beginning teachers most struggled or needed more training. According to their findings, principals reported "methods and planning" as the most difficult areas for novice teachers. For Smiley and Sprague, the results not only legitimated the vocational orientation of schools of education but called for increased attention in these areas.[174]

The actions of many faculty members at schools of education during these years did little to ease the criticisms over their work. Instead, the chasm over the preparation of the professional teacher only widened with the space between the two disparate visions, one revolving around a broadening toward the liberal arts and another rooted in a vocational orientation, growing nearly impossible to bridge. The aura of criticism that surrounded teachers and schools of education carved out critical space for the rise of regulation and accreditation of teacher preparation programs. Nationwide, as commentators of various stripes derided schools of education and linked their shortcomings directly to struggling public schools, policymakers demanded some mechanism of quality control and standardization. In 1952, Commissioner of Education McGrath and the Office of Education published *Proposed Minimum Standards for State Approval of teacher Preparing Institutions* and pushed states to set minimum standards for the preparation of teachers in the hopes of "upgrading the quality of instruction in institutions of higher learning which engage in the education of teachers and of promoting a greater degree of uniformity." Among the areas that needed greatest standardization, according to the report, was admissions. "Perhaps no single index of an institution's caliber is more significant that its admissions policies." the committee composed of federal and state education leaders warned In addition, the report encouraged a broad curriculum rooted in general learning, pedagogy, and clinical ethics.[175]

Stemming from the federal government's 1952 report, in 1954 the National Council for the Accreditation of Teacher Education (NCATE) "became the official body for the specific accreditation of teacher education institutions and programs," responsible for setting the "standards which teacher education programs must meet in order to be accredited."[176] By 1957, NCATE and its national board had crafted seven core standards: "objectives of teacher education," "organization and administration of teacher education," "student personnel programs and services for teacher education," "faculty for professional education," "curricula for teacher education," "professional laboratory experiences for prospective teachers," and "facilities and instructional materials for teacher education."[177] The initial impact of NCATE was modest: "a majority of the twelve hundred" institutions of teacher preparation remained "outside its ranks." Nevertheless, the broader goal to weed out "mediocrity" and "inferiority" in education through standardization set in motion a project that would accelerate over the twentieth century.[178] The rise of the accreditation of teacher preparation programs is also a history shrouded in irony. Calls to dislodge the professional preparation of teachers from schools of education and ground it in the liberal arts fueled the accreditation engine. However, the nature of the standards had the opposite impact as they rooted the preparation of teachers in schools of education, both complicating and disincentivizing intra-university partnerships.

On the surface, the postwar years were a time of consensus. Uniform concerns about international competition, national security, and domestic welfare generated agreement about the significance of the schools and their shortcomings. Policymakers and social commentators, as their predecessors had, looked directly from struggling schools to teachers. Fueled by the discourse of blame, as they had before, Americans saw a teacher corps afflicted with quality problems, but this time they also saw significant quantity problems. The teacher shortages brought new urgency to reform initiatives and linked teachers and the fate of schools more directly than ever before. In search of merit and motivated by fears of mediocrity, reformers of various backgrounds identified teacher professionalization as the silver bullet.

However, the consensus ended there as organized teachers, teachers of various school levels, policymakers, school leaders, and teacher educators fashioned competing definitions of merit that gave way to fractured ideas about the professional teacher and professionalization reforms. In the first camp, ideas of merit and professionalization led to calls for a broadening of teachers' professional preparation and increased competition. In the second camp, similar calls for merit and professionalization led instead to increased regulation, standardization, and an emphasis on the vocational aspects of teachers' work lives. In many regards, what the first camp envisioned mirrored the organization of other professional occupations, but without reforming the actual structures of teachers' work lives, these calls for change remained provocative ideas that were largely impossible to implement. The second created the groundwork for the ascendancy of teacher unionization, discussed in the next chapter. Rather than a specific and calculated strategy, the genesis of union power during these years reflected the nature of public school teaching which, in spite of the present discourse of professionalism, resembled mid-century industrialized workplaces in terms of size, regulation, and worker autonomy.

5

"A Brave New Breed"

Teacher Power and Isolation, 1960–1980

In the spring of 1970, United Federation of Teachers (UFT) president Albert Shanker traveled north to Syracuse University to deliver a speech. "Administrators and Boards of Education," he explained to this audience of teacher educators and future teachers, "use the word professional as a weapon with teachers." In Shanker's estimation, the word professional emerged "as a sort of 'naughty-naughty,' a scolding" when applied to teachers. Advancing a vision of teacher power through union power, Shanker explained to his audience that union leaders saw through these tactics and would no longer stand for it. "A professional is not merely obedient," Shanker demanded. Drawing on traditional, masculine definitions, Shanker explained, "a professional is a person who is an expert in a particular field and because of his expertise, he has a high degree of decision-making power."[1]

By the early 1960s, a new, assertive voice joined discussions about schools, the quality of the teacher corps, and reform: union leaders. Though teachers organized as early as the 1890s, affiliated with labor in 1902, formed the American Federation of Teachers in 1916, and maintained a constant presence in school politics over the ensuing decades, the rise of teacher militancy and collective bargaining during the early 1960s changed the role of teachers unions in public schools and American society. For influential labor leaders like Shanker, Charles Cogen, and David Selden, New York City high school teachers who gained national prominence, the vision of the professional teacher was inseparable from the union's institutional interests. In the estimation of big-city union leaders, the conditions of teachers' work lives, including oppressive administrative structures, high poverty schools, and out-of-touch teacher education programs, contributed in equal measure to teachers' deprofessionalization. The only answer, they argued, was to take power back from administrators, communities, and teacher educators.

School leaders, social critics, and union leaders of these years maintained their historical ambivalence about teachers, simultaneously casting them as the hope of the schools and blaming them for the schools' failures. Commissioner of Education Harold Howe II explained in his 1968 report, "We are asking our schools to compensate for past social injustices, to ameliorate the effects of rapid social change, and to improve upon their performance of traditional academic functions." In Howe's estimation, the nation's public schools were at their "breaking point" not only because of these converging demands but also because of the "exodus of talented people" from the schools.[2] Echoing that criticism in his oral history, Shanker reflected that most teachers "shouldn't be teaching . . . but a lot of them can't find anything else because they were at the bottom of their class."[3]

The realities of urban schooling shaped the discourse of blame and ideas about the professional teacher. In May 1965, Martin Mayer shared a conversation between two New York City school officials with readers of the *New York Times*. "'Your problem . . . is that you think it's a minute to midnight,'" one New York City official supposedly said to the other. "'Relax,'" the more senior leader reassured, "'it's after midnight.'"[4] By the 1960s, social commentators, education reformers, and union leaders agreed that schools in the city and in urban areas around the country were in trouble. "The school system is not fulfilling any function for which it might be thought responsible," one writer offered.[5] Agreeing, Abraham Lass, a former New York City teacher and administrator, described public schools as "places of fear, invaded by vandals, muggers, rapists, gangs, disturbed and dangerous students and outsiders."[6] In addition to crumbling infrastructure and soaring crime and poverty rates, school expenditures climbed as test scores fell. And in spite of the *Brown v. Board of Education* decision of 1954 and the outward-facing liberal orientation of the urban North, schools and neighborhoods remained deeply segregated and unequal. "Public confidence in the school system is fearfully low and dropping," Mayer wrote. "White children are leaving the city schools at a rate of 40,000 a year," and "even worse, the Negro middle class has almost entirely disappeared." As racial tensions in the city mounted, New York City's school bureaucracy grew. By 1970, New York City's school system served one million students and employed over seventy-five thousand teachers and fifty-five thousand administrators.[7] For writers like Mayer, who closed his article by telling readers that he wrote to them from Switzerland, "which is far away—only a little closer than school headquarters to the realities of life in the New York schools," at least one obstacle to school improvement was clear.[8]

During these years, local teachers unions grew into national organizations with political and economic power.[9] However, very little of that authority extended to ordinary classroom teachers. Instead, teachers in New York City remained targets of reform, spoken about and blamed. The vision of teacher power as union power that animated teachers' organizations isolated teachers to their classrooms and inflamed tensions with the communities of color they served. This chapter begins with "'Fighting Mad': The HSTA-Guild Merger and Rise of Collective Bargaining," which explores the merger between the High School Teachers Association (HSTA) and the Teachers Guild that created the United Federation of Teachers, a harbinger of the teacher labor movement and point of emulation for locals around the nation. The merger represented a labor victory and critical step toward collective bargaining but also highlights the paradox of unionization. Powered by the mantra of collective action and strength in numbers, unification came at the expense of women elementary school teachers and their recently won single salary schedule.

The next section, "Smashing 'The Old Stereotype': The UFT and the New Professional Teacher,'" chronicles the vision of the professional teacher that surfaced in New York City following the rise of collective bargaining. Even as history reveals the ascendency of organized labor to have been a gradual evolution, teacher union leaders in New York City understood their work as a revolutionary break from the past. Teaching remained a female-dominated occupation during these years, and women joined the union in unprecedented numbers. But male high school teachers made their way to the helm of the unions; relying on stereotypical depictions of women workers as weak and uncommitted, UFT leaders cast their presence in the schools as a turning point.

Teacher power meant union control; in this framework, administrators, community members, and teacher educators surfaced as meddlers. For union leaders like Cogen and Shanker, the first step on the pathway to professionalism centered on breaking free from managerial control, chronicled in the next section, "'Not Merely Obedient': The UFT and School Leaders." As examined in the next section, "'The Controlling Voice': Teacher Expertise or Community Authority?," unionized teachers also sought to wrest control from communities of color who, animated by the growing Black Power movement, maintained that representation, voice, and authority were essential to equitable institutions. Union leaders called upon ingrained racialized ideas that conflated professional authority and Whiteness and found themselves at odds with the communities of color they served, standing as a barrier to racial justice in the city. In their bid for authority, union leaders also argued for a controlling voice in the professional preparation of teachers. As tracked in the next section, "'Woefully Inadequate': The Quest for Control over Teachers' Preparation," union leaders sought to cleave teachers' professional preparation from traditional moorings in the university. University-based schools of education, similarly compelled by their own institutional interests, ceded control in exchange for partnership. The result was a cacophony of preparation models that adhered to the whims of funders but deprived teachers of a shared body of knowledge and professional cohesion.

Following the militancy of the 1960s, Shanker branded himself as an education reformer and an expert about teachers rather than a teacher himself. More and more, as the final section, "The 'Elder Statesman': Expertise, Authority, and Bureaucracy," explores, teachers' place in labor organizations mirrored their position in the school bureaucracy. The discourse of teacher blame that surfaced during these years unfolded against ideological debates about the function of public schools in an increasingly complex urban landscape marred by inequality. Attempts to reform struggling schools produced tangible structures that shaped how teachers were managed, represented, and educated, and all of this sprang from gendered and racialized ideas that cast masculine Whiteness as authority.

"Fighting Mad": The HSTA-Guild Merger and the Rise of Collective Bargaining

Teachers from across the city's public schools did not perceive their working conditions in a uniform way nor speak with a singular voice, as evidenced by the array of teacher organizations that existed within cities following World War II. As more men entered the high schools, the divide only widened: women of the elementary schools and male high school teachers found themselves at odds, particularly over the city's salary schedules. Even as salary scales based on sex had fallen out of favor by the 1920s, pay schedules in New York City and elsewhere offered higher pay to teachers in high schools, where the majority of men who entered the occupation resided. In 1935, a first year high school teacher earned two and a half times as much as a starting elementary school teacher.[10] As discussed in the previous chapter, the single salary schedule outlined in the 1947 Feinberg Law represented a corrective measure and a way to lure teachers to elementary schools during the teacher shortages immediately following World War II. For Rebecca Simonson, Guild president and elementary school teacher, the new pay schedule was a triumph. Explaining the core issues, a Guild flyer from the early 1950s stated, "at the heart of the matter is status." For Guild members, "the pre-1947 New York City staff was governed by a status system which had almost the force of caste. High school teachers *knew* themselves to be an elite group." In contrast, a document titled "What All the Shouting's About" explained that "elementary teachers were regarded as the peons in the educational vineyards." Revealing the extent to which they were aware of the gendered dynamics of the schools, Guild leaders like Simonson observed that "the contrasting status of high school and elementary school teachers was further emphasized by the fact that teaching younger students traditionally had been a job for women." The 1947 remuneration policy portended to right past inequities. "Tradition, male superiority, moral and legal approval, and the sweet rewards of family and cultural respect," one Guild leaflet explained, "all reinforced each other to put the high school teacher in a special class—if not classroom—both in fact and in his own mind."[11]

As for high school teachers, they were "fighting mad" and threatened to boycott all extracurricular activities.[12] Leaders of the HSTA blasted that "the results to the morale of the high school staff have been devastating"—nothing short of a crisis (figure 6).[13] One article in the HSTA's journal, *High School Teacher*, quoted HSTA leader Samuel Hochberg as stating, "9 out of 10 teachers in the elementary division are women." "Her work," he explained, "is to teach them a few simple fundamental concepts each year. . . . For this, she needs a general and superficial content in various subject fields."[14] In contrast, for Hochberg and the HSTA, the path into the high schools was more arduous; men found their way there both because of the prestige associated with the work and the superior intellect needed. But, they warned, salary equalization would stem the tide of recruits, sending "qualified personnel who might otherwise enter the teaching field . . . to more lucrative endeavors."[15] Throughout much of the 1950s, salary equalization remained a source of discord that pitted elementary school teachers and the Teachers Guild against high school teachers and the HSTA. However, by 1959, Guild president and high school teacher Charles Cogen set his sights on expansion and, along with other Guild leaders, proposed a merger with the HSTA to form one organization to represent all city teachers in place of the dozens of small ones that existed at the time. However, as David Selden of the Guild realized, talks of unification with the high school organization would only proceed if "the Guild accepts the principal of a differential" and agreed to negate the single salary schedule.[16] Affirming that position and noting his skepticism, Emil Tron, the president of the HSTA, wrote to Cogen. "In order that there will be no doubt in anyone's mind about my question, I want to state that as long as I can remember, the Guild has always espoused the cause of single salary for ALL teachers. As long as single salary has been in effect the High School Teachers Association has always violently opposed it." In closing, Tron offered, "If the Guild is willing to abandon its policy of a single-salary schedule for all teachers, and is willing to support a policy of a differential in salaries for all high school teachers, then we will be willing to meet and to discuss a future program."[17]

Even as Cogen maintained support for the single salary in his speeches, he also began to work with Guild leaders to develop a promotional increment plan

FIG. 6 High School Teachers Association, "Crisis in New York City Public High Schools," 1956. (*Source*: New York City Board of Education Collection, Municipal Archives, New York City Department of Records.)

that would once again disproportionately distribute financial rewards to high school teachers. Ultimately, as Guild leaders explained in a newsletter distributed to current and prospective members, there was a "stronger . . . argument for unity among all the divisions."[18] Speaking to Helen Emory of the *World Telegram* in 1959, Cogen explained, "Although the Guild's prime objective in the current negotiations is equalization of increments, we believe an acceptable compromise could be worked out in the future." Continuing, he offered, "We do not intend to depart from our basic principle that a teacher in any division must be able to reach the top salary, but within this framework some adjustment might be possible, especially if this could unite the teaching staff into one powerful organization."[19] Cogen's stance marked a distinct departure from the Guild's long-standing policy and in 1959, his predecessor, Rebecca Simonson, wrote to remind him of that. Speaking of the proposed merger with the HSTA, she explained, "it is shocking to note that a committee undertook to offer terms which are contrary to Guild policy." "Above all," she warned, "let's understand what we are for."[20]

In spite of Simonson's objections, in March 1960 the Guild and the HSTA merged to form the UFT. One early poster presented a picture of the members of the UFT organizing committee; in the center, standing side by side, were Cogen and Hochberg. Aimed at high school teachers, the flyer explained that the unity at the core of this new organization would lead to "immediate salary justice—for all High School teachers."[21] At the base of the merger was Cogen's "promotional increment" proposal, which he presented as a way to balance elementary school teachers' calls for a single salary with high school teachers' calls for a differential salary. In practice, though, the new plan abandoned the gains of the single salary schedule. According to a UFT document, "The promotional increment is the UFT plan for rewarding and encouraging specialized competence by teachers in various subject matter areas. . . . It would grant an added $1000 to high school and junior high school teachers, and others who hold licenses for which five years of training are required. The same $1000 would also go to all elementary school teachers who meet similar requirements."[22] At the base of this plan was the appraisal that teaching at these higher levels was more difficult and required more training. Elementary school teachers could qualify for the raise, but they would need education above and beyond that required by their teaching licenses. Moreover, increased education would not immediately qualify these teachers for the raise. Instead, "all future elementary school teachers who receive regular licenses after the promotional increment has been established will be required to pass a test in their respective academic specialty areas in order to obtain the promotional increment."[23]

The promotional increment proposal, which ceded single salary schedule gains, was a critical stepping-stone in the teacher power movement. In New York City, upon the HSTA-Guild merger, union leaders sent demands to members of the Board of Education and scheduled a strike for collective bargaining for May 17, 1960, Teacher Appreciation Day in the city. City officials averted that strike by promising negotiations, but when those talks failed to materialize, teachers walked out of the schools on November 7, 1960. Two thousand teachers called in sick and other unions, including the International Ladies Garment Workers, stood alongside teachers.[24] The 1935 National Labor Relations Act gave collective bargaining rights to private sector workers, ensuring that union representatives and employers together would negotiate the terms of employment, but until 1960, public sector workers had no such protections. By the early 1960s, following the lead of New York City's unionized teachers, teacher militancy and calls for collective bargaining erupted across the United States. During the AFT's national conference held in Dayton, Ohio, during the summer of 1960, labor leaders "mapped a nation-wide effort to gain collective bargaining rights and representation for teachers."[25]

That first New York City strike led to the formation of the UFT and laid the groundwork for collective bargaining for teachers and public sector employees nationwide. From Chicago to Gary to Louisville, teachers used the strike as the "ultimate weapon" and walked out of the schools demanding higher pay, decreased in-school duties, and a voice for labor in education policy discussions.[26] According to Wesley Wildman, a researcher from the University of Chicago, "the spring of 1965 has been the most turbulent period the nation has ever seen in the increasingly militant and aggressive drive of public school teachers for control over the conditions under which they will teach."[27] Even in cities like Baltimore, where local officials ruled that collective bargaining was illegal, teachers persisted. As Charles Laubheim, an executive secretary in the local union, explained, "In every city where the union has asked for collective bargaining, they said it was illegal, but when the teachers wanted it, it was made legal. We're going to make it legal in Baltimore."[28] From 1960 to 1974, teacher militancy exploded across the United States as teachers walked out in more than one thousand separate strikes.[29] By 1966, one study estimated that more than 1,500 written agreements between teacher organizations and local school boards existed in the United States.[30] As U.S. Commissioner of Education Howe observed, "What has happened to American schoolteachers, once the most docile of public servants, is that they have formed ranks in unions and teachers' organizations and joined in the battle that is raging in our schools today."[31]

Criticism of striking teachers swelled across the county and U.S. Commissioner of Education Francis Keppel characterized "a strike that closes schools" as a "dramatic and sure sign of a very sick community."[32] Even as policymakers and the general public urged teachers to find other means to resolve their conflicts, the power and attention they garnered from these demonstrations were undeniable. Legislation like the Condon–Waldin bill in New York that promised severe punitive measures made many teacher groups hesitant to call a work stoppage throughout the 1950s. However, once the public witnessed teachers in places like New York City return to work after striking, teachers nationwide realized that local policymakers had neither the political will nor resources to follow through with the most severe threats. In spite of efforts to curb union behavior by issuing hefty fines to the organization following strikes and barring the union from collection dues, as officials in New York City did following the 1975 strike, and jailing leaders, such as Shanker in 1967, union participation and militant behavior only grew—largely because teachers' efforts were successful.[33] Across the United States, salaries increased as nonteaching tasks decreased. Teachers in Taylor Township, Michigan, received full medical insurance and life insurance plans, as teachers in San Francisco called for a "data processing center to fill out report cards, registration forms and monthly attendance records," and in Philadelphia, teachers won a "once-a-month 'professional consultation' period" with school leaders.[34] According to Cogen, "Collective bargaining has created . . . a new climate of freedom and professionalism in our schools. The spirit of freedom is the outcome of the procedural innovations in the contract. Its components are emancipation, self-expression and self-determination."[35]

Principles of collective action and the notion of a greater good defined by union leaders sustained the teacher power movement, but as teachers soon learned, these labor concepts and the bureaucratic organizations that sprang from them were neither contingent on unanimity nor oriented around the individual. Theoretically, all teachers had the potential to earn the same amount of money, but in practice the new plan that led to the creation of the UFT and thus was the cornerstone of collective bargaining replicated an uneven salary distribution that favored the upper levels and, implicitly, male teachers. Elementary school teachers from around the city wrote to Cogen, pointing out that the promotional increment abolished a single salary, bewildered by what happened to their short-lived gains. For instance, with the close of the 1962 school year May Itkin wrote to Cogen: "the promotional differential puzzles me." "If given to junior and high school teachers who do not possess the M.A.," she asked, "doesn't it break the single salary schedule?"[36] Cogen responded to her nearly one month later in a brief note. "Dear Miss Itkin," he offered, "We do not consider that the promotional differential is a break in the single salary principle." Before closing his letter "Yours very truly, Charles Cogen, President," he wrote, "We hope you decide to become a member of the UFT."[37] By June 1962, the UFT's membership committee found that eighty-two schools were completely "dead" in terms of membership and all were elementary schools. Ignoring the frustration teachers like Itkin and Simonson expressed and the legacy of activist elementary school teachers tracing back to the women of the Chicago Teachers Federation, leaders of the newly formed Federation interpreted this gap as a lack of activism and professional commitment on the part of these women teachers.[38] By 1964, five of the seven members of the Federation's elementary school executive committee were men, whereas nearly 90 percent of elementary school teachers were women.[39] The formation of the UFT was a critical turning point in the history of union power. That victory, however, came at the expense of female elementary school teachers.

Smashing "The Old Stereotype": The UFT and the New Professional Teacher

Despite the UFT's strong links to past New York City teacher unions, its leaders conceived of their task in decidedly new terms. Not only were they different from past unionists, but union leaders maintained that their work marked a distinct break from that of their predecessors. Through a combination of disregard and criticism, the leaders of the UFT distanced themselves from their forerunners. In creating a dividing line between past and present unionists, and therefore between past and present teachers, the leaders of the UFT framed professional authority and expertise through traditional, masculine terms. A majority of the UFT's most visible leaders, including Charles Cogen, Samuel Hochberg, David Selden, Sol Jaffe, Alice Marsh, and many others, had been members of the union's predecessors. By 1960, these individuals combined had logged decades of work with the Teachers Guild, the High School Teachers Association, and various smaller associations. However, in their many private letters, union publications, speeches, meeting minutes, and interviews they never looked back. Rather than a continuation of the work of earlier unionists, the UFT marked a distinct break from the past, at least in the estimation of union leaders. According to Cogen, the UFT and the advent of collective bargaining "revolutionized our school system."[40]

The consensus among most early UFT leaders was that the work of earlier unionists had been largely unproductive. In an article published in the union's newspaper, *The United Teacher*, Deputy President Samuel Hochberg characterized the work of past teachers unions as "years of unprofessional squabbling."[41] Recording his oral history decades later, Selden affirmed the perception of the Guild "as rather pink tea and not very aggressive."[42] Cogen echoed similar sentiments in a speech delivered to the Detroit Teachers' Union in 1963. Though teachers had always cried out for professionalism, he contended, their lack of strength and action had reduced the concept to a "high sounding word for the books but a mirage in reality."[43] In a later interview, he reaffirmed his assessment, stating that the Teachers Guild and its previous presidents "lacked the force to fight."[44] By all counts, these leaders agreed that the work of past teacher unionists had been irrelevant to their own crusade and that the teachers who had come before them, along with some currently in their midst, were not professionals.

Instead, aligning with a different legacy, in his oral history Cogen viewed his work as an outgrowth of that of Samuel Gompers. Despite the complex and acrimonious relationship between Gompers, teachers, and women workers, Cogen looked to him longingly.[45] "Samuel Gompers played a very important role. He encouraged the organization of teachers. He attended meetings of various kinds and he was quite dynamic in his support, no question about it."[46] Right before the merger, Cogen posed to teachers in the *Spring Conference Journal*, "have [teachers] finally learned from organized labor?" In aligning with trade unionists over teachers, the UFT's leadership embraced an image of robust masculinity and muscular militancy that made earlier unionized teachers squeamish. Even as Rebecca Simonson had been a union leader and worked for teacher rights, she employed a different strategy. Reflecting on her time at the helm of the Guild, she likened her work to "opening a flower one petal at a time."[47] This sort of juxtaposition helped to solidify the perception of the UFT and its members as revolutionary rather than evolutionary. A poster printed shortly after the Federation's formation asked, "Is the UFT really a new organization?" "Definitely YES!" it exclaimed.[48] The UFT, as imagined by its leaders, would be a new type of organization, populated by a new type of teacher.

In addition to creating a new image of the union centered on a departure from past approaches, early leaders of the UFT also created a new image of the teacher. A video produced jointly by the UFT and the American Federation of Labor and Congress of Industrial Organizations (AFL-CIO), *The UFT Story*, encapsulated the imagined differences between teachers of the Federation and their predecessors. The film opened with images of female teachers from the past, the "long-suffering, docile schoolmarms" of yesteryear, surrounded by children. Then, with a flash, the video shifted to the early 1960s and to "today's teachers." A group of men and one woman, the UFT's executive board, sat around a conference table. With the exception of the woman, Alice Marsh, the chairman of the Legislative Committee, who wore a dress, the men wore dark business suits, crisp white dress shirts, and ties. Never pictured in front of a classroom and never surrounded by children, these so-called new teachers, "a brave new breed," were professionals. The UFT, the video proudly asserted, "smashed the old stereotype" of the nurturing female teacher and replaced that with a masculinized image that conformed to popular perceptions of the professional.[49]

The UFT branded this image everywhere it could, presenting it to current members, future members, administrators, teacher educators, and the general public. For instance, the first several pages of the 1961 Spring Conference pamphlet were devoted to a "Portrait of the UFT." The photos presented nearly all men, clad in business suits, holding meetings and organizing; absent from all pictures were children and schools. Likewise, at the 1963 Spring Conference, the pamphlet boasted the year's proudest achievement, the opening of UFT headquarters: "an office of beauty and dignity—a place of pride for all teachers."[50] The new teacher, as these leaders constructed him, embodied fundamentally masculine characteristics, as the 'old' teacher was stereotypically feminine. "There was a time, not too long ago," Cogen told a group of fellow unionists in Detroit, "when . . . [New York City's] 43,000 teachers were docile, passive and cynical." Those teachers, he continued, "were timid [and] fearful"; they were "too conservative." "Along with the enhanced professionalism of the teacher has come an emancipation of the teacher that has made him a new personality," Cogen triumphantly explained.[51] The new teacher was "self-confident" where the old was "timid"; teachers of the UFT were "responsible and proud" while others had been servile and meek.[52] An essay in *High Points*, the journal for teachers sponsored by the New York City Board of Education, amplified this binary. Explaining "how teachers get hurt," Frederick Shaw offered that female teachers were most likely to get injured on school grounds by falling down stairs, a likely byproduct of their "arthritis and eye troubles." In his analysis, injuries to female teachers were "more closely linked with the personal element. They appeared to be largely associated with the physical and emotional difficulties of the middle and advanced years of life." In contrast, the injuries sustained by male teachers stemmed from active pursuits such as "lifting heavy objects, using machinery or tools, or directing physical activities."[53] In this formulation, female teachers were old and delicate, a liability on school grounds. Male teachers, in contrast, were active and strong; if they did incur injury they did so in the service of the schools.

Not only did the UFT's "new" teacher have traditional male characteristics, but, as the organization's video and many publications revealed, the new UFT teacher was a man. In addition to gendered adjectives when writing about teachers, these unionists often also used gendered pronouns. Describing the importance of professionalization and increased teacher autonomy, Cogen explained, "The teacher, by becoming personally involved in the day-to-day decisions affecting his work, naturally tends to become more involved in every aspect of his teaching activity." This sort of formulation marks a distinct break from the past. In 1942 for instance, addressing the members of the League of Industrial Democracy, Simonson warned her audience, "Unless the teacher is bolstered by respect and confidence, unless she is given time and opportunity to experience democracy and personal dignity, her participation in the program for democracy must remain limited."[54] Not until the 1960s did the leaders of teachers unions begin to universally refer to teachers as men.

A look at *High Points* suggests that, more than accidental slips or a reflection of the gendered linguistics of the day, such pronoun usage denoted an active choice. Teachers, these teacher-authored articles suggest, were aware of the language they used. To be sure, many articles, especially those written by males, referred to teachers with male pronouns. However, many articles did not. In 1961 in one example of many, Eleanor Capson wrote to her fellow teachers about the challenges of teaching gifted children. "The teacher has a syllabus to cover," she reminded readers. "While she doesn't wish to frustrate the child, she cannot let the class discuss a particular point for the entire period."[55] Several years later, Irving Gerber wrote to teachers in a more equitable way. Describing the value of a merit-based system, he wrote, "in New York, a probationary teacher . . . has to exhibit unusual or bizarre behavior before he or she is considered ineligible for a regular license."[56] And in his satirical essay "The Best Teacher I Ever Had," James Cunningham wrote about a machine, and offered "I always tried hardest when I was in (her, his) *its* class."[57]

In their endeavor to both create and support the image of the new professional teacher, UFT leaders forged a male-dominated network. Members of the executive board wrote to each other, to male New York City officials, and to union leaders of traditionally male-dominated industries. Explicitly, these letters in their abundance appear largely unnecessary and superfluous. They did not discuss crucial union business nor did they plan specific engagements. Instead, these letters were cordial. Members of the executive board wrote to other men to congratulate them on promotions, to extend their condolences upon deaths, and to thank them for thinking of the UFT. In August 1963, for instance, Cogen wrote to Michael Quill, the president of the Transportation Workers Union of America. "Dear Brother Quill," he began, "I have seen a transcript of the interview which you had on August 4th. Your remarks about the UFT and myself are deeply appreciated. We know that we can always count on you as one of our devoted friends in the labor movement." Cogen signed the letter, "Sincerely and Fraternally, Charlie."[58]

Implicitly, however, these letters carried significance as they forged ties that reached beyond the traditional feminine confines of the field and created new boundaries that sifted male from female teachers. A language of exclusivity bolstered these alliances. While friendly and informal, these letters inducted the "new" teacher into a much larger fraternal labor organization. Authors often addressed each other by their first name and, in some instances, by nicknames, and each letter began with the salutation "Dear Brother" and closed with some form of "Fraternally." However, Cogen and the other members of the executive board reserved such language for their "brothers" in the network. On April 4, 1962, Genevieve Gideon, president of the Granite City Federation of Teachers, wrote to Cogen to congratulate him on the UFT's successes over the past years. Fourteen days later, Cogen replied. "Dear Mrs. Gideon," he began, "Thank you for your belated congratulations. Our objective in bargaining with the school board is to obtain a contract that will meet the demands of the children, teachers and school system. We are doing all within our power to achieve this. . . . Sincerely," he ended the brief note in a tone and style distinct from his correspondences with male unionists, "Charles Cogen."[59]

The alliances and boundaries forged by these informal communications constructed new male-only spaces within the teaching profession and added further distance between the new manly teacher and the old feminine one. In all of this, UFT leaders created a new understanding of the unionized teacher. Where teachers of the previous periods grappled with their place in a labor union, such was not the case for the leadership of the UFT. "We consider ourselves workers in the classroom," Cogen proudly asserted in an interview.[60] Whereas the efforts of union leaders to fight for professionalism by turning to the tried and true playbook of workers seemed ironic to some, for union leaders, muscular militancy was essential to the vision of teacher power that undergirded the UFT's concept of teacher professionalism.

In the spring of 1963, Joseph Giacobbe, a member of the UFT, wrote to Cogen questioning his tactics. "I wonder," he asked, "are we to be considered as respected teachers or as union members?"[61] Cogen wrote back within the week. "Your concluding sentence indicates a dichotomy . . . I think the two are, in our case, synonymous."[62] An image printed in the September edition of *The United Teacher* captured this duality as a man in overalls shakes hands with another in a cap and gown. Beneath them read "Labor and the Intelligentsia."[63] Rather than oppositional, these two figures were fused, embodying the Federation's ideal teacher-member. Whereas teachers of the Depression and war years went to great lengths to reconcile professionalization with unionization, discussed in chapter 3, by the early 1960s the relationship was complementary for union leaders. In a speech to Detroit teachers, Cogen offered, "We have proven that militancy pays off. . . . Membership must be involved in fighting for their rights; nothing will be handed to them on a silver platter."[64] For Cogen and the other leaders of the UFT, the use of force to protect their professional rights was an expression of their very masculinity and, as such, an affirmation of their professionalism. As one teacher from Pawtucket, Rhode Island, asserted, "Teachers are not timid, shy Milque-toasts any more—they've got spunk!"[65]

Though women comprised the vast majority of the city's teaching force and at least half of the UFT's rank-and-file membership, men dominated the UFT's leadership structure. In 1960, while over 70 percent of the state's teachers were female, 75 percent of the Federation's executive board was male, and by 1964, male leadership rose to 88 percent.[66] Despite the large presence of men at the helm of the union, a handful of women made their way onto the executive board. Alice Marsh, the chairman of the Legislative Committee, was the highest-ranking woman from 1960 to1964, as well as the most visible. Throughout this period, her peers selected her to represent the union at various non-union functions. Moreover, her correspondence simultaneously set her apart from the general membership and her fellow female teachers and incorporated her into the exclusive and expanding brotherhood. However, even when these highest-ranking women were present, the gendered language of the meeting minutes rendered them absent. For example, in 1960, thirty-three members comprised the executive board; nine of them were women. In an endeavor to reach more members, they resolved, "each board member and officer will have to talk with a dozen or more people. Each member can choose from a master list those people he wishes to contact. From then on he will be responsible for the results."[67]

Marsh described herself as different from the other women she grew up with. When interviewed later in her life and reflecting on her work at the helm of the union, she felt compelled to note that she had full-time help at home, which gave her "greater flexibility" to participate in union activities without worry for her child and home.[68] Fredda Richmond, another union member, highlights the complex place of women in the UFT's leadership structure. Like Marsh, Richmond was also a member of the executive board, but she stepped down in the spring of 1961. In that year's conference journal, titled *A Professional Organization's Vision and Mandate*, fellow leaders wished her farewell and noted, "We're sorry to lose Fredda Richmond to motherhood."[69] The nature of working women's lives was complex during these years and perhaps doubly so for teachers, who, in addition to social mores, were hemmed in by long-standing perceptions of the woman teacher. Even as more and more women entered the workplace, the notion of the stay-at-home mother remained central to the myth of the middle-class American dream. In 1962, George Gallup and Evan Hill conducted a poll for the *Saturday Evening Post*. Upon questioning 2,300 women from across the United States, Gallup and Hill asserted, "Our study shows that few people in the nation are as happy as a housewife." Women across the nation responded that "being subordinate to men is part of being feminine" and "a woman's prestige comes from her husband's opinion of her." "Apparently," the pollsters concluded, "the American woman has all the rights she wants."[70]

With few exceptions, the women of the UFT remained anonymous. Though they joined committees alongside men and played a role in organizing various events, their presence lingers unnamed in the background of historical records. For instance, a majority of women headed and populated the organizing committee for the Spring Conferences in these early years. However, no woman actually delivered a speech in one of these meetings until 1964.[71] One union activity, though, remained in the distinctive realm of the woman: social activities. Despite the female leadership of the social committee and the obvious opportunities for recognition, their meeting minutes and intra-union correspondences diverged from those produced by male-dominated committees. Rather than signing their letters "Fraternally," as did all other committees, they concluded theirs with "Sincerely." Additionally, while nearly all of the documents produced by the UFT's other committees and boards carried the name of the chairman, these women chose instead to maintain their anonymity, authoring letters in the name of "the social committee." These organized women planned house parties, bridge tournaments, singles mixers, summer outings, and weekend trips, among other events, to build community and increase membership. As the rhetoric of teacher power emerged during the early years of the UFT, so too did notions of distinct male and female spaces rooted in Victorian gender norms. These separate spaces, sometimes physical, in terms of leadership roles and committee membership, and at other times rhetorical, played a central role in the vision of teacher professionalism and the mantra of teacher power: the general subordination of women within the union enabled the Federation to claim a large membership but at the same time keep a male face on it.

Even as the number of men entering the teaching profession outpaced their female counterparts due to recruitment following World War II, by 1960, just 30 percent of all of New York's teachers were men.[72] However, as Superintendent John Theobald's *Annual Report* alerted in 1960, long-standing gender imbalances had grown. Women dominated the whole of the city's teaching population but they were not equally represented throughout the school levels. According to Theobald, "the percentage of women in the day school staff ranged from a low of 30.7% for those engaged in the enforcement of compulsory education laws to 90.1% for those in the elementary schools."[73] By 1970, nearly 70 percent of teachers and teacher aides in the city were women. In the elementary schools, women comprised 80 percent of the teaching force. But at the higher levels, these figures switched. For the first time since the inception of the common schools in the mid-nineteenth century, men outnumbered women, representing 61 percent of high school teachers. This divide was even more pronounced at the administrative level, where 66 percent of elementary and secondary school administrators were male.[74] The union replicated these dynamics, as a male-dominated group led the largely female rank-and-file members. Seventy percent of New York's teachers were women, but in 1960 only two of the UFT's forty-five district chairmen were women.[75]

These gender dynamics emerged in the various demands at the base of the UFT's professionalization project as well as in the idiosyncratic ways they fought for them. Calls for higher pay, for instance, centered on the preservation of male stature. In one televised interview, Cogen explained, "When a young person considers a career he wants to know what he can earn in the immediate future. In teaching, the immediate future is bleak indeed."[76] In another, he offered, "When a man goes into a New York City school system at present and he starts with a $5300 salary; he knows that at the end of the 14th year, he will get $9170. This is part of the entire prospect before him and part of the picture that determines whether or not to take the job."[77] A group of four male teachers shared similar thoughts with colleagues and school leaders in *High Points*. "Salaries are an important part of teacher morale," they began, "because many factors besides the actual amount of money received go into the attitude of the recipient toward his salary. . . . Teachers feel that they have declined relatively in the communities in which they live. Their salaries have not kept pace with those of others in their neighborhood. They feel they are sinking down to an even lower position in the social scale." The importance of teacher salary went beyond mere dollars and cents; it embodied their position in the larger community. "Unfortunately, many people measure a man's standing in his community by the amount of money he earns," the authors explained. "This aspect of salaries," they continued, "may be even more important than the actual salary received. This is particularly true of men teachers. A man who brings his children up on a lower level than the one on which he was raised, is, in popular terms a failure."[78] Extending the Depression-era rationale, for these teachers the problem was especially acute for men.

In addition to higher pay, UFT leaders also advocated for paid leaves for sabbaticals and illnesses. However, the most frequented sort of leave, maternity, was unpaid and conspicuously absent from their list.[79] As one local paper reported, "the AFT adopted its first women's right resolutions [in 1970] amid snickers, sly looks, and boisterous laughter from male delegates who seemed unable to take women seriously."[80] Similarly, after three years of dormancy at the leadership level, Patricia Halpin wrote to Shanker regarding the AFT's participation in the Coalition of Labor Union Women (CLUW). "Olga Madar, CLUW president, called to ask me to run as a vice-president of the organization," she informed Shanker. "I was surprised by the offer but realize that we are by far the union with the most members in CLUW. Do you want the AFT to continue with the organization? If not, I won't run for the v-p slot."[81] Halpin did not pursue the position, and the AFT remained eerily silent on all matters related to women's rights. It was not until 1981 that female teachers banded together to pass a resolution against the paternalism and discrimination within their own organization. They affirmed "whereas, the proportion of women in the AFT staff does not represent that proportion of women wither in the AFT or in the profession; therefore be it resolved, that the AFT, state federations, and locals encourage women to apply for staff vacancies so as to substantially increase the number of women on staffs."[82]

Further widening the divide between union leaders' perceptions of the old and new teacher, between a feminized profession and one that was masculinized, UFT leaders argued that teachers be released from what they classified as "non-teaching duties," the domestic side of teaching. Roll book, attendance sheets, collection of milk money and other funds, record keeping, and bulletin boards, "the endless non-teaching chores," as Cogen termed them in the

1962 preface to the Federation's spring conference, were a waste of the new teacher's time.[83] For Cogen, such activities only added to the "excessive routinization of his [the teacher's] life," and squelched "the free exercise of the professional spirit."[84] In the UFT's formulation, the new teacher, an academic, a professional, and above all, a man, had no time for such tasks and even if he did, such chores were "degrading."[85] Instead, UFT leaders argued, administrators ought to call upon mothers, secretaries, and other aides to complete these daily chores.

In January 1964, members of the UFT and Board of Education signed a sixty-five-page agreement concerning an array of working conditions, including nonteaching chores. In that agreement, UFT leaders bargained for high school teachers to receive 3.5 times more assistance per day in completing such tasks from aides and other support staff than their peers in the elementary schools, articulating clear assumptions about the different natures and responsibilities of these two groups of teachers.[86] In an address delivered at the commencement ceremony of Public School 105 in the spring of 1962, Cogen encouraged students to learn from teachers' recent actions. "Education can make a man of courage out of you," he explained to the graduating boys and girls. "And as you grow up you will need to make use of this moral courage as when a man stands up for his rights as a citizen."[87] For Cogen, this was precisely what the UFT and its new militancy was all about: men asserting their rights. Rugged, not rowdy, the "responsible militancy" that sat at the base of Cogen's conception of the professional teacher hinged from contemporary notions of masculinity.[88]

"Not Merely Obedient": The UFT and School Leaders

In a speech delivered in 1962, Cogen explained, "All too often teachers are popularly depicted as servile, supine species of humanity. In clothing us with the title of the professional, the intent of some people is, often as not—though sometimes unconsciously—to suppress any latent desires among us to stand up for our rights."[89] Concurring, Selden explained, teachers "are dissatisfied with their status" because they have had "little or no control over the conditions under which they practice their profession." For union leaders like Cogen and Selden, local union leaders who gained national prominence, new teachers found the public school working conditions untenable and the result was "a tidal wave of teacher resentment against the educational establishment, and it has generated widespread pressure for teacher reform."[90] With growing class sizes and responsibilities but placed on the lowest rungs of an expanding school hierarchy, teachers complained that they had been "relegated to the status of production workers on an educational assembly line."[91] By the 1960s, the organizational structure of the New York City school bureaucracy had grown increasingly complex (figure 7). To make sense of the growing bureaucracy, the Board of Education produced flow charts depicting the array of offices and levels of authority connected by intersecting lines. So removed were they from the work of running the city's schools, teachers were nowhere on the chart. For UFT leaders, these dynamics represented one primary barrier to teacher power and professionalism.

Standing in the way of teacher professionalism, these leaders concurred, was what they characterized as the overbearing paternalism of school and city leaders. One poster calling teachers to the 1961 strike pictured the current relationship: the teacher, depicted as a small boy in man's clothing, cowered, as the mayor, drawn as a large man, placed a coin in his hand and warned him to "run along like a good boy!"[92] (figure 8). "I started in a very tough elementary school," Shanker recalled, "and I had great doubts that I would make it." "After a couple of weeks, the assistant principal appeared at my door," he explained in "Forty Years in the Profession." "I remember thinking," he continued, "'Thank God! Help has come.'" But instead of offering Shanker the support he expected, the principal motioned to the floor and said before leaving, "'Mr. Shanker, I see a lot of paper on the floor in the third aisle. It's very unsightly and very unprofessional.'"[93] Cogen argued that in their dealings with administrators, teachers must demand "respect," "equality," and, above all, "a new professional dignity which is long overdue."[94] Faced with Superintendent Theobald's claims to fire strikers, Cogen defiantly replied, "he can't run the schools without teachers!"[95] Explaining the sentiments at the base of the UFT's first strike, Cogen recalled, "We were determined that the basic decisions involving our working lives were no longer to be made unilaterally by a paternalistic administrator. . . . I had to take drastic action to determine that we meant business."[96]

Around the country, teachers agreed that "master-servant relationships" and "dictatorial principals," male and female, who treated teachers like "messenger boys" inhibited the development of a professional voice. "The idea that the teacher and administrator are one big family just isn't true anymore," offered one high school teacher from Denver. "There's much more of a realization today that they're two separate functions."[97] In previous generations, Shanker suggested, the power imbalance between administrators and teachers may have been warranted because "there was educational distance between the teacher and the principal." But for the new UFT teacher, such dynamics made little sense: "we ought to have the power because we know more."[98] At the base of the Federation's vision of teacher power and professionalism was a complete revision of authority and control in the schools.

When defining the professional, Shanker turned to traditional, masculine definitions, explaining that "he is relatively unsupervised." Drawing comparisons to doctors, Shanker reasoned,

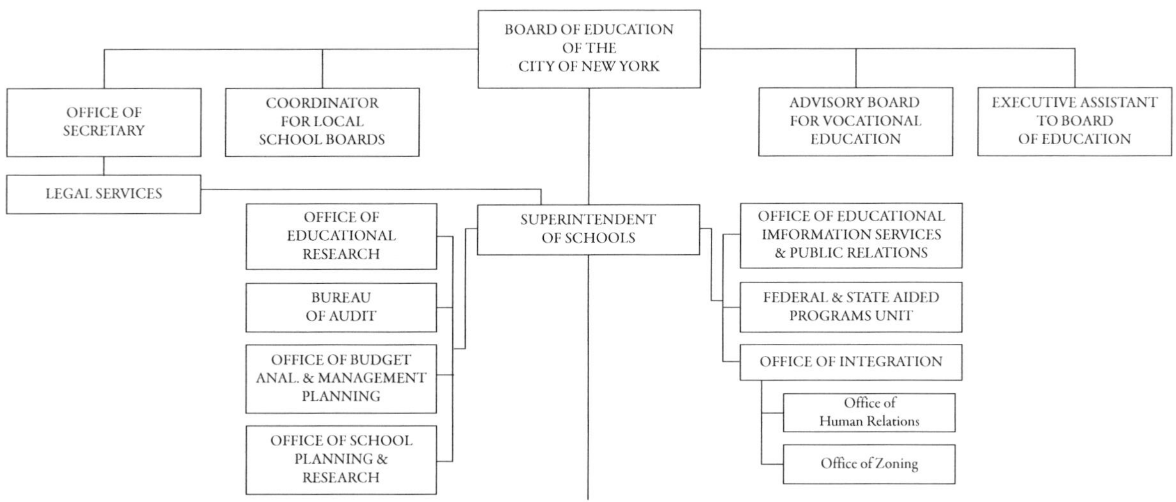
BOARD OF EDUCATION OF THE CITY OF NEW YORK
OFFICE OF SECRETARY
COORDINATOR FOR LOCAL SCHOOL BOARDS
ADVISORY BOARD FOR VOCATIONAL EDUCATION
EXECUTIVE ASSISTANT TO BOARD OF EDUCATION
LEGAL SERVICES
SUPERINTENDENT OF SCHOOLS
OFFICE OF EDUCATIONAL RESEARCH
BUREAU OF AUDIT
OFFICE OF BUDGET ANAL. & MANAGEMENT PLANNING
OFFICE OF SCHOOL PLANNING & RESEARCH
OFFICE OF EDUCATIONAL IMFORMATION SERVICES & PUBLIC RELATIONS
FEDERAL & STATE AIDED PROGRAMS UNIT
OFFICE OF INTEGRATION
Office of Human Relations
Office of Zoning

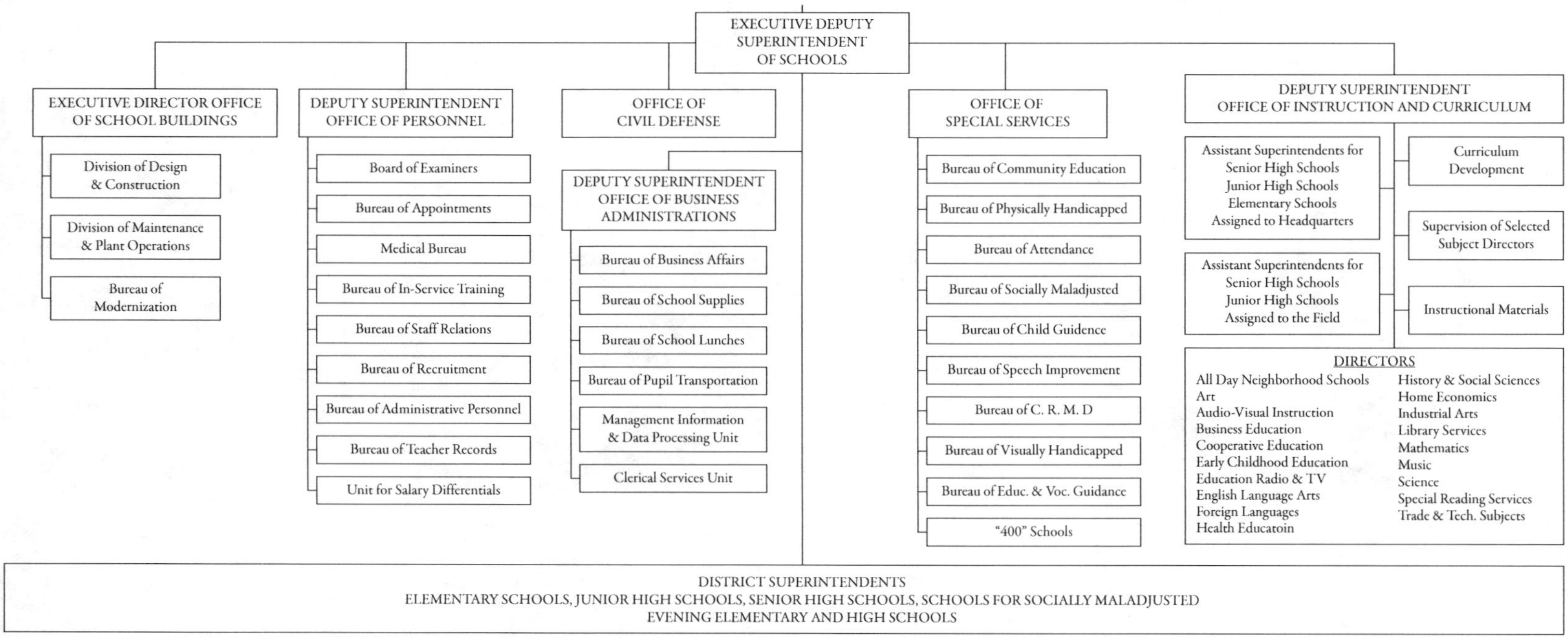

Decentralization of city school system approved by Board of Education has resulted in this new table of organization prepared under direction of Superintendent of Schools. From central headquarters to school district, the table spells out lines of authority leading to objectives of improved administration and supervision of the total educational program.

FIG. 7 "Organization Table of City School System," *Staff Bulletin*, January 31, 1966. (*Source*: New York City Board of Education Collection, Municipal Archives, New York City Department of Records.)

FIG. 8 "The Art of Shortchanging," United Federation of Teachers flyer, ca. mid-1960s. (*Source*: United Federation of Teachers Records, WAG 022, box 17, folder 7, the Tamiment Library/Robert F. Wagner Labor Archives, New York University.)

When a surgeon goes into a hospital or into the operating room, you never have the situation where the president of the board of the hospital or the chief administrator of the hospital walks into the operating rooms and tells the surgeon to cut a little to the left or a little to the right. Not that the administrator of the hospital isn't a professional; not that he doesn't have expertise in his

> own field. . . . As a matter of fact, the surgeon couldn't properly perform his job if the hospital wasn't properly administered. But each of them has a separate type of expertise.[99]

Extending this logic, Shanker called for separate systems and tracks of preparation. During these years, the majority of the city's principals and lower-level administrators began as classroom teachers. Shanker called for an end to this practice, advocating a cohort of "administrators employed from the non-teacher ranks on the basis of administrative competence."[100]

For Shanker and other UFT leaders, teachers' power and professional authority centered on the classroom and curricular matters. Pushing back against calls for building leaders to serve as "instructional leaders," a concept that surfaced during the 1930s and proliferated again during the 1970s and 1980s, UFT leaders advocated a new division of labor. Above all, Shanker explained to an audience at Albion College, "teachers want to deal as equals with administrators."[101] As Shanker made his way around the country giving speech after speech and wrote extensively on the question of teacher professionalism, his James Worley parable became one of his most used examples. "Principals had come and gone in his school, and all had praise for James Worley," Shanker explained in his essay "The Making of a Profession." "Then a new principal arrived." What happened next in the Worley saga changed slightly across Shanker's various retellings. In one of his earliest mentions, Shanker explained to his Syracuse audience in 1971 that Worley's principal declared, "the way a person shows his dedication is by his willingness to make sacrifices, and I want to show the people of this community that our teachers are more dedicated and more willing than other teachers because we are more professional. Therefore I am telling you to go home this weekend and come back on Monday with a detailed hour by hour lesson plan for the entire year in advance."[102] Years later, Shanker modified the tale: "one of [that principal's] first acts was to require all the teachers in the school to submit detailed lesson plans two weeks in advance."[103] The Syracuse audience heard that "Worley went to the principal and said 'I have a good record here; I am not lazy; I am going to write daily plans and submit a very detailed weekly plan and one for a two week period; I will write an essay on what I plan to accomplish over the year.'" Later readers learned that Worley simply refused to comply. In either case, the result was the same: Worley was fired, not because of incompetence but because of insubordination. "The submission of a lesson plan," Shanker explained in "The Making of a Profession," was "an attack on his dignity as a teacher."[104]

By 1961, shortly after the rise of collective bargaining, the UFT removed administrators from their rank-and-file membership. Though small numbers of administrators belonged to the Federation and, before that, the Guild, UFT leaders argued that the presence of administrators within the organization was a violation of basic labor principles.[105] The Federation's stance on administrators was also a key factor that differentiated the organization from the National Education Association (NEA). According to Shanker, "Our non-acceptance of supervisors as a group in the union is certainly in conformity with proper labor practice. Our opposition to the NEA as a company union is based precisely on the role of supervisors within their organization. We must adhere to the principle that unions are for employees and should exclude management and employers no matter how personally liberal, progressive or pro-labor they are."[106] By the mid-1960s, the membership of the NEA had reached 940,000, whereas the AFT counted approximately 110,000. However, as one reporter noted, in spite of its small size, "the AFT's membership has almost doubled in the past five years."[107] Whereas AFT-affiliated teachers opted for militancy, NEA locals derided that approach and instead issued sanctions; both organizations justified their approach in the name of teacher professionalism. Increasingly, the NEA represented suburban and rural teachers, while teachers in the nation's most populous urban centers gravitated toward the AFT. Not interested in joining "company unions dominated by management," teachers in New York City, Philadelphia, Los Angeles, Cleveland, and Detroit, among other cities, chose the AFT as their bargaining agent.[108]

Witnessing the precipitous growth of the AFT, in 1966 the president of the NEA proposed a merger. Responding by telegram, union leaders had little interest in the plan: "The AFT stands for a united teacher organization free from administrator domination and dedicated to the improvement of American society. Our AFL-CIO affiliation has been a great benefit in pursuing this objective. We therefore have no intention of forsaking our affiliation with organized labor."[109] Without the support of labor and with the influence of administrators, leaders of the Federation argued that teachers would be subject to the whims of local leaders and would have to accept "whatever the School Board is willing to give."[110] The professionalism and power organized teachers envisioned centered on freedom from administrative control and interference. Rather than partnership with administrators, union leaders called for control, but on this point, they had no traction. The strong rhetoric by Shanker and others projected power but did little to increase the authority of ordinary classroom teachers in the schools who continued to work in highly managed and routinized environments.

"The Controlling Voice": Teacher Expertise or Community Authority?

In 1963, a report by the city's Board of Examiners highlighted "a still unresolved problem": "The reluctance of new teachers to accept appointments or assignments to schools that they regard as difficult."[111] Throughout the 1960s, as the

Federation negotiated teachers' contracts, one of the primary working conditions union leaders sought to manage centered on so-called disadvantaged schools, a description grounded in deprivationist thinking to characterize schools in high-poverty neighborhoods or those with large populations of children of color. In the 1967 contract negotiations, for instance, unionized teachers requested three critical concessions. First, union leaders called for an end to forced rotations, a practice that administrators maintained was the only way to bring qualified staff to areas of high need. Second, as increasing numbers of teachers moved to the suburbs and many others argued the city was unsafe, organized teachers requested that all new school construction projects include parking lots for teachers. Third, union leaders demanded freedom for teachers to remove the "disruptive child" from their classrooms. As community groups and school leaders cited concerns about equity and social justice, teachers steadfastly maintained that so-called disruptive children impeded their professional work.[112] Thinking back to his first experience as a teacher, Shanker shared impressions of his students. "I was absolutely shocked," he told an interviewer. The sixth graders, he remembered, "were pretty big and tough and using foul street language and screaming and yelling, some of them spoke no language at all." For Shanker, these kinds of kids and the communities that produced them were deprofessionalizing. "One of the driving forces to going to college," he explained in his oral history, "was to get out of that sort of violent life and be in a different kind of neighborhood and be with a different kind of people. And here I was, gone to college, very close to a Ph.D., and there I was locking myself into a room with kids who were exactly the kids I was trying to run away from."[113] Framing the matter in opposite terms, Deputy Chancellor Bernard Donovan, one of the city's highest-ranking Black leaders, maintained that teachers who refused "to serve in 'difficult' ghetto area schools" lacked "professionalism" and "dedication."[114]

These contract negotiations unfolded alongside shifts in the racial politics of the city and nation, amplifying cleavages between city teachers, a predominantly White group, and the communities of color they served. The hope of integration dwindled across the urban North during the late 1960s as the rise of the suburbs amplified long-standing segregation, discrimination, and inequality, prompting grassroots activists around the nation to advocate new strategies for social justice. Calls for community control of police departments, housing boards, and public schools epitomized the sort of shifts in power that were fundamental to the Black Power movement.[115] As one activist explained, White teachers acting in concert with the White-dominated city school system "trapped the black lower class in the tributaries leading to the slums."[116]

In 1967, the Board of Education approved a Ford Foundation–funded community control experiment in the hopes of quelling growing tensions within the city.[117] In the plan, which the UFT signed off on, boards of parents and community members would replace the centralized Board of Education in a series of experimental districts. Initially, Federation leaders understood plans to decentralize the schools by shifting decision-making authority to local boards as a gesture toward partnership that would avoid other more cumbersome busing solutions. However, when local district head Rhody McCoy demanded the transfer of nineteen teachers and administrators out of the Ocean Hill–Brownsville school district, union leaders were enraged and called a strike that stretched into the next school year. On and off for months, UFT teachers picketed the schools alongside Shanker, who argued that the community board's decision ignored "the new power and integrity of the professional teacher."[118] Meanwhile, many Black teachers, representing just 8 percent of the city's teachers and the African American Teachers Association, crossed picket lines to stand with parents and community activists.[119] As one local parent explained to a reporter, "white teachers came into our area and spent practically all of their time studying so that they could get a higher position instead of teaching our children." Pointing to the high number of transfer requests, another parent noted, "They didn't want to teach in neighborhoods such as ours. We don't want those kind of teachers."[120]

The strikes ended in November 1968, largely because the state rolled back all authority that had been granted to communities, but racialized tensions continued to boil over across the schools and city. In an effort to restore the peace, local leaders actively recruited teachers of color for the city's schools through the paraprofessional program and by relaxing certification rules for some teachers. The nature of the hiring policies simultaneously increased the number of teachers of color in the city's schools and entrapped them on the lowest levels of the school bureaucracy. Regardless, the gains were fleeting. As the 1975 fiscal crisis descended on New York City, local policymakers identified mass layoffs of municipal workers as the only way to avoid bankruptcy. Deputy Chancellor Gifford, along with other local leaders, warned that collectively bargained seniority rules would make the firing fall squarely on the backs of the newly hired teachers of color. Shanker, however, was unwilling to bend seniority rules, the crucible of union power, and Gifford's predictions came to fruition as the majority of teachers of color who had made their way into the city's schools were once again displaced.

For many in the city, the firings provided more evidence that White interests trumped those of the Black community. In response, local activists organized a protest at City Hall "to draw attention to the fact that a disproportionate number of Blacks are being excessed or laid off because they lack seniority" and to affirm that the "seniority doctrine is inimical to the economic welfare of Blacks."[121] By 1975, long-standing claims of discriminatory hiring practices made their way to the United States Department of Housing, Education and Welfare's (HEW) Office for Civil Rights (OCR). Shifting the focus from the shortcomings of the South to the endemic racism of the North and West, Martin Gerry, director of OCR, and his staff investigated big cities around the country and found that unions and "teachers themselves" were key barriers to change.[122]

In 1976, Gerry's investigation reached the New York City schools. Finding evidence of widespread discriminatory practices that traced back to collectively bargained contracts, the OCR team called for corrective action within ninety days, explaining, "the laws apply equally North and South and to all school systems, large or small."[123] Shanker excoriated the report as illogical and destructive and promised that it would only further inflame racialized tensions in the city.[124] Nevertheless, local school leaders were compelled by the OCR's threat to withdraw the more than $200 million the city's schools received in federal aid each year, and set out to develop a plan to diversify the city's schools. By September 1977, nearly one year after Gerry released his report, city school leaders generated a plan that met the approval of OCR officials; the solution centered on two boxes. In one were the positions White teachers could apply for, comprised of schools where the proportion of minority teachers exceeded 20 percent, and in the other were positions for Black and Hispanic teachers, in schools where minority teachers comprised less than 10 percent of the teaching staff. "For the first time in the history of the city school system," one reporter alerted readers, "teachers were officially assigned on the basis of race."[125]

New York City had long been a national bellwether for education policy and reform and, as such, it garnered much attention. In 1977, members of Congress debated the merits of the city's hiring plan. Some, like David Tatal, the director of the Office of Civil Rights, characterized the arrangements as a "major step forward" in complying with the Civil Rights Act of 1964 and education amendments of 1972 prohibiting discrimination. Likewise, many members of the local Black community praised the plan as an important step in the right direction. As Velmadette Montgomery, president of Community Schools Board 13, explained to a local reporter, "I'd like to see HEW go even further in their integration demands so the city can deal with the whole problem of segregation."[126] Meanwhile, other local politicians like mayoral candidate Ed Koch and Senator Daniel Patrick Moynihan assailed the race-based hiring plan, calling it a "prescription for division and hostility." For Moynihan, the visual of teachers lining up by race for jobs conjured images of "the sorting out of human beings for the death camps of Hitler's Germany."[127] Echoing those criticisms, for many members of the UFT, concerns about the demographic composition of the teacher workforce and efforts to achieve a more equitable distribution represented the toppling of an imagined merit system. Shanker claimed that in searching for diversity, school leaders had "lowered the standards to a point where a significant number [of teachers come] in below the literacy line."[128] "We want our institutions to be integrated," Shanker explained in his paid "Where

We Stand" installment in the *New York Times*, but "we have worked for a society which will be color blind."[129] From Shanker's vantage point, affirmative action plans undermined the ideals of merit and diversification measures eroded the quality of the profession, offering a rationale that pathologized Blackness and situated teacher professionalism within the realm of Whiteness.

In October 1977, before the hiring plan could be fully realized, it was derailed when leaders of one of the city's majority-White school districts joined with Shanker and the UFT to bring legal action against the city and HEW. The case wound its way through the courts for nearly two years before being decided in favor of the city and HEW. Regardless, local school leaders had already backed off of the plan. On April 7, 1978, School Chancellor Irving Anker announced that the Board of Education had decided to discontinue the race-based hiring practices, in spite of encouragement from OCR to continue. In a closed-door meeting, board members instead opted for a program of voluntary rotation and random selection. According to one board member who wished to remain anonymous, they made the change because the previous plan has been "so distasteful." "I've been walking a tightrope," agreed Frank Arricale, executive director of the Board of Education's Division of Personnel. "I felt I had to go along with the racial placements in order not to lose millions of dollars for youngsters, but at the same time I was revolted and offended by the procedure."[130] A function of historic forces, employment and housing opportunities, and deeply rooted racialized perceptions, there was no simple pathway leading to equity and justice. Union leaders fought for a vision of the professional teacher fueled by the burgeoning institutional interests of their organization. Of course, Federation teachers did not bear responsibility for the circumstances alone. But in their staunch defense of both existing arrangements and the hierarchical vision of power that envisioned professional teachers as separate from and above the communities they served, they simultaneously represented a barrier to change and the intricate ways inequity had woven through the organizational fabric of social institutions nationwide.

"Woefully Inadequate": The Quest for Control over Teachers' Preparation

The mantra of teacher power and expertise, which hinged on control and separation in the name of professionalism, informed the Federation's perspectives on and interactions with school administrators, community members, and teacher educators. While the sort of shift in power Shanker and UFT leaders imagined when it came to school administrators never came to fruition, they were much more successful when it came to teacher preparation, largely because teacher educators and schools of education were vulnerable after fending off decades of criticism. Extending the reproach launched decades earlier, James

Koerner, author of *The Miseducation of American Teachers* and former director of Harvard's Master of Arts in Teaching program, castigated in 1963, "The intellectual capacity of the education faculty is *the* fundamental limitation of the field." In his analysis, self-proclaimed "educationists" taught classes that were "puerile, repetitious, dull and ambiguous—incontestably." Like others before him, Koerner called for greater academic preparation for teachers and the elimination of undergraduate preparation programs.[131] For some, accreditation and the development of the National Council for the Accreditation of Teacher Education (NCATE) during the 1950s represented one way to ensure higher quality and uniformity. But by the early 1960s and preliminary rounds of reviews, critics argued that accreditors were embedded in schools of education and other organizations like the NEA; instead of being a force of change, they argued, accreditation was a manifestation of the core problems with teacher education and would only serve to further entrench problems. A leading voice on the matter was Koerner's colleague and former Harvard president James Conant, who argued that "methods of instruction and accreditation" together "were responsible for the presence of unqualified teachers in the nation's schools" and called on presidents, deans, and professors to close their schools to accrediting teams.[132]

For critics like Conant, the situation at the University of Wisconsin's School of Education provided all of the supporting evidence they needed. Though it was already accredited, Dean Lindley Stiles sought reaccreditation in 1962 for all programs at the school from elementary teacher education to the doctoral program. The result was a "violent disagreement" between the school and NCATE that "led to an academic explosion." In September 1962, NCATE accreditors informed Stiles that while they had approved the graduate program, they were placing the school's undergraduate training program on probation. In addition to ancillary critiques including university infrastructure in need of repair and an overspecialization in the areas of training music and agriculture teachers, which Stiles argued had nothing to do with accreditation, the visiting NCATE team's primary critique centered on the place of liberal arts in the preparation of teachers at the school. According to one report, "The council criticized the fact that there were a number of different avenues and course patterns through which students could satisfy their non-professional, general education and liberal arts requirements." As academics, members of philanthropic organizations, and other critics had called for precisely such circumstances, NCATE's stance on the matter represented a clear line drawn in the sand: NCATE did not represent "the vast army of liberal arts scholars."[133] Stiles lambasted NCATE as "rigid" and "arbitrary," and attributed its shortcomings to the composition of the council: education school professors and representatives from state education organizations and teacher organizations.[134] In an attempt to win over critics, the 1970s standards included "responsible experimentation and innovation" and claimed that "a deliberate attempt has been made in these standards to encourage individuality, imagination, and innovation in institutional planning."[135] The changes, however, were not enough to assuage critics and went largely unnoticed.

As the reach of the federal government extended further into local school districts throughout the 1960s, Commissioner Howe reported potential recruits were "sometimes discouraged from entering the profession by the required training programs, the situation in the schools themselves, and the discontinuity between these two experiences." In addition to discouraging prospective talent, in Howe's assessment, "traditional" approaches sent teachers into the nation's schools "unprepared."[136] During the spring of 1967, Howe sat before a senate subcommittee and testified that "present training programs are not capable of encouraging either the numbers, kinds, or quality of people needed to staff this Nation's educational programs."[137] In response, to encourage improved instruction in the nation's elementary and secondary schools through improved teacher education, in 1967 President Johnson signed the Education Professions Development Act that allocated $6.9 million for fellowships and special programs.[138]

Joining the storm of critics, Federation leaders identified two overarching problems with teacher education. The first and most important deficiency, they decried, was the simple inconsequentiality of the teacher education curriculum. In his speech at Syracuse University, Shanker characterized teacher training as "universally recognized as now being completely irrelevant." Like teachers before him, Shanker contended that the brand of education these programs advanced had little to do with teachers' actual work. In the second related critique, the Federation took aim at the faculty populating schools of education, arguing that they were out of touch with the realities of teachers' work lives. Too many courses in schools of education, Shanker contended, "are given by many people who have never themselves taught in elementary and secondary schools, but rather are scholars and theorists." Instead, he continued, "faculties ought to be leavened by those who have had considerable classroom experience and continue to practice in the classroom."[139]

To support their vision of teachers' professional preparation, the Federation implemented sweeping in-service education programs. Sponsoring Teacher Centers, UFT mini-courses, and programs aimed at promising college seniors, the Federation leadership became an embedded component of teacher education. By the summer of 1969, the city's Board of Education officially recognized the UFT-sponsored in-service curricula, linking course completion to incremental salary increases.[140] Designed to compensate for what teacher training institutions lacked, UFT-created programs directed by classroom teachers focused on "real" knowledge for practitioners. "Each teacher should not have to rediscover the wheel. . . . That is the idea behind the UFT mini-course (which by the way, are not long courses about theory, but two hour sessions about how to do one particular thing or teach one particular concept)."[141] These programs fostered "actual on-the-job" knowledge and were taught by actual classroom teachers; the UFT marketed their work as an alternative to traditional programs and a road to increased pay.[142]

In 1974, for instance, the Federation released an open letter to the city's deans of teacher education and directors of teacher certification. Asserting their authority in the professional education of teachers, the union affirmed that "in order to insure teacher input, the UFT requests representation at all levels of teacher education program development." Leveraging a threat that university officials understood, the letter proclaimed that "unless teachers are involved in program development and implementation at every stage they will not cooperate."[143] In addition to establishing curricula, Federation leaders demanded an active and visible role for the organization in the preparation and training of teachers. In an effort to "break down the barrier between the classroom and the university," the Federation called for "classroom teachers [to] serve as professors of education."[144]

During these years, the faculty at schools of education in the city turned to the union in new ways. For instance, in February 1968, Joseph Grannis, director of the Division of Instruction at Teachers College, Columbia University, wrote to Shanker. "For several months now a number of us at Teachers College have been considering how we might orient our teacher training programs to the needs and realities of urban education," he began his note. Candidly, he continued, "it will be agreed by all around that the College should have been thinking about this some time ago, and it is not going to be any easier now for having waited." Soliciting Shanker's advice and support, Grannis explained, "We are considering a two year MA program in which the candidate would be gradually initiated into various aspects of urban teaching during the first year, and in which he would be a paid intern in a secondary school . . . during the second year." Promising "a basic revision of much of the existing program at Teachers College," Grannis asked for the "support of the United Federation of Teachers. Can we meet soon?"[145] Happy to oblige, in his years at the helm of the UFT and the AFT, Shanker traveled across the city and around the country meeting with college faculty and delivering speeches.

The financial realities gripping university-based schools of education, including negligible endowments, cost-sharing plans, and tuition dependency, informed how faculty at schools of education responded to criticism and the Federation. Even as select institutions like the Graduate School of Education at Harvard University opted for "a smaller student body in view of dwindling financial aid and the need for more individual attention" under the leadership of Dean Paul Ylvisaker, a former officer at the Ford Foundation, such was not a course of action other institutions could afford.[146] Instead, the majority of schools of education around the country reached outward in search of new partnerships that would yield new streams of tuition revenue. At New York University, for instance, school officials created new programs in partnership with the UFT, the federal government, and the Board of Education. Even as these groups each levied significant criticism at New York University, in particular, and at teacher preparation, generally, faculty and school officials there barely shrugged. For instance, in 1972, Sandra Feldman, a rising star in the UFT and one of its future presidents, shared her impressions of New York University's teacher education program with faculty there: "For the most part teacher training is inadequate to the actual needs of the teachers." She devoted the rest of her letter to enumerating possible changes and closed by stating, "I hope this gives you some notion of where emphasis I would like to see placed" [*sic*].[147] Similarly, the UFT's proposal for Teacher Centers blasted the inadequacy of teacher education programs. In response, Dean Griffiths of New York University gently cautioned that relying too heavily on teachers as professors might lead the "course work to degenerate into a show and tell," but affirmed that the proposal was "very good" and that "we would certainly be very pleased to work with you."[148]

At the same time that schools of education like New York University's created new programs with the union grounded in their perception of what teachers' professional preparation ought to look like, they also engaged in similar conversations with other groups, resulting in an array of disparate programs. In 1968, the federally funded National Teacher Corps partnered with New York University and other schools around the nation. Designed as an alternative to traditional teacher education programs, the school gladly embraced the program. In a progress report on the first two cycles of the corps at New York University, Frederick Rodgers, director of the program, focused on how much money the initiative generated for the school. "The grand total of contracts awarded to the New York University Teacher Corps Project for the first two academic years and three summer sessions amounted to $538,594." He closed his report by stating the obvious to the school's leadership. "It becomes evident," he wrote, "that the Teacher Corps Program at New York University has been a major contributor to the financial and programmatic growth of the School and Education in particular and the University in general."[149] Whereas students who enrolled in programs supported by the UFT learned about the practical aspects of classroom management, Corps students spent their time with community members learning about the social contexts of prospective students.

Following yet another discrete path and amplifying the emerging institutional incoherence apparent during these years, the school of education at New York University also initiated a close relationship with the Board of Education. Creating a pipeline between the school and the city's classrooms, in 1978, New York University and the board entered into a historic partnership. Frank

Arricale, the executive director of the board's Division of Personnel, explained the type of training administrators would like future "personnel" to have. New York University, represented by Associate Dean Arnold Spinner, agreed to run particular classes at board-approved times. In turn, the board would pay for the courses. A financial contract more than anything else, the proposal stated, "It is to be understood that confirmation of this agreement obligates the Board of Education of the City of New York to compensate New York University for the total amount of this agreement regardless of enrollments. Payment is scheduled to be 50 percent upon execution of this agreement, 25 percent on 1 December 1978 and a final payment of 25 percent on 1 June 1979."[150] The total amount of money at play was $126,792, but beyond a financial pact, the agreement had real consequences for the shape of education at the school. For instance, before printing the 1980 course bulletin, Dean Griffiths wrote to members of the board inquiring if the proposed offerings would be acceptable. Monica Blum responded to Griffith, stating that "New York University's three-week 1980 Summer Session Courses are acceptable toward meeting eligibility requirements for salary differentials and promotional incrementals."[151] They were not alone in this sort of outreach; in 1984, James M. Cooper, dean of the Curry School of Education at the University of Virginia, announced to local school districts that he would offer a warranty on the teachers the school prepared. Referring to a television commercial from the time, he stated, "I'll be like the Maytag repairman, who will sit by the phone, but get no calls. We have confidence in our product." What would happen in the event of a complaint? Cooper committed to "dispatch a professor to correct the problem."[152]

As numbers in the teacher education programs began to dwindle, administrators at the school of education at New York University, accustomed to large student enrollments, turned their sights elsewhere. "Though teacher education programs continue to be offered," officials noted in a report from 1980, "it has been through the imaginative moves into new areas of study, especially in the emerging health-related and arts professions, that the School has been able to maintain its financial soundness."[153] In 1974, emphasizing this new situation, New York University's School of Education changed its name to the School of Education, Health, Nursing, and Arts Professions (SEHNAP), comprised of four distinct and equal divisions. Around the country, motivated by similar pressures, schools of education changed their names and reached beyond the preparation of teachers. For example, in 1971, California State University merged its school of education with programs in speech, criminal science, and social work to create a new school devoted to professional and applied studies. According to University President Donald L. Shields, "I see it as an opening up of the vistas for our education program, allowing it to expand and broaden into areas other than just the training of teachers."[154] As schools of education ceded their role in the professional preparation of teachers, they further deprived teachers of the sort of academic training and place in the university in which other professional occupations grounded their claims of expertise. In asserting their authority, leaders of the Federation gained unprecedented control over teacher education. However, even as they did so in the name of professional authority, in prioritizing the vocational aspects of training and isolating teachers from the university, union leaders distanced teachers from the status they sought.

By the late 1970s, mounting criticism of formal education programs and the rising power of organized teachers lifted calls for Teacher Centers to the top of federal reform agendas. According to one report from 1977, "all of us have known for decades that teacher education has never been adequate. . . . For too long, teachers and teacher education have proclaimed their professional status, knowing that it was more aspirational than reality."[155] As local UFT leaders asserted, teacher education was "woefully inadequate" and those deficiencies had sweeping implications. "It is the firm belief of the UFT leadership," the proposal stated, "that the failures of teacher education thus far are closely related to the profession's lack of ability to influence its own development." Teacher Centers would "offer teachers the first opportunity to determine the form of their own professional development."[156] By 1978, the federal government allocated $45 million to support three hundred centers around the country. According to Myrna Cooper, a Center leader in New York City, the program brought "bits of success to the attention of others who are demoralized." At its base, the Teacher Center model focused on teachers teaching teachers. Even as conservative groups like the Heritage Foundation derided the centers as "tax-payer financed union halls," supporters maintained that such initiatives were central to teacher improvement. "A district board may set a new priority and, for instance, order everybody to individualize the reading program, and then the board members go home and to bed." According to Cooper, "we try to help teachers do it—to select materials, diagnose and evaluate the children."[157] According to an AFT report, through Centers—which took multiple forms across the United States—"teachers will finally be given the major responsibility for determining the kinds of changes and improvements that are needed in their classrooms."[158] In the assessment of Roy Edelfelt, a former director of the Teacher Center program, "despite problems of poor working conditions, low salaries, and inadequate public esteem, [teachers] are hanging onto the teacher center because that is where they find support, trust, freedom, stimulation, and help in doing a better job."[159] Union-supported initiatives like Teacher Centers cropped up across the nation, giving teachers the opportunity to sidestep university-based programs and talk about their work outside of their classrooms. Even as these initiatives were received warmly, reformers were unclear if they had any measurable impact on student learning. In the end, even as new initiatives and lofty rhetoric abounded, the fundamental circumstances of teachers' work lives changed little as the hierarchical power structures of the school remained largely intact.

The "Elder Statesman": Expertise, Authority, and Bureaucracy

Following the strikes and demonstrations of teacher militancy during the 1960s, Shanker recalled, "we demonstrated our tremendous power . . . we didn't have to demonstrate it anymore."[160] Instead, as Shanker assumed the presidency of the AFT in 1974, holding that post along with the presidency of the UFT until 1986 as well as taking on new positions within the AFL, he carved out a different space for himself. "A crucial issue in education is the extent to which teachers are to share in the policy-making," Shanker explained to a crowd in Michigan in 1965.[161] Shanker, along with other UFT leaders, claimed over and over again during these years that the only way for teachers to achieve the prestige of professional expertise was for teachers to have equal standing with administrators and teacher educators. To an extent, they achieved this. Over this time, the teachers union gained enormous power on the local and national levels, seemingly becoming a branch of the educational system, and Shanker became a revered educational statesman. For instance, at a memorial service in Shanker's honor in 1997, President Clinton heralded him as "one of the most important teachers of the twentieth century."[162] Later, Secretary of Education Arne Duncan offered a similar sentiment, recalling Shanker as a "legendary" reformer and leader.[163] However, while the Federation, as an institution, and Shanker, as an individual, ascended, teachers attained little additional authority.[164] Furthermore, in Shanker's speeches and writings, he spoke about teachers, as other reforms had. As it had for others across the educational landscape, the discourse of teacher blame propelled Shanker's brand of gendered and racialized benevolent paternalism.

For instance, in an essay reflecting on his years in the Federation, Shanker mused about the schools' shortcomings and blamed teachers. Why were students not learning as much as they should? According to Shanker, poor teaching was to blame. Comparing two scenarios, he wrote, "If I had learned about birds in school, my teacher probably would have had flashcards and pictures of birds all over the room. Eventually we would have had a bird test. . . . I know I would have forgotten the birds within three weeks of taking the test—and that would have been no loss because I probably would have learned to hate them anyway." Thankfully, Shanker recalled, he did not learn about birds from a teacher but instead from a troop leader when he was a boy scout. "I don't know of anybody who got a bird-study merit badge who didn't maintain an interest in birds for many years after that," he concluded.[165] Despite the fact that by the late 1960s he represented 97 percent of the city's public school teaching population, Shanker still maintained that the problem with the profession rested on its consistent inability "to attract and keep teachers of any caliber."[166] Even as earlier union leaders and teachers pointed to their preparation and certification as markers of their professional credibility, Shanker characterized both as a "joke" in 1985. Undermining teachers' claims, for Shanker, the barriers to enter the teaching profession would "be the equivalent of licensing doctors on the basis of an examination in elementary biology or licensing accountants and actuaries on the basis of some type of elementary mathematics examination."[167]

In joining the union leadership, work he described as "an exhilarating intellectual experience," Shanker transformed himself from a teacher into an "elder statesman."[168] In "The Making of a Profession," Shanker outlined his transformed image.

> The day after that speech, I went out to Utah, where we are organizing teachers. The morning I arrived in Utah, the local headline said, "Union Boss Supports Teacher Tests." I spoke at a couple of places in Salt Lake City; and the next day the headline said, "Speaker Reiterates Support for National Test." By the third day, the headline said, "Educator Supports Teacher Testing." Within three days I went from being a union boss to being an educator; and that's what this is all about—what our role is going to be and how the public sees us.[169]

Shanker's role as reformer brought a new interest and relevance to the Federation and to locals around the country, even as he derided those already in the profession.

Pictured with mayors, governors, presidents, and foreign dignitaries, but rarely ever in a classroom, Shanker's meteoric rise was well planned. Following the Ocean Hill–Brownsville strikes in the fall of 1968, Shanker hired a public relations advisor to mend his image. The advice he received formed the impetus of his "Where We Stand" column in the *New York Times*. In this weekly advertisement designed to look like an editorial, Shanker wrote on a variety of issues. Though it was paid for by the Federation, Shanker saw the column as his own, maintaining that if it was a "house organ . . . nobody is going to read it." Instead, Shanker reflected, "that means you have to be allowed to say what you want, even though the organization is paying for it." Appealing to a public far wider than teachers, Shanker used the space to talk about "educational debates, political, social, human rights, [and] labor issues"—that is, anything that piqued his interest. Though inextricably writing on behalf of teachers as their president, he was clear that he was not writing to them. In an effort to appease teachers, he explained, "every second or third or fourth [column] there is something which will be appealing to teachers, even though I wasn't mostly writing it for them." As a result of the column, Shanker received various invitations to review manuscripts and to deliver paid speeches. Recalling one evening in Thailand, he reminisced, "I received a note in my hotel letter box saying that the Prime Minister, Kreingsak, was inviting us to dinner. So we got to this hotel, and as we walked in to the Prime Minister's dinner—the Prime Minister wasn't there but there was a little musical combo that was playing and here were five or six members of congress and a few members of the military. We were having cocktails and in came the Prime Minister . . . and he walked right past the Members of Congress and came up to me." Meanwhile, when considering the impact his column had on the teachers who paid for it, he explained that they experienced a sort of notoriety by association. "Teachers," Shanker shared with his interviewer, "would find that their [family and friends] would talk with them about what Shanker wrote last week or two weeks ago, and usually they said something like 'I agreed with what Shanker said,' and that got members to realize the powerful impact." Shanker understood his work as a matter of balancing the needs of "a number of different audiences and constituencies." Teachers were just one group of many he was concerned with.[170]

As president of the UFT and later the AFT as well, Shanker had little tolerance for dissent within the ranks. For instance, in February 1965, teachers at the evening high school scheduled a strike under the leadership of Roger Parente. Shanker rightly understood the threat of a wildcat strike as union busting and, in response, called a meeting at one evening school. "Roger was sitting there," he remembered. "Somebody said, we have Mr. Parente here to debate with Mr. Shanker and each one will have ten minutes. Then somebody stuck a tape recorder and said Mr. Shanker will go first." Refusing to be recorded and demanding the floor for the entire time, Shanker explained to the group, "This is my meeting. Meet with him if you like, but not at this meeting." He then proceeded to explain to the assembled teachers that they did not have the support of the UFT. "You will end up cutting your own throats. . . . I will personally enlist thousands of teachers to take your jobs and I will be one of them," he recalled saying.[171] Taking his threats seriously, the evening teachers chose to fall in line with the rest of the city's teachers behind Shanker.

Shanker argued that "a professional is a person who is an expert and [as such] is permitted to operate fairly independently, to make decisions, to exercise discretion, to be free of most direct supervision," but few teachers experienced this, least of all in their new union.[172] As the union grew, so too did its leadership structure, becoming more distant from rank-and-file members. "That is not exciting for a member," Shanker admitted. Where previously members mobilized through collective action, in a nod towards the Federation's increasing bureaucratic structure, Shanker noted "now most of those things are handled quietly."[173] To keep track of teachers, the UFT produced "record of professional growth forms" and "request for approval of professional growth credit forms," reproducing the bureaucracy of the school system.[174] Teachers flocked to the union in historic numbers during these years in search of representation and power. Voiceless within the bureaucratic structure of the schools, teachers optimistically looked to the union as a mechanism to support complaints regarding administrators. Because of the sheer size of the membership, however, the Federation quickly implemented procedures "to sift and weed out those grievance complaints which are clearly unfounded or insignificant."[175] Lines and levels of authority defined the bureaucratic structure of the Federation, clearly demarcating the leadership, which was mostly male, from the rank-and-file membership, which was mostly female. Communicating this very divide, Shanker explained, "We who lead teachers were once only a handful of believers with a vision."[176]

Not all Federation teachers agreed with Shanker or supported his actions, but even as the union leadership called for teacher power and voice, rank-and-file members found that they had little of either within their own organization. Following the 1967 strike, for example, teachers sent angry letters to Shanker, feeling that he accepted Mayor Lindsey's proposal too quickly. One letter of many sent to Shanker in September argued, "You asked us to have courage and then you sold us out."[177] In a letter to all members later that month, Shanker declared, "WE HAVE WON," looking past the criticism and setting the terms for victory on his own.[178] Shanker inhabited a difficult space at the helm of the Federation because of the size of the organization and the diverse viewpoints and expectations of members. Just as some teachers thought he folded too easily, many others wrote in and sent telegrams begging him to end the 1967 work stoppage. "Must end strike now—I want to teach," Seymour Samuels wrote to Shanker.[179] "Please stop haggling," Lilian Marks and Frances Rose told Shanker via telegram. "Settle contract so that pupils and teachers can get back to schools."[180] Following the 1975 strike, another torrent of angry letters filled the UFT headquarters. "I would like to express my deepest dissatisfaction concerning the contract, as I was not allowed to express it in the Felt Forum through voting," teacher-member Mark Durbin wrote. "Why weren't the polls opened till late at night, as they were on the day we voted to strike?" he continued. "Were you afraid all the rank and file would vote to continue the strike? I was not given enough notice to get there. . . . I am considering leaving the UFT. And did we really get that pay hike where there are so many teachers being laid off. . . . Our union is dead. It is no longer great and powerful. I pray that one day a new phoenix will rise from the ashes.[181]

Many teachers accused Shanker of joining with the governor and mayor for his own political gain, charging yet again that he "sold out the teachers."[182] Another wrote, "You have certainly earned yourself a place in labor history as a betrayer of the rank and file."[183] Though perhaps not the response they desired, thanks to a highly efficient bureaucratic structure, each author received a form letter issued by Shanker's assistant: "Albert Shanker has asked me to thank you for your letter of ____. You are not alone in your frustration; many other UFT members, as you know, are also upset.... UFT members have become accustomed to strikes producing almost miraculous results that few of us can accept the reality that, in the city's present crisis, the strike is simply not a miracle worker.... Yours Sincerely, Ned Hopkins, Assistant to President."[184] As the Federation's power grew, so too did its internal bureaucracy. In representing teachers, labor organizations were also representing their own institutional interests, which, while related, were not always the same. By the early 1980s, both the structure of teachers' labor organizations on the local and national level and the place of teachers within it undermined the fundamental calls for teacher power and professionalism that propelled the union from the start.

The mantra of teacher power as professionalism instigated the development of teachers' muscular militancy and the ascendancy of the union during these years. Even as teachers had affiliated with organized labor since the turn of the twentieth century, the rise of collective bargaining in the 1960s fundamentally altered existing arrangements. Union leaders of the time explained the growth of the movement as a victory of personality and a function of the entrance of men following World War II. However, other important factors were also at play that carved out space for teacher militancy. In addition to a steady historical evolution, perhaps above all factors were the conditions under which teachers worked. By the 1960s, teachers in New York found themselves teaching inside crumbling schools with overcrowded classrooms in a city where crime and poverty rates soared. Meanwhile, the bureaucracy of the schools had expanded to such a degree that there was no longer space for teachers on visual depictions of the schools' organizational structure. The number of administrators in the district compared to the number of teachers yielded a near 1:1 ratio as teachers found their work lives regulated and managed.[185] The rise of the teachers union and the labor playbook that set its strategy matched the industrialized nature of public school teaching.

Even as more men entered the city's schools by the 1960s than before, teaching in New York and elsewhere remained a female-dominated profession; those women who joined the Federation in historic numbers as rank-and-file members sustained the organization's claims of authority. However, in the leadership ranks, gender dynamics switched and men predominated. Rather than challenge the stereotypical image of female teachers that disempowered them for more than a century, male leaders used those images as a foil to affirm that they represented something new and different. In Federation leaders' calls for power and authority, they argued that teachers, rather than administrators, community members, or teacher educators ought to have control, amplifying existing racial tensions and crafting a vision of professionalism rooted in Whiteness. However, rank-and-file teachers experienced neither power nor voice, either in the schools or in their union, which, in an effort to keep pace with growth, developed its own bureaucratic organization. By the 1980s, local and national union leaders had become fixtures in education policy debates and the union an embedded component of the structures of public schooling. Nevertheless, the structures that standardized, regulated, and disempowered teachers remained intact. The discourse of teacher blame gave life to and strengthened the bureaucratic organization of municipal public schools systems, university-based teacher education programs, and teacher unions.

Epilogue

Dan Lortie oriented his 1975 sociological study *Schoolteacher* around "a search for the nature and content of the ethos of the occupation."[1] In that work he described the structural stability and cellular organization of public schools, famously characterizing teachers' workspaces as egg crates that left them socially and intellectually isolated. For Lortie and others, the circumstances of teachers' working conditions, beginning with the nature of their preparation and extending to administrative hierarchies, delimited them as semiprofessionals.[2] In many accounts, including Lortie's, the problems plaguing public school teachers, ranging from low pay to low voice, centered on their collective lack of professional stature and stemmed from that isolation. Teachers' shared plights, in this formulation, were the unintended consequences of the historic development of the modern school bureaucracy, but teachers' shared professional destiny was in their own hands. Teachers, Lortie argued, "must choose which functions they will agree to perform and which they will leave to others."[3] Continuing, he suggested that the pathway to improvement for the occupation and public schools hinged on teachers' "collegial responsibility": teachers ought to trust one another, exert their voice, and play a part in the operation of the schools. "To expect teachers to contribute to the development of their occupational knowledge," he offered in closing, "seems reasonable; to the extent that they do, their future standing and work circumstances will benefit."[4] An embodiment of the bootstrap ideology, in this policy story, the problems schools and teachers faced and their persistence traced back to teachers who, collectively, have not done enough to change their lot.

Even as elements of that essential policy story rooted in blame and the reforms that narrative yielded changed over time along with the social, economic, and political circumstances of the moment, the fundamental plotline remained consistent. Like a thread weaving throughout history, that policy story has set the tenor of education reform in the twenty-first century as well. Speaking before a group gathered at the National Board of Professional Teaching Standards in the summer of 2011, Secretary of Education Arne Duncan noted the importance of the nation's public school teachers but also lamented that "bright, committed young Americans—the very people our students need in the classroom—do not answer the call to teach." In Duncan's estimation, though "teaching must be one of our nation's most honorable professions," it simply was not. Identifying "an amazing chance to modernize the teaching profession and expand the talent pool" in forecasted retirements, Duncan called for "dramatic changes in the way we recruit, train, support, evaluate and compensate teachers." The stakes were high, Duncan explained to his audience. Professionalized teachers would not only close persistent achievement gaps but would also support technological innovation and international competition. Echoing Lortie, Duncan at once cast teachers as the solution and potential barrier to improvement: "Change," he cautioned, "can only come from the men and women who do the hard work every day in our classrooms." Duncan urged, "We must remake the teaching profession itself . . . our children, our parents, our teachers, and our country deserve better."[5] To readers of this book, the reforms that sprang from Duncan's calls, including teacher evaluation systems, alternate pathways into the profession, tighter controls over teacher preparation, and merit pay, will all sound familiar. Even as Duncan and many others have cast their calls for change as radical, new experiments, they have reiterated the same policy story that blames teachers. From that narrative, a predictable package of professionalization-as-rationalization reforms has sprung.

The history chronicled in this book challenges the persistent trope of the problem teacher. Far more than historical accidents, reforms levied in the name of teacher improvement for school improvement isolated teachers within the schools to the lowest levels of a growing bureaucracy, curtailed their expertise, silenced their voices, and circumscribed their ability to make decisions and act autonomously. Policymakers introduced teacher professionalization reforms as ways to standardize, regulate, and improve the efficiency of the public schools, as the historical mantra of professionalism built easy consensus. Professionalization was a metaphor for stature and authority, but the teacher reforms levied in its name bore little resemblance to the processes that shaped other professional occupations. The vocabulary of profession generated consensus as it carried fundamentally positive connotations, but in substance, teacher professionalization, systematization, and rationalization were one and the same—all propelled by the discourse of blame in the service of increasing the efficiency and efficacy of public school systems. Ideologies about the social value of public schooling combined with the institutional interests of various groups of reformers defined professionalization initiatives for teachers.

Teaching, this history reveals, was not merely an occupation predominated by White women but an occupation designed as such. Policymakers, school leaders, teacher educators, and union leaders viewed the schools through a racialized and gendered lens; those perceptions produced policies and practices that cast public school teaching as work for White women by ushering some in and keeping others out. In short, the composition of the teacher workforce and the nature of public school teaching were by design.

This book demonstrates that, regardless of whether we are aware of it or not, history extends all around us with no clear dividing line between then and now. In making history visible, we gain a lens to make sense of the present and chart the future.[6] At a first level is an origination story: an understanding of the past helps us understand where the problems and challenges we face came from and how others have tried to address them. Related to that, historical knowledge shakes off our illusion of newness, alerting us instead to evolution: even amid change we are part of a broader legacy, a bigger story. Most important of all, an understanding of the past ought to be disruptive: taking history seriously means questioning the fundamental assumptions and standard tropes we have come to accept as fact.

If the central thesis of this book, that teacher professionalization reforms not only impeded professional stature for teachers but amplified calls for more professionalization reforms, is fundamentally Sisyphean, then how can we get the proverbial rock up the hill once and for all? Core contributions of this book include identifying the historic policy story of blaming teachers; tracking how policymakers, teacher educators, union leaders, and social commentators together created, contested, and maintained that story over time; and, finally, recovering the competing reforms those policy stories gave way to. The good news is that policy stories can change. Rather than objective facts, these narratives are social creations, reflections of how we want to see the world. However, the more difficult news is that even as those policy stories are products of our imagination, they have tangible consequences.

Twenty-first-century corporate school reform has pushed teachers further to the periphery, isolating them as problems to be managed and setting them adrift in a sea of competing reforms. Teacher preparation continues to garner attention as a culprit of underperforming teachers. One package of reform targeting university-based preparation programs pushes for greater accountability and standardization. The Council for the Accreditation of Education Preparation, a descendant of the National Council for the Accreditation of Teacher Education, calls on programs to furnish evidence that they are preparing teachers to work in the nation's public schools and to track their progress once in the classroom. Meanwhile, programs explicitly created in opposition to university-based programs, like the Relay Graduate School of Education, purport to deliver real-time vocational training and have spread nationwide. At the same time, alternate pathways into the profession continue to widen as initiatives like Teach for America, the New York City Teaching Fellows, programs for career switchers, and many others proliferate. Beyond the racket of reform, all of this experimentation deprives teachers of a shared body of professional knowledge. Accreditors, teacher educators, and reformers clash over the nature of teacher preparation, their advocacy fundamentally driven by competing institutional interests. Without a shared body of knowledge, teachers walk into the nation's schools as reflections of reform debates.

Likewise, teacher organizations are under siege as the reason for poor teachers. In California and New York, critics turned to the courts to overturn tenure practices, a major component of union-bargained agreements, identifying those policies as barriers to reform. In the summer of 2018, the Supreme Court ruled that public sector unions, including those representing teachers, could no longer levy mandatory fees on all workers, members or not. A press release from United Federation of Teachers president Michael Mulgrew described the decision as the culmination of "years of scheming by forces desperate to destroy workers' rights and to undermine public education."[7] Threats to dismantle teacher organizations combined with the realities of teachers' work lives, including low pay and under-resourced, crowded schools, ignited a new wave of militancy as teachers from Los Angeles to Chicago to Oklahoma walked out of the schools. Union leaders maintain that labor organizations provide essential protections for teachers. Antilabor school leaders maintain that unions inhibit reform. In the end, one exists because of the other and both undermine teachers' professional authority.

Long in place, the push toward teacher evaluation, testing, and canned curricula has only accelerated, emerging as a critical bolster of twenty-first century style school reform. As much about teacher-proofing the schools as closing any "achievement gaps," private companies have joined the reform movement, identifying profitable markets. In 2013, for instance, Pearson sponsored a conference on teaching titled "The Professionalization of Teaching: The Next Generation." Sessions centered on discussions of assessment tools for sale like edTPA, a metric branded as a way to objectively determine whether a new teacher is "ready for the job."[8] The policy story of teacher blame generated industries and organizations that exist because of and profit from the maintenance of that narrative.

Since the 1980s, reformers have fretted over the demographic composition of the teacher workforce. In the face of a rapidly diversifying student population, local and national policymakers have wondered why teaching has remained so White even as researchers documented what many families of color knew already: same-race role models are important for children; representation matters. Extending the policy story of blame, policymakers highlight supply as the culprit: there are simply not enough teachers of color who want to teach or who are qualified to do so, or so this narrative goes. In this formulation, the problem centers on individuals of color who select other career options or communities of color who have not prepared enough of their own for the public schools. This framing turns a blind eye to history and the specific policies and practices that created barriers inhibiting the entrance of teachers of color and establishing teaching as the work of White women.[9]

Over the years, many scholars and reformers have argued that teachers need to speak up and play a role, that their shared apathy is the cause for their shared lack of professionalism. This line of reasoning, however, assumes that teachers have not tried to do just that over this long history. That assumption springs directly from the policy story of blaming teachers and, as this book has chronicled, it is a myth. Teachers have sought to exert their voice, often risking punishment, but they have also been met with powerful barriers that have silenced them and delegitimized their voices. Reforms stemming from the policy stories of blaming teachers produced the modern public schools, university-based schools of education, and teacher unions, one not more culpable for teachers' shared plight than the other. Those institutions owe their survival and success to the discourse of blame as teachers, saddled with the weight of competing institutional interests, faced a history of colliding policies.

The teachers we have are the ones we have created over more than a century of a reform. If we as a society are unhappy with that, we have only ourselves to blame. Professionalizing teachers cannot merely be a matter of listening to teachers and including them in decision-making processes. Instead, the balance of power that characterizes the public education landscape must shift. Indeed, teachers must press for authority, but power is not limitless. If professionalization as other fields have experienced it is the goal for the nation's public school teachers, then policymakers, school leaders, teacher educators, and union leaders must be willing to cede their authority.

Acknowledgments

I began my doctoral work at New York University just months after my father, Thomas F. D'Amico, died and twenty years after he earned his PhD from the same institution. As I walked down Greene Street and through Washington Square Park, I retraced his steps. As I sat in the stacks at Bobst and searched through the collections housed in Tamiment, I developed this project, feeling him beside me. In many ways he was. This book began in a labor seminar I took with Danny Walkowitz during my first or second year in the program, but its roots traced back much farther. In *Silencing the Past* (Beacon Press, 1995), Michel-Rolph Trouillot wrote that he "grew up in a family where history sat at the dinner table." That was my experience as well. In the books that filled our home and the conversations and stories that shaped my childhood, I developed a love for the past and an understanding of its relevance. I remember summer drives in our blue Dodge Aspen with my mother, Franca D'Amico, as we rode across the Bronx to bring my nonna, Dolores Paniccia, back to her home. Lured by the promise of an ice cream cone at Carvel, I listened to my mother translate my nonna's stories about immigrating to the United States with her young children and hiding in Italy's caves during World War II as I stretched my hand out the window, playing with the warm city air. Sometime in the late 1980s, my dad brought home a pack of pencils from work for my sister and me with the words "Write Women Back into History" embossed in gold down the barrel. I used those pencils to do my homework and to write a school project about my nonna that I titled "Herstory." Today one remaining unsharpened burgundy pencil from that collection sits on my bookshelf, a reminder of my father and the fact that he had me thinking about what would become my life's work long before I knew it.

As I reflect on this project and prepare to share it with the world, I am overwhelmed with appreciation for the people who have unwaveringly supported me. It was not lost on me as I wrote this book about the long history of blaming teachers that, like so many others, I owe any success I might claim to my own teachers. After my family, my greatest debt of gratitude goes to Jonathan Zimmerman. I first met Jon when I was still in college, and my first impression of him remains today, nearly twenty years later: a more generous person I've yet to meet. Jon shared his love of history and writing with me early on and remains my most trusted critic. At Franklin and Marshall College in Lancaster, Pennsylvania, I am especially thankful to the late John Andrew, Patricia O'Hara, Louise Stevenson, and Phyllis Whitesell. At Teachers College, Columbia University, where I earned a master's degree in history and education, I am grateful to Margret Crocco, V. P. Franklin, and Cally Waite. And at New York University, I remain indebted to James Fraser, Paul Mattingly, Danny Walkowitz, Jon Zimmerman, and the late Harold Wechsler, whose advice and critiques were abundant and kind.

I owe a special debt of gratitude to my colleagues. I was fortunate to begin my career in academia with a postdoctoral year as visiting assistant professor in the Education Department at Brown University: I am thankful to Carl Kaestle for his warm welcome and our lunch conversations, Tracy Steffes for her friendship and advice, and Ken Wong for his mentorship and sustained interest in and support of my research. At George Mason University, I am grateful to have had the opportunity to learn from and work with Betsy Levine Brown, Meagan Call-Cummings, Betsy DeMulder, Penny Earley, Becky Fox, Toya Frank, Gary Galluzzo, Mark Ginsberg, Angie Hattery, Margret Hjalmarson, Bethany Letiecq, Bev Shaklee, Rob Smith, Michelle Van Lare, Colleen Vesley, and Shelly Wong, among many others. In particular, I have been energized and inspired by the mentorship, friendship, and research of Rodney Hopson, Sonya Horsford, and Jenice View. I moved my family across the country to Grand Forks, North Dakota, for the quality of life and opportunity to collaborate with a corps of engaged, dedicated, and creative faculty around a range of initiatives that I care deeply about. For how they have so generously welcomed us, I am especially grateful to Tamba-Kuii Bailey, Virginia Clinton, Bonni Gourneau, Sherry Houdek, Cheryl and Josh Hunter, Gail Ingwalson, Cindy Juntunen, Andre Kehn, Tricia and Jamie Lunski, Jim Mochoruk, Rachel Navarro, Casey Ozaki, Donna Pearson, Cindy Prescott, Rob Stupnisky, Becky and Marcus Weaver-Hightower, Deb Worley, and many others at the University of North Dakota. It has been a privilege to work with my doctoral students, and this book has directly benefited from the questions, interest, and engagement of Khaseem Davis, Rebecca Diemer, Andrea Guiden, and Tiffany Mitchell Patterson, among many others. In particular, I am grateful to Katherine Bowser, Dee Delfin, and Heather Keenan, who provided first-rate research support.

In addition to the colleagues with whom I have shared institutional affiliations, this project has benefited immeasurably from the feedback and advice I have received from outside readers. Though any flaws with the book are mine alone, credit for any of its strengths must also go to the collection of scholars who have read various parts of this book in different phases of its development, including Barbara Beatty, whose creative insights led to the title of this book; Jackie Blount; Zoe Burkholder; Patricia Graham; Jon Hale; Nick Juravich; Chris Ogren; Jonna Perrillo; Bill Reese; Kate Rousmaniere; Wayne Urban; and Tim Williams. Likewise, I have benefited from thoughtful audience members at the annual meetings of the American Educational Research Association, the American Historical Association, the History of Education Society, and the Organization of American History, as well as Harvard University's School of Education and UCLA's Graduate School of Education and Information Studies, whose questions about and excitement for the project have propelled me forward. I had the rare opportunity to write some of this book while away at a writing residency. The weeks I spent writing at The Porches rekindled my joy for writing and enthusiasm for this project; special thanks go to Trudy Hale for welcoming me into a space that was nothing short of magical. Finally, I am especially appreciative of Ben Justice for his careful reading of the entire manuscript and thoughtful suggestions, and to Lisa Banning and the editorial team at Rutgers University Press for shepherding this book through the publication process.

This book would not exist were it not for the rich archival sources that fill its pages. The masterful research assistance and knowledge of archivists and librarians at the Chicago Historical Society, the City College of New York Archives, the Gottesman Libraries at Teachers College, the Hunter College Library, the Kheel Center at Cornell University, the Library of Congress, the Municipal Archives of the City of New York, the New York Historical Society, the New York Public Library, the Tamiment Library and Special Collections at New York University's Bobst Library, the Walter P. Reuther Library of Labor and Urban Affairs at Wayne State University, and several others have enabled me to unearth this important history. In particular, I am thankful to Dan Golodner, Gail Malmgreen, and David Ment for their time and expertise.

In addition to the generosity of individuals, I have benefited from a range of institutional supports. At New York University, a generous funding package along with smaller grants and awards gave me the ability to study full-time and to travel to archives and conferences. A fellowship from the NAEd/Spencer Dissertation Program supported the writing of my dissertation and connected me with a cohort of engaged scholars. My dissertation received the Politics of Education Society's Outstanding Dissertation Award and that recognition, along with the helpful feedback from the award committee, ignited the process of transforming my dissertation into a book. Support from Brown University, George Mason University, and the University of North Dakota further supported the research and writing of this project, granting me both the time and financial support to travel to archives, conferences, and writing residencies.

But in the end, above all the debts I have incurred, it is to my family that the largest is owed, for they have sustained me. My parents, Thomas and Franca, raised me in a home full of love and laughter. My father taught me to be curious and to take risks; as he battled a long-term illness, he was a model of strength, persistence, and bravery. My mother taught me to protect fiercely, and she has been a model grandmother, showering my children with endless love. My sister, Gina D'Amico, is caring and funny, a teacher who puts creativity and justice above everything and an aunt who puts all others to shame. My four children—Grace, Ella, Thomas, and Robert—fill my life with happiness, humor, and fun. I could fill a book with what makes each of them unique, special, and important but will save them that embarrassment. Watching them grow has been the greatest joy of my life, and it is for them that I do all things. I would not trade the chaos and silliness of our days for anything; it is from that mixture of messy love that this book has emerged, not in spite of it. My deepest appreciation goes to my husband, Robert Pawlewicz, for his selfless support and encouragement. Rob and I met in college; by all measures we were children still, but I knew then what I know now: our lives were meant to be entwined. Together we have grown up, dreamed, built careers, had children, and made a home. It is to Rob, for the life we have built together and the adventures yet to come, that I dedicate this book.

Notes

Introduction

1 "School Reform Probable," *New York Times*, January 18, 1891, 14.
2 "Teachers Who Teach Note," *New York Times*, April 27, 1891, 5.
3 "A Teacher's Protest," *New York Times*, April 29, 1891, 9.
4 Caroline B. LeRow, "Essentials of a Good Teacher," *Ladies' Home Journal* 7, no. 9 (August 1890): 11.
5 For one example, refer to "Closing the Opportunity Gap: Remarks of U.S. Secretary of Education Arne Duncan at the *Brown v. Board of Education* National Historic Site, Topeka, Kansas," September 18, 2012, U.S. Department of Education, https://www.ed.gov/news/speeches/closing-opportunity-gap.
6 Mortimer Smith, *And Madly Teach* (Chicago: Henry Regnery, 1949), vii.
7 Frederick Hess, "The Work Ahead," *Education Next* 1, no. 4 (Winter 2001): 12.
8 Department of Education, *Report of the Commissioner of Education Made to the Secretary of the Interior* (Washington, DC: Government Printing Office, 1870), 62.
9 Quoted in a speech delivered by Richard Dowling, "The Teacher's Position in Our Present Social Status," *Vital Speeches of the Day*, November 15, 1938, 66–68.
10 "Teachers and Task-Masters," *The Century Magazine*, December 1879, 303.
11 Arne Duncan, "Change Is Hard: Remarks of U.S. Secretary of Education Arne Duncan at Baltimore County Teachers Convening," August 12, 2012, U.S. Department of Education, http://www.ed.gov/news/speeches/change-hard; "The RESPECT Project Vision Statement," U.S. Department of Education, 2015, http://www.ed.gov/teaching/national-conversation/vision.
12 "Trump Jr. Tells Young Conservatives Don't Let Teachers 'Indoctrinate' You with Socialism," *Washington Post*, February 17, 2019, https://www.washingtonpost.com/video/politics/trump-jr-tells-young-conservatives-dont-let-teachers-indoctrinate-you-with-socialism/2019/02/17/e9bb78d3-20ea-43a9-a399-4b9f42ca159d_video.html.
13 Deborah Stone, *Policy Paradox: The Art of Political Decision Making* (New York: W. W. Norton, 2012); Murray Edelman, *The Symbolic Uses of Politics* (Urbana: University of Illinois Press, 1985); John W. Kingdon, *Agendas, Alternatives, and Public Policies* (New York: Harper Collins, 1984); David Rochefort and Roger

Cobb, eds., *The Politics of Problem Definition: Shaping the Policy Agenda* (Lawrence: University Press of Kansas, 1994); Mark K. McBeth, Michael D. Jones, and Elizabeth Shanaham, "The Narrative Policy Framework," in *Theories of the Policy Process*, ed. Paul A. Sabatier and Christopher M. Weible (Boulder, CO: Westview Press, 2014), 225–266; Anne L. Schneider, Helen Ingram, and Peter deLeon, "Democratic Policy Design: Social Construction of Target Populations," in Sabatier and Weible, *Theories of the Policy Process*, 105–150.

14 W. Lance Bennett and Murray Edelman, "Toward a New Political Narrative," *Journal of Communication* 35, no. 4 (December 1985): 159.

15 U.S. Bureau of the Census, *Eleventh Census: Occupational Statistics* (Washington, DC: Government Printing Office, 1895).

16 U.S. Bureau of the Census, *1970 Census of Population: Occupation by Industry* (Washington, DC: Government Printing Office, 1972).

17 Andrew Abbott, *The System of Professions: An Essay on the Division of Expert Labor* (Chicago: University of Chicago Press, 1988); Eliot Freidson, *Professionalism Reborn: Theory, Prophecy, and Policy* (Chicago: University of Chicago Press, 1994); Eliot Freidson, *Professionalism: The Third Logic* (Chicago: University of Chicago Press, 2001). For one discussion of the role of university-based education in professionalization, refer to Rakesh Khurana, *From Higher Aims to Hired Hands: The Social Transformation of American Business Schools and the Unfulfilled Promise of Management as a Profession* (Princeton, NJ: Princeton University Press, 2010).

18 Amitai Etzioni, *The Semi-Professions and Their Organization: Teachers, Nurses, Social Workers* (New York: Free Press, 1969); Dan C. Lortie, *Schoolteacher: A Sociological Study* (Chicago: University of Chicago Press, 1975); Richard M. Ingersoll and Gregory J. Collins, "The Status of Teaching as a Profession," in *Schools and Society: A Sociological Approach to Education*, ed. Jeanne H. Ballantine, Joan Z. Spade, and Jenny M. Stuber, 6th ed. (Los Angeles: Sage Publications, 2018), 199–213; Jal Mehta, *The Allure of Order: High Hopes, Dashed Expectations, and the Troubled Quest to Remake American Schooling* (New York: Oxford University Press, 2013); Bureau of Labor Statistics, "Labor Force Statistics from the Current Population Survey," January 18, 2019, https://www.bls.gov/cps/tables.htm#charemp.

19 Burton J. Bledstein, *The Culture of Professionalism: The Middle Class and the Development of Higher Education in America* (New York: W. W. Norton, 1978); Thomas L. Haskell, *The Emergence of Professional Social Science: The American Social Science Association and the Nineteenth-Century Crisis of Authority* (Baltimore: Johns Hopkins University Press, 2001); Nathan A. Hatch, *The Professions in American History* (Notre Dame, IN: University of Notre Dame Press, 1988). For important work on the gendered meanings of professionalism, refer to Daniel J. Walkowitz, *Working with Class: Social Workers and the Politics of Middle-Class Identity* (Chapel Hill: University of North Carolina Press, 1999); Dee Garrison, *Apostles of Culture: The Public Librarian and American Society, 1876–1920* (New York: Macmillan Information, 1979); Barbara Melosh, *"The Physician's Hand": Work Culture and Conflict in American Nursing* (Philadelphia: Temple University Press, 1982); Nel Noddings, "Feminist Critiques in the Professions," *Review of Research in Education* 16, no. 1 (January 1, 1990): 393–424; Anne Witz, *Professions and Patriarchy* (London: Routledge, 1992); Joan Jacobs Brumberg and Nancy Tomes, "Women in the Professions: A Research Agenda

for American Historians," *Reviews in American History* 10, no. 2 (June 1, 1982): 275–296.

20 "The Status of the Teaching Profession: Report of the Committee of the State Teachers' Association of South Carolina, 1917," *Bulletin of the University of South Carolina*, no. 61 (October 1917): 3.

21 Mehta, *The Allure of Order*, 28.

22 "Educational Interests of the State Will Be There," *Daily Capital Journal*, December 16, 1916, 7.

23 "Code of Ethics Being Prepared for Boston Teachers' Guidance," *Boston Daily Globe*, July 3, 1927, A3.

24 "Teacher Is Tried for Her Criticism," *New York Times*, May 16, 1922, 15.

25 Smith, *And Madly Teach*, 3–4.

26 Mary Holman, *How It Feels to Be a Teacher* (New York: Bureau of Publications, Teachers College, Columbia University, 1950), 156, 2.

27 Lois MacFarland and David G. Wittens, "I'm Through with Teaching," *Saturday Evening Post*, November 9, 1946.

28 Jack Mabley, "Teacher's Plea: Don't Blame Us," *Chicago Tribune*, July 18, 1977, 4.

29 JoAnne Brown, *The Definition of a Profession: The Authority of Metaphor in the History of Intelligence Testing, 1890–1930* (Princeton, NJ: Princeton University Press, 1992).

30 Eliot Freidson, *Professionalism Reborn: Theory, Prophecy, and Policy* (Chicago: University of Chicago Press, 1994).

31 John Field, "Medical Education in the United States: Late 19th and 20th Centuries," in *The History of Medical Education*, ed. C. P. O'Malley (Berkeley: University of California Press, 1970), 501–530; Kenneth M. Ludmerer, *Learning to Heal: The Development of American Medical Education* (Baltimore: Johns Hopkins University Press, 1996); Regina Markell Morantz-Sanchez, *Sympathy and Science: Women Physicians in American Medicine* (New York: Oxford University Press, 1985); Steven G. Brint, *In an Age of Experts: The Changing Role of Professionals in Politics and Public Life* (Princeton, NJ: Princeton University Press, 1994); Harold L. Wilensky, "The Professionalization of Everyone?," *American Journal of Sociology* 70, no. 2 (1964): 137–158.

32 Across the American South during the *Plessy* era of separate but equal and double taxation, Black teachers assumed pivotal social roles as they taught in community-based schools often separate from municipal school systems. In addition, Black teachers made inroads into some large municipal school systems in areas like Washington, DC, even as they were largely prevented from entering districts like New York City's, discussed further in this book. In important regards, the *Brown* decision was the death knell for Black teachers as the courts mandated the integration of public schoolchildren but said nothing of the public school workforce. As districts reluctantly complied with the federal mandate, Black teachers were fired en masse. For more on the history of Black teachers, refer to James D. Anderson, *The Education of Blacks in the South, 1860–1935* (Chapel Hill: University of North Carolina Press, 1988); Vanessa Siddle Walker, *Their Highest Potential: An African American School Community in the Segregated South* (Chapel Hill: University of North Carolina Press, 1996); Michele Foster, *Black Teachers on Teaching* (New York: New Press, 1997); and Adam Fairclough, *A Class of Their Own: Black Teachers in the Segregated South* (Cambridge, MA: Harvard University Press, 2007). For more on the firing of Black teachers following the

Brown decision, refer to Adam Fairclough, "The Costs of *Brown*: Black Teacher and School Integration," *Journal of American History* 91, no. 1 (2004): 43–55; Michael Fultz, "The Displacement of Black Educators Post-*Brown*: An Overview and Analysis," *History of Education Quarterly* 44, no. 1 (April 1, 2004): 11–45; Linda C. Tillman, "(Un)Intended Consequences? The Impact of the *Brown v. Board of Education* Decision on the Employment Status of Black Educators," *Education and Urban Society* 36, no. 3 (May 1, 2004): 280–303; and Sonya Douglass Horsford and Kathryn Bell McKenzie, "'Sometimes I Feel Like the Problems Started with Desegregation': Exploring Black Superintendent Perspectives on Desegregation Policy," *International Journal of Qualitative Studies in Education* 21, no. 5 (September 1, 2008): 443–455. For one contemporary study on discrimination and teacher hiring, see Diana D'Amico et al., "Where Are All the Black Teachers? Discrimination in the Teacher Labor Market," *Harvard Educational Review* 87, no. 1 (2017): 26–49.

33 Tracy Steffes, *School, Society, and State: A New Education to Govern Modern America, 1890–1940* (Chicago: University of Chicago Press, 2012); David Tyack, *The One Best System: A History of American Urban Education* (Cambridge, MA: Harvard University Press, 1974); Carl Kaestle, *Pillars of the Republic: Common Schools and American Society, 1780–1860* (New York: Hill and Wang, 1983); Michael Katz, *The Irony of Early School Reform: Educational Innovation in Mid-Nineteenth Century Massachusetts* (Cambridge, MA: Harvard University Press, 1968).

34 David F. Labaree, *The Trouble with Ed Schools* (New Haven, CT: Yale University Press, 2006); Jurgen Herbst, *And Sadly Teach: Teacher Education and Professionalization in American Culture* (Madison: University of Wisconsin Press, 1989); James W. Fraser, *Preparing America's Teachers: A History* (New York: Teachers College Press, 2007); Geraldine Jonçich Clifford and James W. Guthrie, *Ed School: A Brief for Professional Education* (Chicago: University of Chicago Press, 1990).

35 Jackie M. Blount, *Fit to Teach: Same-Sex Desire, Gender, and School Work in the Twentieth Century* (Albany: State University of New York Press, 2005); Patricia Anne Carter, *"Everybody's Paid but the Teacher": The Teaching Profession and the Women's Movement* (New York: Teachers College Press, 2002); Myra H. Strober and David Tyack, "Why Do Women Teach and Men Manage? A Report on Research on Schools," *Signs* 5, no. 3 (April 1, 1980): 494–503; Joel Perlmann and Robert A. Margo, *Women's Work? American Schoolteachers, 1650–1920* (Chicago: University of Chicago Press, 2001); Geraldine Jonçich Clifford, "Man/Woman/Teacher: Gender, Family and Career in American Educational History," in *American Teachers: Histories of a Profession at Work*, ed. Donald R. Warren (New York: Macmillan, 1989), 293–343; Jo Anne Preston, "Gender and the Formation of a Women's Profession: The Case of Public School Teaching," in *Gender Inequality at Work*, ed. Jerry Jacobs (Thousand Oaks, CA: Sage Publications, 1995), 379–407.

36 Geraldine J. Clifford, *Those Good Gertrudes: A Social History of Women Teachers in America* (Baltimore: Johns Hopkins University Press, 2014); Kate Rousmaniere, *City Teachers: Teaching and School Reform in Historical Perspective* (New York: Teachers College Press, 1997); Doris Hinson Pieroth, *Seattle's Women Teachers of the Interwar Years: Shapers of a Livable City* (Seattle: University of Washington Press, 2004); Janet Nolan, *Servants of the Poor: Teachers and Mobility in Ireland and Irish America* (Notre Dame, IN: University of Notre Dame Press,

2004); Larry Cuban, *How Teachers Taught: Constancy and Change in American Classrooms, 1890–1980* (New York: Longman, 1984); Richard J. Altenbaugh, *The Teacher's Voice: A Social History of Teaching in Twentieth-Century America* (London: Falmer Press, 1991); Carter, *"Everybody's Paid but the Teacher."*

37 Jonna Perrillo, *Uncivil Rights: Teachers, Unions, and Race in the Battle for School Equity* (Chicago: University of Chicago Press, 2012); Jon Shelton, *Teacher Strike! Public Education and the Making of a New American Political Order* (Urbana: University of Illinois Press, 2017); Marjorie Murphy, *Blackboard Unions: The AFT and the NEA, 1900–1980* (Ithaca, NY: Cornell University Press, 1992); Wayne J. Urban, *Why Teachers Organized* (Detroit: Wayne State University Press, 1982); Wayne J. Urban, *Gender, Race, and the National Education Association: Professionalism and Its Limitations* (New York: Routledge Falmer, 2000); Jon Shelton, *Public Education and the Making of a New American Public Order* (Urbana: University of Illinois Press, 2017).

38 For more on the history of federal education reform refer to Maris Vinovskis, *From a Nation at Risk to No Child Left Behind: National Education Goals and the Creation of Federal Education Policy* (New York: Teachers College Press, 2008); Gareth Davies, *See Government Grow: Education Politics from Johnson to Reagan* (Lawrence: University Press of Kansas, 2007).

39 "New York Mixed Schools," *The Sun*, March 5, 1903, 2; "Topics in New York: White Pupils Object to a Negro Teacher," *The Sun*, April 30, 1903, 7.

Chapter 1 "A Chaotic State"

1 Lawrence A. Cremin, ed., *The Republic and the School: Horace Mann on the Education of Free Men* (New York: Teachers College Press, 1957), 79–112.

2 Horace Mann, *A Few Thoughts on the Powers and Duties of Woman: Two Lectures* (New York: Hal, Mills and Company, 1853), 84.

3 Lorraine S. Pangle and Thomas L. Pangle, *The Learning of Liberty: The Educational Ideas of the American Founders* (Lawrence: University Press of Kansas, 1993).

4 For more on common schools and early public schools, refer to Carl Kaestle, *Pillars of the Republic: Common Schools and American Society, 1780–1860* (New York: Hill and Wang, 1983); Michael Katz, *The Irony of Early School Reform: Educational Innovation in Mid-Nineteenth Century Massachusetts* (Cambridge, MA: Harvard University Press, 1968); and Lawrence A. Cremin, *The Transformation of the School* (New York: Knopf, 1961). For more background on the history of public schools in New York City, refer to Diane Ravitch, *The Great School Wars: A History of the New York City Public Schools* (Baltimore: Johns Hopkins University Press, 1974); Thomas Boese, *Public Education in the City of New York: Its History, Condition, and Statistics; An Official Report to the Board of Education* (New York: Harper and Bros., 1869); and William Oland, *History of the Public School Society of the City of New York: With Portraits of the Presidents of the Society . . .* (New York: W. Wood & Co., 1873).

5 Department of Education, *Report of the Commissioner of Education Made to the Secretary of the Interior* (Washington, DC: Government Printing Office, 1870), 62–63.

6 Joseph M. Rice, "Substitution of Teacher for Text-Book," *The Forum*, August 1895, 681.

7 Jon A. Peterson, *The Birth of City Planning in the United States, 1840–1917* (Baltimore: Johns Hopkins University Press, 2003); Edwin G. Burrows, *Gotham: A History of New York City to 1898* (New York: Oxford University Press, 1999).

8 Joseph C. G. Kennedy, *Population of the United States in 1860: Compiled from the Original Returns of the Eighth Census under the Direction of the Secretary of the Interior* (Washington, DC: Government Printing Office, 1864), iv.

9 "No. 22: Address of the President," in *Documents of the Board of Education of the City of New York for the Year 1855* (New York: Wm. C. Bryant & Co. Printers, 1855), 5.

10 Kennedy, *Population of the United States in 1860*, xxix, xxxii.

11 "Slumming in This Town: A Fashionable London Mania Reaches New-York. Slumming Parties to Be the Rage This Winter—Good Districts to Visit—Mrs. Langtry as a Slummer," *New York Times*, September 14, 1884, 4.

12 Eric Homberger, *Mrs. Astor's New York: Money and Social Power in a Gilded Age* (New Haven, CT: Yale University Press, 2002); Burrows, *Gotham*.

13 Matthew Frye Jacobson, *Whiteness of a Different Color: European Immigrants and the Alchemy of Race* (Cambridge, MA: Harvard University Press, 1999).

14 Linda Kerber, *Women of the Republic: Intellect and Ideology in Revolutionary America* (Chapel Hill: University of North Carolina Press, 1980).

15 Cremin, *The Republic and the School*, 79–112.

16 Ira Mayhew, *Popular Education: For the Use of Parents and Teachers and for Young Persons of Both Sexes* (New York: Daniel Burgess & Company, 1855), 411.

17 *Fourteenth Annual Report of the Board of Education of the City and County of New York for the Year Ending January 1, 1856* (New York: Wm. C. Bryant & Co. Printers, 1856), 23.

18 Paul Mattingly, *The Classless Profession: American Schoolmen in the Nineteenth Century* (New York: New York University Press, 1975).

19 Geraldine Jonçich Clifford, "Man/Woman/Teacher: Gender, Family and Career in American Educational History," in *American Teachers: Histories of a Profession at Work*, ed. Donald R. Warren (New York: Macmillan, 1989); Jackie M. Blount, "Spinsters, Bachelors, and Other Gender Transgressors in School Employment, 1850–1990," *Review of Educational Research* 70, no. 1 (March 1, 2000): 83–101; Kimberley Tolley, "Music Teachers in the North Carolina Education Market, 1800–1840: How Mrs. Sambourne Earned a 'Comfortable Living for Herself and Her Children,'" *Social Science History* 32, no. 1 (February 20, 2008): 75–106; James C. Albisetti, "The Feminization of Teaching in the Nineteenth Century: A Comparative Perspective," *History of Education* 22 (1993): 253–263; John G. Richardson and Brenda Wooden Hatcher, "The Feminization of Public School Teaching: 1870–1920," *Work and Occupations: An International Sociological Journal* 10 (1983), 81–99; Myra H. Strober and Audri Gordon Lanford, "The Feminization of Public School Teaching: Cross-Sectional Analysis, 1850–1880," *Signs: Journal of Women in Culture and Society* 11 (1986), 212–235; Joel Perlmann and Robert A. Margo, *Women's Work? American Schoolteachers, 1650–1920* (Chicago: University of Chicago Press, 2001); John L. Rury, "Who Became Teachers? The Social Characteristics of Teachers in American History," in Warren, *American Teachers*, 9–48; John L. Rury, *Education and Women's Work: Female Schooling and the Division of Labor in Urban America, 1870–1930* (Albany: State University of New York Press, 1991).

20 "No. 1: Remarks of Erastus C. Benedict, Esq., on His Re-election as President of the Board of Education, at Its Organization, January 11, 1854," in *Documents of the Board of Education of the City of New York for the Year 1854*, 2.
21 Department of Education, *Report of the Commissioner of Education* (Washington, DC: Government Printing Office, 1870), 58.
22 *Fourteenth Annual Report of the Board of Education*, 25–28.
23 Catharine E. Beecher, *The True Remedy for the Wrongs of Woman: With a History of an Enterprise Having That for Its Object* (Boston: Phillips, Sampson & Co., 1851), 57.
24 "No. 3: Monthly Report of City Super," in *Documents of the Board of Education of the City of New York for the Year 1855*, 2.
25 "No. 14: Annual Report of the City Superintendent of Schools," in *Documents of the Board of Education of the City of New York for the Year Ending December 31, 1861* (New York: C. S. Westcott & Co. Printers, 1862).
26 Department of Education, *Report of the Commissioner of Education with Circulars and Documents Submitted to the Senate and House of Representatives on June 2, 1868* (Washington, DC: Government Printing Office, 1868).
27 Briscoe E. Man, "Personality of Teachers," *The North American Review* 146 (June 1888): 711.
28 *Report of the Commissioner of Education* (Washington, DC: Government Printing Office, 1868), 833–848.
29 *Report of the Commissioner of Education* (Washington, DC: Government Printing Office, 1870), 38.
30 U.S. Bureau of the Census, *Eleventh Census: Occupational Statistics* (Washington DC: Government Printing Office, 1895).
31 "The Color Line," *Chicago Tribune*, April 20, 1883, 2.
32 U.S. Bureau of the Census, *Eleventh Census: Occupational Statistics* (Washington DC: Government Printing Office, 1895).
33 "Schools in Baltimore," *New York Times*, December 27, 1880, 1.
34 "No. 1: Remarks of Andrew H. Green," in *Documents of the Board of Education of the City of New York for the Year 1856* (New York: Wm. C. Bryant & Co. Printers, 1858), 2.
35 Richard Larremore, *Address of Richard Larremore, Esq. on his Election as President of the Board of Education of the City of New York: Delivered January 8, 1868* (New York: Wm. C. Bryant & Co. Printers, 1868).
36 *Fortieth Annual Report of the Board of Education of the City, and County of New York for the Year Ending December 31, 1881* (New York: Hall of the Board of Education, 1882), 36.
37 John D. Philbrick, *City School Systems in the U.S.* (Washington, DC: Government Printing Office, 1885), 127.
38 *Manual of the Board of Education of the City of New York* (New York: Hall of the Board of Education, 1889), 48.
39 "The Salaries of Public School Teachers," *New York Times*, April 4, 1867, 4.
40 "No. 15: Report from the Committee on Teachers," in *Documents of the Board of Education of the City of New York for the Year Ending December 31, 1859* (New York: Joseph Russell, 1860), 2.
41 "Dissatisfied School Teachers," *New York Times*, April 22, 1884, 8.
42 *Journal of the Board of Education of the City of New York, 1883* (New York: Wm. A. Wheeler, 1883), 592–593.

43 Refer, for instance, to Prism Gardner, "Pay the Teachers at Once," *Chicago Daily Tribune*, June 5, 1879, 12; "Pay Up the Teachers," *Atlanta Constitution*, July 9, 1890, 5.
44 "The Salaries of Public School Teachers," 4.
45 William H. Neilson, *Remarks of Wm. H. Neilson, Esq. on Assuming the Presidency of the Board of Education: January 14, 1874* (New York: Cushing & Bardua, Steam Printers, 1874), 7.
46 "No. 1: Inaugural Address of Andrew H. Green, Esq., President, Department of Public Instruction, Board of Education, City of New York February 4, 1857," in *Documents of the Board of Education of the City of New York, for the Year Ending December 31, 1857* (New York: Pudney & Russell, Printers, 1858), 5.
47 "No. 34: Annual Report of the Board of Education," in *Documents of the Board of Education of the City of New York, for the Year Ending December 31, 1856* (New York: Wm. C. Bryant & Co. Printers, 1858), 41.
48 "No. 3: Monthly Report of the City Superintendent of Schools," in *Documents of the Board of Education of the City of New York for the Year 1855*, 3.
49 *Journal of the Board of Education of the City of New York* (New York: Wm. C. Bryant & Co. Printers, 1883), 863.
50 *Thirteenth Annual Report of the Board of Education of the City of New York for the Year Ending January 1, 1855* (New York: Wm. C. Bryant & Co. Printers, 1855), 6.
51 P. R. Burchard, "Our Educational Outlook," *Scribner's Monthly*, May 1872, 97–103.
52 *Report of the Commissioner of Education for the Year 1879* (Washington, DC: Government Printing Office, 1881), xxi.
53 "No. 34: Annual Report of the Board of Education," 38.
54 "No. 34: Annual Report of the Board of Education," 52.
55 "No. 14½: Remarks of Wm. H. Neilson, Esq., at the Inauguration of the Daily Normal School," in *Documents of the Board of Education of the City of New York, for the Year Ending December 31, 1856*, 5.
56 *A Manual of Discipline and Instruction for the use of Teachers of the Grammar Schools Under the Charge of the Board of Education of the City of New York* (New York: J. S. Babcock, 1884), 11, series 49, New York City Board of Education Collection, Municipal Archives, New York City Department of Records (hereafter Municipal Archives).
57 "Live Teachers," *New York Daily Times*, January 29, 1855, 4.
58 Burchard, "Our Educational Outlook," 103.
59 *Report of the Commissioner of Education* (Washington, DC: Government Printing Office, 1868), 16.
60 J. G. Schurman, "Teaching—A Trade or a Profession?," *The Forum*, April 1896, 171; "Live Teachers," 4.
61 "Two Ways of Teaching English," *The Century Magazine*, March 1896, 793–794.
62 Rice, "Substitution of Teacher for Text-Book," 681; "Pedagogical Law: The Law as to the Teacher's Morality," *American Educational Monthly*, January 1867, 15–20.
63 B. G. Northrop, *Examination of Teachers* (New Haven, CT: Tuttle, Morehouse & Taylor, 1880), 6; *Fourteenth Annual Report of the Board of Education*, 27.
64 "Live Teachers," 4.
65 "The Teachers' Association," *Atlanta Constitution*, August 18, 1886, 7.
66 Schurman, "Teaching," 176–177.
67 Burchard, "Our Educational Outlook," 102.
68 Beecher, *The True Remedy for the Wrongs of Woman*, 26.

69 Diana D'Amico, "An Uneasy Union: Women Teachers, Organized Labor, and the Contested Ideology of Profession during the Progressive Era," *LABOR: Studies in Working-Class History of the Americas* 14, no. 3 (September 2017): 35–54; Cathy N. Davidson and Jessamyn Hatcher, eds., *No More Separate Spheres! A Next Wave American Studies Reader* (Durham, NC: Duke University Press Books, 2002); Joan W. Scott and Debra Keates, *Going Public: Feminism and the Shifting Boundaries of the Private Sphere* (Urbana: University of Illinois Press, 2005); Joan B. Landes, "Further Thoughts on the Public/Private Distinction," *Journal of Women's History* 15 (2003): 28–39.

70 Horace Mann, *A Few Thoughts on the Powers and Duties of Woman: Two Lectures* (Syracuse, NY: Hall, Mills and Co., 1853), 105–106, 125.

71 *Fourteenth Annual Report of the Board of Education*, 26.

72 "Teachers' Associations," *New York Times*, May 27, 1858, 5.

73 "No. 15: Report from the Committee on Teachers," 3.

74 Philbrick, *City School Systems in the U.S.*, 7–8.

75 Christine A. Ogren, *The American State Normal School: An Instrument of Great Good* (New York: Macmillan, 2005); Barbara M. Solomon, *In the Company of Educated Women: A History of Women and Higher Education in America* (New Haven, CT: Yale University Press, 1985). For more on the early education of women, refer to Margaret A. Nash, *Women's Education in the United States, 1780–1840* (New York: Palgrave Macmillan, 2007).

76 Ogren, *The American State Normal School.*

77 Christine Ogren, "The History and Historiography of Teacher Preparation in the United States: A Synthesis, Analysis, and Potential Contributions to Higher Education History," in *Higher Education: Handbook of Theory and Research*, ed. Michael B. Paulson (Dordrecht, Netherlands: Springer, 2013), 405–458.

78 Katherina Kroo Grunfeld, "Purpose and Ambiguity: The Feminine World of Hunter College, 1869–1945" (EdD diss., Teachers College, Columbia University, 1991).

79 "No. 10½: Annual Report of the City Superintendent of Schools," in *Documents of the Board of Education of the City of New York for the Year Ending December 31, 1860* (New York: George Russell, 1861), 8.

80 *Manual of the Board of Education of the City and County of New York, 1856* (New York: Edward O. Jenkins, 1856), 12.

81 "No. 18: Annual Report of the Board of Education for the Year Ending December 31, 1860," in *Documents of the Board of Education of the City of New York for the Year Ending December 31, 1860*, 44.

82 "No. 2: Report from the Executive Committee on Normal Schools," in *Documents of the Board of Education of the City of New York for the Year Ending December 31, 1859*, 18.

83 "Teachers and the Normal Schools," *New York Daily Times*, October 12, 1853, 4.

84 "On Grading the Salaries of the Teachers of the Common Schools," *New York Daily Times*, July 18, 1854, 3.

85 A. Teacher, "Proposed Re-Examination of School Teachers—City Normal Schools," *New York Daily Times*, July 13, 1854, 3.

86 "Article 17: Normal Schools," in *By-Laws and General Rules and Regulations of the Board of Education*, 1856, 107, series 35, box 9, Municipal Archives.

87 Grunfeld, *Purpose and Ambiguity.*
88 Grunfeld, *Purpose and Ambiguity*; "25th Anniversary," *New York Press*, February 15, 1895.
89 Linda M. Perkins, "African-American Women and Hunter College: 1873–1945," *Echo: Journal of the Hunter College Archives* (1995): 16–25.
90 "Appendix: Dedication of the New York Normal College, October 29, 1873," *Journal of the Board of Education of the City of New York, 1873* (New York: School Journal Print, 1873), 1.
91 James Richardson, "Our New Normal College," *Scribner's Monthly*, September 1874, 535–537.
92 *Fortieth Annual Report of the Board of Education of the City, and County of New York*, 181.
93 "Appendix: Dedication of the New York Normal College," 42.
94 "Appendix: Dedication of the New York Normal College," 32.
95 *Fortieth Annual Report of the Board of Education of the City, and County of New York*, 188.
96 Joseph Mayer Rice, "Our Public School System: Evils in Baltimore," *The Forum*, October 1892, 145–158.
97 *Fortieth Annual Report of the Board of Education of the City, and County of New York*, 46–47.
98 *Fortieth Annual Report of the Board of Education of the City, and County of New York*, 182–183.
99 *Report of the Commissioner of Education for the Year 1885–1886* (Washington, DC: Government Printing Office, 1887), 653.
100 "A Bill Granting Aid for the Establishment of Free Common Schools and for the Professional Education of Public School Teachers," H.R. 3327, 50th Cong., 1st sess. (January 9, 1888), in *Report of the Secretary of the Interior*, vol. 1 (Washington, DC: Government Printing Office, 1887), 10.
101 "School Matters in New York," *The Outlook*, June 20, 1896, 1140–1141.
102 "Our Schools," *New York Daily Times*, March 12, 1856, 3.
103 "Report of the City Superintendent," in *Documents of the Board of Education of the City of New York for the Year Ending December 31, 1859*, 28.
104 B. G. Northrop, *Examination of Teachers* (New Haven, CT: Tuttle, Morehouse & Taylor, 1880), 2.
105 Philbrick, *City School Systems in the U.S.*
106 *Manual of the Board of Education of the City and County of New York, Hall of the Board of Education* (New York: Wynkoop and Hallenbeck, 1879), 130–133, series 35, box 10, Municipal Archives.
107 *Forty-Ninth Annual Report of the Board of Education of the City of New York* (New York: Hall of the Board of Education, 1891), 122.
108 *Fortieth Annual Report of the Board of Education of the City, and County of New York*, 126.
109 Isaac Stone, *The Elementary and Complete Examiner; or Candidate's Assistant: Prepared to Aid Teachers is Securing Certificates from Boards of Examiners, and Pupils in Preparing Themselves for Promotion, Teachers in Selecting Review Questions from Normal Schools, Institutes, and in All Drill and Class Exercises* (New York: A. S. Barnes & Company, 1864), iii.
110 Andrew S. Draper, *Uniform Examination Questions for Teachers' Licenses, in the State of New York* (Rochester, NY: Educational Gazette, 1888).

111 Reprinted from the *New York School Journal* as "Not Too Many Teachers," in *Eclectic Teacher and Southwestern Journal of Education*, September 1879, 6.
112 "Appendix: Dedication of the New York Normal College, October 29, 1873," 9.
113 "No. 28: Department of Public Instruction, State of New York. Board of Education, City of New York, October 3, 1855," in *Documents of the Board of Education of the City of New York* (New York: Wm. C. Bryant & Co. Printers, 1855), 3.
114 "No. 18: Annual Report of the Board of Education," 28.
115 *Manual of the Board of Education of the City and County of New York, Hall of the Board of Education, 1856* (New York: Wm. C. Bryant and Co. Printers, 1856), 69, series 35, box, Municipal Archives.
116 "Politics in the Schools," *New York Times*, December 10, 1888, 8.
117 "A Bill Granting Aid for the Establishment of Free Common Schools," 5.
118 John N. Fain, "Examination of Public School Teachers," *Atlanta Constitution*, May 25, 1890, 24. For other selected examples, refer to "Examination of Howard County Teachers," *The Sun*, July 1, 1887, 4; "Examination of Teacher," *Chicago Press and Tribune*, February 18, 1860, 1; "Teachers' Examination: How Applicants will be Put on the Gridiron," *Los Angeles Times*, July 11, 1885, 5.
119 "Rejected Negro Teachers," *New York Times*, July 23, 1884, 5.
120 "No. 11: Board of Education, Remarks of E. C. Benedict, Esq., President of the Board of Education, on Laying before the Members the Act Revising the School Laws Relating to the City, June 16, 1851," in *Documents of the Board of Education of the City of New York for the Year Ending December 31, 1851* (New York, 1851), 8.
121 "No. 18: Annual Report of the Board of Education," 56.
122 "No. 18: Annual Report of the Board of Education," 36.
123 "No. 18: Annual Report of the Board of Education," 56.
124 For more on the rise of testing, refer to William J. Reese, *Testing Wars in the Public Schools: A Forgotten History* (Cambridge, MA: Harvard University Press, 2013).
125 "No. 18: Annual Report of the Board of Education," 36.
126 "Charges Against a Teacher," *New York Times*, June 30, 1881, 8.
127 "Teachers Who Teach Not," *New York Times*, April 27, 1891, 5.
128 Man, "Personality of Teachers," 712.
129 Department of Education of the City of New York, *First Annual Report of the City Superintendent of Schools to the Board of Education for the Year Ending July 31, 1899* (New York: John Polhemus Printing Company, 1900), 39.
130 "Individuality in Teaching," *The Century Magazine*, September 1888, 790.
131 William Desmond, "Open Letters: The Evolution of the Educator," *The Century Magazine*, December 1889, 318.
132 Man, "Personality of Teachers," 711.
133 A. Teacher, "Proposed Re-Examination of School Teachers-City Normal Schools," *New York Daily Times*, July 13, 1854, 3.

Chapter 2 To "Raise Teachers' Profession to a Dignity Worthy of Its Mission"

1 "East Side Parents Storm the Schools," *New York Times*, June 28, 1906, 4.
2 "Throat-Cutting Rumors Revive School Mob," *New York Times*, June 29, 1906, 9.
3 Ossian Lang, "Educational Events," *The Forum*, July 1902, 105.
4 "Topic of the Time: The New Movement in Education," *The Century Magazine*, May 1890, 151–152.

5 J. H. Van Sickle and John Whyte, "The Larger Cities," in *Biennial Survey of Education, 1916–18*, vol. 1 (Washington, DC: Government Printing Office, 1921), 115.

6 "How to Strengthen the Schools," *Journal of the National Education Association* 14 (January 1925): 3–4.

7 Joseph Mayer Rice, "Our Public School System: Evils in Baltimore," *The Forum*, October 1892, 151. For more on the scholarly debates surrounding Americanization, refer to Gary Gerstle, "Liberty, Coercion, and the Making of Americans," *Journal of American History* 84, no. 2 (September 1997): 524–558; David Hollinger, "National Solidarity at the End of the Twentieth Century: Reflections on the United States and Liberal Nationalism," *Journal of American History* 84, no. 2 (September 1997): 559–569. For more on the cultural meanings of professionalism, refer to Burton J. Bledstein, *The Culture of Professionalism: The Middle Class and the Development of Higher Education in America* (New York: W. W. Norton, 1978); Magali S. Larson, *The Rise of Professionalism: A Sociological Analysis* (Berkeley: University of California Press, 1979); and JoAnne Brown, *The Definition of a Profession: The Authority of Metaphor in the History of Intelligence Testing, 1890–1930* (Princeton, NJ: Princeton University Press, 1992).

8 David Tyack, *The One Best System: A History of American Urban Education* (Cambridge, MA: Harvard University Press, 1974); Tracy Steffes, *School, Society, and State: A New Education to Govern Modern America, 1890–1940* (Chicago: University of Chicago Press, 2012); Jal Mehta, *The Allure of Order: High Hopes, Dashed Expectations, and the Troubled Quest to Remake American Schooling* (New York: Oxford University Press, 2015); Herbert M. Kliebard, *The Struggle for the American Curriculum, 1893–1957* (New York: Routledge, 2004).

9 William O'Shea, "Inaugural Address," May 13, 1924, folder 426A, box 25, series 6, James Earl Russell Papers, Gottesman Libraries, Teachers College, Columbia University.

10 Campbell Gibson and Emily Lennon, "Table 19. Nativity of the Population for the 50 Largest Urban Places: 1870–1990," U.S. Census Bureau, Population Division, https://www.census.gov/population/www/documentation/twps0029/tab19.html, last revised October 31, 2011.

11 U.S. Immigration Commission, *The Children of Immigrants in Schools* (Washington, DC: Government Printing Office, 1911).

12 Niles Carpenter, *Immigrants and Their Children, 1920: A Study Based on Census Statistics Relative to the Foreign Born and the Native White of Foreign or Mixed Parentage* (Washington, DC: Government Printing Office, 1927).

13 For more on the "ideal" teacher, refer to Kate Rousmaniere, *City Teachers: Teaching and School Reform in Historical Perspective* (New York: Teachers College Press, 1997), 33–53; Jonna Perrillo, "Beyond 'Progressive' Reform: Bodies, Discipline, and the Construction of the Professional Teacher in Interwar America," *History of Education Quarterly* 44, no. 3 (2004): 337–363.

14 William Ettinger, "Address to the Teachers of New York City," September 20, 1918, series 392, box 3, scrapbook vol. 13, New York City Board of Education Collection, Municipal Archives, New York City Department of Records (hereafter Municipal Archives).

15 William Vlyman, "The Teaching of English in Classes other than English Classes," *Bulletin of High Points in the Work of the High Schools of New York City*, May 1924, 3.

16 *Biennial Survey of Education, 1916–18*, vol. 3 (Washington, DC: Government Printing Office, 1921), 8–12.
17 Nicholas Murray Butler, "The Educational Progress of the Year," *The Outlook*, August 5, 1899, 755–766.
18 Frederick Harrison, "Thoughts about Education," *The Forum*, December 1891, 488.
19 William Burnham, "Some Aspects of the Teaching Profession," *The Forum*, June 1898, 481.
20 Nicholas Murray Butler, "The Unity of Education," *The Outlook*, January 13, 1896, 94–95.
21 Rice, "Our Public School System," 151.
22 U.S. Bureau of the Census, *Census Statistics of Teachers* (Washington, DC: Government Printing Office, 1905), 16; see also Janet Nolan, *Servants of the Poor: Teachers and Mobility in Ireland and Irish America* (Notre Dame, IN: University of Notre Dame Press, 2004).
23 U.S. Bureau of the Census, *Twelfth Census of the United States: Statistics of Occupations, 1900* (Washington, DC: Government Printing Office, 1907), 350–351. It is likely that these proportions were even larger than indicated in this report, as the *Twelfth Census* paired teachers with college professors, forming a single occupational group.
24 Verne McGuffey, "Some Elements of the Cultural Background of Students in One of the New York City Training Schools for Teachers," *Educational Administration and Supervision Including Teacher Training* 4 (April 1928): 279–282. For other sources on the composition of the teaching profession of this time, refer to John L. Rury, "Who Became Teachers? The Social Characteristics of Teachers in American History," in *American Teachers: Histories of a Profession at Work*, ed. Donald R. Warren (New York: Macmillan, 1989), 9–48; and Rousmaniere, *City Teachers.*
25 McGuffey, "Some Elements of the Cultural Background of Students," 281.
26 U.S. Bureau of the Census, *Eleventh Census: Occupational Statistics* (Washington, DC: Government Printing Office, 1895); U.S. Bureau of the Census, *Fourteenth Census of the United States: Occupations* (Washington, DC: Government Printing Office, 1920).
27 "New York Mixed Schools," *The Sun*, March 5, 1903, 2.
28 "New York Mixed Schools," 2; "Topics in New York: White Pupils Object to a Negro Teacher," *The Sun*, April 30, 1903, 7.
29 David M. Kennedy, *Over Here: The First World War and American Society* (New York: Oxford University Press, 2004).
30 U.S. Department of the Interior, U.S. Bureau of Education, *Proceedings Americanization Conference: Held under the Auspices of the Americanization Division* (Washington, DC: Government Printing Office, 1919), 22 (hereafter *Proceedings Americanization Conference*).
31 *Proceedings Americanization Conference*, 25.
32 *Proceedings Americanization Conference*, 108.
33 *Proceedings Americanization Conference*, 27.
34 *Proceedings Americanization Conference*, 78
35 *Proceedings Americanization Conference*, 109–111.
36 Stephen Petrina, "The Medicalization of Education: A Historiographic Synthesis," *Higher Education Quarterly* 46, no. 4 (February 24, 2017): 503–531; Barbara

Beatty, Emily D. Cahan, and Julia Grant, eds., *When Science Encounters the Child: Education, Parenting, and Child Welfare in 20th-Century America* (New York: Teachers College Press, 2006).

37 "Teaching Is Not Attractive," February 14, 1919, series 392, box 3, scrapbook vol. 13, Municipal Archives.

38 "Opposes Socialists in the City's Schools," *New York Times*, April 27, 1919, 6.

39 William Ettinger, "Work of the Teachers' Association," *School* 11, no. 7 (1899): 54.

40 "The Week: Dr. Maxwell on the American Teacher," *The Outlook*, December 27, 1902, 968–969.

41 John Gilmer Speed, "Higher Pay and Better Training for Teachers," *The Forum*, October 1895, 247.

42 Rice, "Our Public School System," 151.

43 Joseph M. Rice, "The Futility of the Spelling Grind—II.," *The Forum*, June 1897, 419.

44 Rice, "Our Public School System," 151.

45 "Opposes Socialists in the City's Schools," 6.

46 Joseph M. Rice, "Educational Research: Talent vs Training in Teaching," *The Forum*, April 1893, 588–607.

47 Rice, "Our Public School System," 148.

48 Andrew S. Draper, "Common Schools in the Larger Cities," *The Forum*, June 1899, 391. For more on working conditions, see Rousmaniere, *City Teachers*.

49 Robert H. Weibe, *The Search for Order, 1877–1920* (New York: Hill and Wang, 1966), 42.

50 Rice, "Our Public School System," 147.

51 William J. Reese, *Power and the Promise of School Reform: Grass Roots Movements during the Progressive Era* (New York: Teachers College Press, 2002).

52 Joseph M. Rice, "Obstacles to Rational Educational Reform," *The Forum*, December 1896, 389.

53 Weibe, *The Search for Order*; Tyack, *The One Best System*; Steffes, *School, Society and State*; Mehta, *The Allure of Order*; Michael McGerr, *A Fierce Discontent: The Rise and Fall of the Progressive Movement in America, 1870–1920* (New York: Free Press, 2003).

54 Edward Thorndike, "The Measurement of Educational Products," *School Review: A Journal of Secondary Education* 20, no. 5 (May 1912): 289.

55 Edward L. Thorndike, "The Nature, Purposes, and General Methods of Measurements of Educational Products," in *The Seventeenth Yearbook of the National Society for Study of Education: Part II. The Measurement of Educational Products*, ed. G. M. Whipple (Bloomington, IL: Public School Publishing, 1918), 16.

56 John Dewey, "My Pedagogic Creed," *School Journal* 54 (January 1897): 77–80.

57 Ellen Condliffe Lagemann, "The Plural Worlds of Education Research," *History of Education Quarterly* 29 no. 2 (Summer 1989): 183–214.

58 "The Week: The New York Schools," *The Outlook*, September 24, 1898, 213–214.

59 For more on the professionalization of school leaders, refer to Steffes, *School, Society, and State*.

60 Nicholas Murray Butler, "The Educational Progress of the Year," *The Outlook*, August 5, 1899, 755–766.

61 Samuel Haber, *The Quest for Authority and Honor in the American Professions, 1750–1900* (Chicago: University of Chicago Press, 1991); Bledstein, *The Culture of Professionalism*.

62 "A Question of Humor," *School* 11, no. 13 (1899): 100.
63 Rice, "Obstacles to Rational Educational Reform," 385–395.
64 Committee on By-Laws and Legislation, June 15, 1897, series 48, Municipal Archives.
65 Teacher, "Correspondence: Politics vs. Education," *The Outlook*, March 14, 1903, 648.
66 John Dewey, "Professional Spirit among Teachers," in *The Middle Works of John Dewey*, vol. 7, *1899–1924*, ed. J. A. Boydston (Carbondale: Southern Illinois University Press, 1979), 109–112.
67 Alice Thompson, "The Superintendent from the Primary Teacher's Point of View," *The Forum*, March 1901, 47–55.
68 E. N. P., "Grievance of Teachers," *New York Times*, June 28, 1903, 8.
69 "The Week: Education and Teachers," *The Outlook*, April 10, 1897, 966–967.
70 "School Bills Attacked," *New York Times*, February 17, 1899, 3.
71 "The School Budget," *School* 11, no. 7 (1899): 54.
72 "The Week: The Ahearn Bill," *The Outlook*, April 1, 1899, 714.
73 "The Week: Teachers' Salaries," *The Outlook*, April 15, 1899, 855.
74 "Teachers' Suits Begun," *School* 11, no. 14 (1899): 110.
75 "A Question of Humor," 100.
76 "The Week: Educational Progress," *The Outlook*, November 17, 1900, 681.
77 National Education Association of the United States, *Report of the Committee on Salaries, Tenure, and Pensions of Public School Teachers in the United States to the National Council of Education, July, 1905* (n.p.: National Education Association, 1905), 73–75.
78 "Wants Negro Teachers Paid Same as Whites," *The Sun*, February 26, 1920, 20; "Black Teachers Paid Same as White," *New York Times*, August 23, 1905, 6.
79 "The Public School Teacher," *New York Times*, February 9, 1883, 8.
80 "Teachers Protected in Their Positions," *Los Angeles Daily Herald*, January 11, 1890.
81 "Teachers' Tenure," *Boston Daily Globe*, March 27, 1885, 5.
82 "No Tenure for Teachers," *The Sun*, June 13, 1883, 1.
83 "The Public School Teacher," 8.
84 John D. Philbrick, *City School Systems in the U.S.* (Washington, DC: Government Printing Office, 1885), 110–112.
85 E. L. Cowdrick, "Notes and Comments: The Tenure of the Teacher's Office," *The North American Review*, October 1897, 507.
86 Lee Russell, "The Crisis in Education," *Scribner's Monthly*, January 1921, 60.
87 Cowdrick, "Notes and Comments," 507.
88 "Tenure of Teachers," *Atlanta Constitution*, February 4, 1922, 4.
89 "Teachers' Term to Be Permanent," *Chicago Daily Tribune*, February 24, 1902, 9.
90 Ellwood Cubberly, "Appointment, Tenure, Pay, and Pensions," in *State School Administration: A Textbook of Principals* (Boston: Houghton Mifflin, 1927), 643.
91 E. C. Broome, "Advantages and Disadvantages of the Permanent Tenure Law in New Jersey," in *Ninth Annual Schoolmen's Week Proceedings, April 20–22, 1922* (Philadelphia: The Press of the University of Pennsylvania, 1922), 226.
92 "Court Cases Affecting Teacher Tenure," *Research Bulletin* (Washington, DC: Research Division of the National Education Association of the United States, 1925), 156.

93 "Court Cases Affecting Teacher Tenure," 147–169; Joseph Brady, "Tenure of Teachers: Tenure Laws in the United States," in *Ninth Annual Schoolmen's Week Proceedings, April 20–22, 1922*, 215–220.
94 Broome, "Advantages and Disadvantages of the Permanent Tenure Law," 226–227.
95 "Asks for Removal of Unfit Teachers," *New York Times*, December 23, 1917, 12.
96 Joseph Adna Hill, U.S. Bureau of the Census, *Statistics of Women at Work: Based on Unpublished Information Derived from the Schedules of the Twelfth Census: 1900* (Washington, DC: Government Printing Office, 1907), 36.
97 U.S. Bureau of the Census, *Statistics of Women at Work*, 109.
98 Frances M. Abbott, "A Generation of College Women," *The Forum*, November 1895, 377–384; Charles Thwing, "What Becomes of College Women," *The North American Review*, November 1895, 546–553.
99 For more on the links between salary and citizenship, refer to Diana D'Amico, "An Uneasy Union: Women Teachers, Organized Labor, and the Contested Ideology of Profession during the Progressive Era," *LABOR: Studies in Working-Class History of the Americas* 14, no. 3 (September 2017): 35–54; Alice Kessler-Harris, *In Pursuit of Equity: Women, Men, and the Quest for Economic Citizenship in 20th Century America* (New York: Oxford University Press, 2001), 4; Lara Vapnek, *Breadwinners: Working Women and Economic Independence, 1865–1920* (Champaign: University of Illinois Press, 2009).
100 E. R. S., "Married Women as Teachers," *California Blue Bulletin* 3 (March 1917): 6–7.
101 Annie Nathan Meyer, "Married School Teachers: Cannot Properly Perform Their Duties as Mothers," *New York Times*, October 11, 1913, 14.
102 "Married Teachers Not Wanted Here," *New York Times*, June 23, 1913, 1.
103 "Mothers as Teachers," *Washington Post*, May 30, 1913, 6.
104 Jackie M. Blount, "Spinsters, Bachelors, and Other Gender Transgressors in School Employment, 1850–1990," *Review of Educational Research* 70, no. 1 (2000): 83–101; Jackie M. Blount, *Fit to Teach: Same-Sex Desire, Gender, and School Work in the Twentieth Century* (Albany: State University of New York Press, 2004).
105 Kate Gannett Wells, "Why More Girls Do Not Marry," *The North American Review*, February 1891, 175–181.
106 Patricia Anne Carter, *"Everybody's Paid but the Teacher": The Teaching Profession and the Women's Movement* (New York: Teachers College Press, 2002).
107 "Teacher-Mothers' Ally," *New York Times*, November 14, 1914, 11.
108 Blount, *Fit to Teach*, 75.
109 "Asks Repeal of Rule 45," *Washington Post*, April 4, 1915, 15.
110 "Concealed Marriages of Women Teachers," *New York Times*, March 23, 1913, C6.
111 "Hunt for Teachers Newly Married," *New York Times*, October 10, 1913, 2.
112 "Dismiss Women Teachers," *New York Times*, December 28, 1911, 3.
113 "Epidemic of Marriage Robs Schools of Their Teachers," *Chicago Daily Tribune*, December 4, 1904, G4.
114 E. R. S., "Married Women as Teachers," 6–7.
115 David M. Donahue, "Rhode Island's Last Holdout: Tenure and Married Women Teachers at the Brink of the Women's Movement," *History of Education Quarterly* 42, no. 1 (Spring 2002): 50–74.
116 William H. Maxwell, *17th Annual Report of the City Superintendent of Schools for the Year Ending July 31, 1915*, series 401, Municipal Archives.
117 Henrietta Rodman, "Sporting Note," *New York Tribune*, November 10, 1914, 8; for more on Rodman, refer to Patricia A. Carter, "From Single to Married:

Feminist Teachers' Response to Family/Work Conflict in Early Twentieth-Century New York City," *History of Education Quarterly* 56, no. 1 (2016): 36–60; June Sochen, "Henrietta Rodman and the Feminist Alliance: 1914–1917," *Journal of Popular Culture* 4, no. 1 (1970): 57–65; and Julie C. Laible, "Henrietta Rodman and Other Modern Feminists: Redefining the New Professional Teacher," *Journal of the Midwest History of Education Society* 22 (1955): 229–239.

118 "Dismissal of the Appeal of Henrietta Rodman De Fremery," *School and Society*, June 26, 1915, 924–925.

119 "The Teacher-Mother Question in New York," *Educational Review*, March 1915, 285–294.

120 "Teacher to Appeal Motherhood Case," *New York Times*, May 29, 1913.

121 I. N. Edwards, "Marriage as a Legal Cause for Dismissal of Women Teachers," *Elementary School Journal* 25, no. 9 (May 1925): 692–695.

122 "The Case of the Teacher Mothers," *The Outlook*, December 6, 1913, 729–730.

123 "The Teacher-Mother Question in New York," 285–294.

124 Marjorie Murphy, *Blackboard Unions: The AFT and the NEA, 1900–1980* (Ithaca, NY: Cornell University Press, 1992).

125 Letter from Henry Linville to Sullivan, April 10, 1912, Henry Linville Collection, box 2, folder 1912, Walter P. Reuther Library, Archives of Labor and Urban Affairs, Wayne State University, Detroit, MI (hereafter Reuther Library).

126 "The Indignity of Teaching," *American Teacher*, October 1918, 161.

127 "Questionnaire," *American Teacher*, November 1916, 152.

128 "What Is the Teachers Union Going to Do?," January 20, 1917, series VI, box 1, AFT Collection, Reuther Library.

129 American Association of University Professors, "Declaration of Principles," *AAUP Bulletin*, December 1915.

130 "Teacher Tenure," *American Teacher*, October 1926, 14–15.

131 "Board Will Hear Accused Teachers," *New York Times*, November 18, 1917, 4.

132 "Board Will Hear Accused Teachers," 4.

133 "Why the De Witt Clinton Teachers Were Dismissed," *American Teacher*, January 1918, 12–14.

134 Thomas Mufson, *The Trial of the Three Suspended Teachers of the De Witt Clinton High School* (New York: Teachers Defense Fund, 1918), 44–47.

135 "Charges out in Case of Ousted Teachers," *New York Times*, November 20, 1917, 6.

136 "Teachers Guilty in Disloyalty Trial," *New York Times*, December 11, 1917, 15; "Dismiss Teachers after Hot Debate," *New York Times*, December 20, 1917, 1.

137 "Teachers Lose Appeal," *New York Times*, November 5, 1918, 12.

138 "Drop Two Teachers for Views on War," *New York Times*, June 20, 1918, 24; "The Union 'Literature' That Stirred New York School Authorities to Action: Terrorism in Our Public Schools," *American Teacher*, April 1919, 90–91.

139 "Fight to Reinstate Glassberg in School," *New York Times*, December 8, 1924, 19.

140 "Teachers Uphold Demands of Union," *New York Times*, April 13, 1919.

141 Correspondence, 1920, folder 2, box 42, collection 5015, Kheel Center, Catherwood Library, Cornell University (hereafter Kheel Center).

142 "A Proposal to Establish an Experimental School," 1924, folder 3, box 50, collection 5015, Kheel Center.

143 "Dr. Finley Urges Loyalty in Schools," *New York Times*, November 25, 1917, 7.

144 "Academic Freedom," *Detroit Educational Bulletin*, December 1921, 1.

145 *Proceedings Americanization Conference*, 127.

146 "Attack Disloyalty at Teachers' Rally," *New York Times*, November 28, 1917, 6.
147 "Wilcox in Loyalty Talk," *New York Times*, November 9, 1917, 8.
148 "Attack Disloyalty at Teachers' Rally," 6.
149 "Disloyal Teachers Must Go, Says Wade," *New York Times*, November 21, 1917.
150 "Attack Disloyalty at Teachers' Rally," 6.
151 "Will Union Be Barred," *American Teacher*, April 1919, 91.
152 New Jersey State Board of Education, *Annual Report of the State Board of Education and the Commissioner of Education of New Jersey with Accompanying Documents for the School Year Ending June 30, 1917* (Union Hill, NJ: Hudson Printing Company, 1918), 20–24.
153 "Governor Approves Two Loyalty Bills," *New York Times*, May 10, 1921, 5; "The Lusk Bills," *The Outlook*, March 21, 1923, 523.

Chapter 3 Teacher Education and the "National Welfare"

1 "Hits Teachers' Incompetency," *Daily Boston Globe*, November 7, 1937, A2.
2 Claude C. Crawford, Louis P. Thorpe, and Fay Adams, *The Problems of Education: A First Course for the Orientation of Prospective Teachers* (Los Angeles: Southern California School Book Depository, 1938), 67.
3 Dennis H. Cooke, *Problems of the Teaching Personnel* (New York: Longmans, Green, 1933).
4 *National Survey of the Education of Teachers: Bulletin 1933, No. 10*, vol. 1, *Selected Bibliography on the Education of Teachers*, compiled by Gilbert Betts, Benjamin W. Frazier, and Guy C. Gamble (Washington, DC: Government Printing Office, 1932), ix.
5 *National Survey of the Education of Teachers: Bulletin 1933, No. 10*, vol. 2, *Teacher Personnel in the United States*, compiled by Edward S. Evenden, Guy C. Gamble, and Harold G. Blue (Washington, DC: Government Printing Office, 1935), 63.
6 *National Survey of the Education of Teachers: Bulletin 1933, No. 10*, vol. 3, *Teacher Education Curricula*, compiled by Earle U. Rugg, Wesley E. Peik, Frank K. Foster, Walton C. John, and Robert B. Raup (Washington, DC: Government Printing Office, 1935), xii.
7 Rugg et al., *National Survey of the Education of Teachers: Bulletin 1933, No. 10*, vol. 3, *Teacher Education Curricula*, xii.
8 "Lehman Stresses Teacher Training," *New York Times*, October 19, 1934, 24.
9 Christine A. Ogren, *The American State Normal School: An Instrument of Great Good* (New York: Macmillan, 2005); Christine Ogren, "The History and Historiography of Teacher Preparation in the United States: A Synthesis, Analysis, and Potential Contributions to Higher Education History," in *Higher Education: Handbook of Theory and Research*, ed. Michael B. Paulson, vol. 28 (Dordrecht: Springer, 2013), 405–458; James W. Fraser, *Preparing America's Teachers: A History* (New York: Teachers College Press, 2007).
10 Ogren, *The American State Normal School*, 202–203.
11 Christopher Jencks and David Riesman, *The Academic Revolution* (Garden City, NY: Doubleday, 1968), 232.
12 Herbst described the transformation as a treasonous "retreat from teaching": Jurgen Herbst, "Teacher Preparation in the Nineteenth Century: Institutions and Purposes," in *American Teachers: Histories of a Profession at Work*, ed. Donald R. Warren (New York: Macmillan, 1989), 231. Refer also to Herbst, *And Sadly Teach:*

Teacher Education and Professionalization in American Culture (Madison: University of Wisconsin Press, 1989). Geraldine Clifford and James Guthrie offer a similar critique: Geraldine Jonçich Clifford and James W. Guthrie, *Ed School: A Brief for Professional Education* (Chicago: University of Chicago Press, 1990).

13 To different degrees, scholars have established the presence of market pressures, exogenous policies, and gendered assumptions in teacher education. But we have yet to consider the ways in which these contextual forces interacted or how they fundamentally transformed teachers' professional preparation curriculum. See, for instance, David Angus, *Professionalism and the Public Good: A Brief History of Teacher Certification*, ed. Jeffrey E. Mirel (Washington, DC: Thomas Fordham Foundation, 2001); Jo Anne Preston, "Gender and the Formation of a Women's Profession: The Case of Public School Teaching," in *Gender Inequality at Work*, ed. Jerry Jacobs (Thousand Oaks, CA: Sage, 1995), 379–407; David F. Labaree, *Trouble with Ed Schools* (New Haven, CT: Yale University Press, 2004); Linda Eisenmann, "The Influence of Bureaucracy and Markets: Teacher Education in Pennsylvania," in *Places Where Teachers Are Taught*, ed. John I. Goodlad, Roger Soder, and Kenneth A. Sirotnik (San Francisco: Jossey-Bass, 1990), 287–329; John I. Goodlad, "Connecting the Past to the Present," in Goodlad, Soder, and Sirotnik, *Places Where Teachers Are Taught*, 3–39; Fraser, *Preparing America's Teachers*; and Herbst, *And Sadly Teach*.

14 "New-York Normal College," *New York Times*, July 11, 1870.

15 *Catalogue and Course of Study of the Normal College of the City of New York*, 1913, box 1, folder 1, Archive and Special Collections, Hunter College Library (hereafter Hunter College Archives).

16 Report by James Kieran to George Davis, 1912, box 1, folder 1, Hunter College Archives.

17 *Annual Report of the President of Hunter College of the City of New York*, 1914, 11, box 7, folder 3, Hunter College Archives.

18 Teachers College was founded as the Kitchen Garden Association in 1880. The school changed its name to Teachers College in 1892. It was not until 1898 that Teachers College affiliated with Columbia University. For more on the history of Teachers College, refer to Lawrence A. Cremin, *A History of Teachers College, Columbia University: The Bicentennial History of Columbia University* (New York: Columbia University Press, 1954). For more on the history of the education schools at New York University, refer to John Payne and Elsie Hug, *Response to Change: The School of Education, Health, Nursing and Arts Professions of New York University, 1890–1980* (New York: Priority Press, 1981).

19 *New York University School of Pedagogy Bulletin*, 1912–1913, New York University Archives, New York University (hereafter NYU Archives).

20 *New York University School of Pedagogy Bulletin*, 1900, NYU Archives; *Teachers College Bulletin: School of Practical Arts Announcement, 1916–1917* (New York: Teachers College, Columbia University, 1917), Gottesman Libraries, Teachers College, Columbia University (hereafter Gottesman Libraries).

21 *New York University School of Pedagogy Bulletin*, 1900, NYU Archives.

22 The Graduate School of Education, *Reports of the President and the Treasurer of Harvard College, 1920–1921*, 177, Harvard University Archives.

23 Edward R. Shaw, "The University Professional Training of Teachers," *The Outlook*, May 23, 1896, 932–933.

24 Fraser, *Preparing America's Teachers*, 159; Katherina Kroo Grunfeld, "Purpose and

Ambiguity: The Feminine World of Hunter College, 1869–1945" (EdD diss., Teachers College, Columbia University, 1991), 68–69.

25 *New York University School of Pedagogy Bulletin*, 1900 and 1903, NYU Archives.

26 Teachers College, School of Education, School of Practical Arts Announcement, 1916–1917.

27 *Catalogue and Course of Study of the Normal College of the City of New York*, 1913, Hunter College Archives.

28 Teachers College, School of Education, School of Practical Arts Announcement, 1916–1917.

29 Letter from James Russell to George Ryan, March 3, 1919, James Earl Russell Papers, series 6, box 25, folder 426A, Gottesman Libraries (hereafter James Earl Russell Papers).

30 *Report of Teachers College, Columbia University*, 1924, Gottesman Libraries.

31 Paul Monroe, *Reflections of Twenty-Five Years at Teachers College*, 1922, Gottesman Libraries.

32 William H. Maxwell, *17th Annual Report of the City Superintendent of Schools for the Year Ending July 31, 1915*, series 401, New York City Board of Education Collection, Municipal Archives, New York City Department of Records (hereafter Municipal Archives).

33 George Ryan to James Russell, March 12, 1920, James Earl Russell Papers.

34 James Russell to George Ryan, March 19, 1920, James Earl Russell Papers.

35 James E. Russell, *Confidential Report to the Trustees of Teachers College* (New York: Teachers College, 1912), 14.

36 Barbara M. Solomon, *In the Company of Educated Women: A History of Women and Higher Education in America* (New Haven, CT: Yale University Press, 1985).

37 James E. Russell, *Confidential Report to the Trustees of Teachers College*, Appendix A.

38 Maxwell, *17th Annual Report of the City Superintendent of Schools for the Year Ending July 31, 1915*, table V.

39 *New York University School of Pedagogy Bulletin*, 1909–1910, NYU Archives.

40 *Teachers College Bulletin: School of Practical Arts Announcement, 1915–1916* (New York: Teachers College, Columbia University, 1916), Gottesman Libraries.

41 *Teachers College Bulletin: School of Practical Arts Announcement, 1915–1916.*

42 The Graduate School of Education, *Reports of the President and the Treasurer of Harvard College, 1920–1921*, 179, Harvard University Archives.

43 James E. Russell, *Confidential Report to the Trustees of Teachers College* (New York: Teachers College, 1912), 6.

44 *Report of the Dean of the School of Pedagogy for the Years 1918–1919*, in *NYU Report of Officers*, 131–132, NYU Archives.

45 *Teachers College Bulletin, Teachers College Report of the Dean for the Year Ending June, 1921* (New York: Teachers College, Columbia University, 1921); *Teachers College Bulletin, Teachers College Report of the Dean for the Year Ending June, 1922* (New York: Teachers College, Columbia University, 1922), Gottesman Libraries.

46 The Graduate School of Education, *Reports of the President and the Treasurer of Harvard College*, 1922–1923, 161, Harvard University Archives.

47 *Teachers College Report of the Dean for the Year Ending June 1928* (New York: Teachers College, Columbia University, 1928), 10, Gottesman Libraries.

48 *Teachers College Bulletin: School of Practical Arts Announcement, 1915–1916.*

49 "Teachers Tell Board to Pay Up or Get Out," *Chicago Daily Tribune*, June 16, 1931, 3;

"Teachers' Pay Raise to Wait," *Los Angeles Times,* June 5, 1931; "Lost Pay of Teachers," *Atlanta Constitution*, June 5, 1931, 10; "School Pay Kept Up Despite Hard Times," *New York Times*, December 27, 1931.

50 *32nd Annual Report of the Superintendent of the Schools of the Board of Education of the City of New York, Year Ending July 31, 1930*, 180, series 401, Municipal Archives.

51 *Selection and Appointment of Teachers in America's High Schools: Special Release of the National Survey of Secondary Education*, March 18, 1935, United Federation of Teachers Collection, WAG 022, box 10, the Tamiment Library/Robert F. Wagner Labor Archives, New York University (hereafter Tamiment).

52 Evenden, Gamble, and Blue, *National Survey of the Education of Teachers: Bulletin 1933, No. 10*, vol. 2, *Teacher Personnel in the United States*, 105.

53 Evenden, Gamble, and Blue, *National Survey of the Education of Teachers: Bulletin 1933, No. 10*, vol. 2, *Teacher Personnel in the United States*, ix.

54 Board of Education of the City of New York, *Supervision in the Elementary Schools*, 1938, collection 5279, box 6, folder 11, Kheel Center, Catherwood Library, Cornell University (hereafter Kheel Center).

55 Board of Education of the City of New York, *Supervision in the Elementary Schools*.

56 Evenden, Gamble, and Blue, *National Survey of the Education of Teachers: Bulletin 1933, No. 10*, vol. 2, *Teacher Personnel in the United States*, 40, 103.

57 Christopher J. Lucas, *American Higher Education: A History*, 2nd ed. (New York: Palgrave Macmillan, 2006), 185–223. Similarly, Ludmerer contends that the "goal of medical training was to foster critical thinking": Kenneth M. Ludmerer, *Learning to Heal: The Development of American Medical Education* (Baltimore: Johns Hopkins University Press, 1996), 5.

58 For more on the role of the state in teacher professionalization, refer to Preston, "Gender and the Formation of a Women's Profession." Also refer to Barbara Beatty, "Teaching Teachers in Private Universities," in Goodlad, Soder, and Sirotnik, *Places Where Teachers Are Taught*, 224.

59 William G. Rothstein, *American Medical Schools and the Practice of Medicine* (New York: Oxford University Press, 1987), 140; Jerold S. Auerbach, *Unequal Justice: Lawyers and Social Change in Modern America*, 2nd ed. (New York: Oxford University Press, 1977); Robert Stevens, *Law School: Legal Education in America from the 1850s to the 1980s* (Chapel Hill: University of North Carolina Press, 1983), 176–177, 192–199; Alfred S. Konefsky and John Henry Schlegel, "Mirror, Mirror on the Wall: Histories of American Law Schools," *Harvard Law Review* 95, no. 4 (February 1982): 833; William R. Johnson, *Schooled Lawyers: A Study in the Clash of Professional Cultures* (New York: New York University Press, 1978), 154–179.

60 Rakesh Khurana, *From Higher Aims to Hired Hands: The Social Transformation of American Business Schools and the Unfulfilled Promise of Management as a Profession* (Princeton, NJ: Princeton University Press, 2010). For examples from other fields, refer to Ludmerer, *Learning to Heal*; Rothstein, *American Medical Schools and the Practice of Medicine*, 107, 143; Konefsky and Schlegel, "Mirror, Mirror on the Wall," 833–851; Johnson, *Schooled Lawyers*, 121; and Stevens, *Law School*, 176.

61 For more on the importance of self-determination in the creation and maintenance of professional stature, refer to Andrew Abbott, *The System of*

Professions: An Essay on the Division of Expert Labor (Chicago: University of Chicago Press, 1988); Eliot Freidson, *Professionalism: The Third Logic* (Chicago: University of Chicago Press, 2001). Daniel M. Fox argues that faculty members, rather than external policymakers, shaped the nature of doctors' professional preparation: Daniel M. Fox, "The New Historiography of Medical Education," *History of Education Quarterly* 26, no. 1 (Spring 1986): 117–124. Similarly, Khurana argues that organizations like the Association to Advance Collegiate Schools of Business shaped the nature of professional preparation in this field and were populated by professors and members of the occupation: Khurana, *From Higher Aims to Hired Hands*. For more on the move toward specialization in medical and legal education, refer to Martin Kaufman, *American Medical Education: The Formative Years, 1765–1910* (Westport, CT: Greenwood Press, 1976), 150–151; Stevens, *Law School*; Ludmerer, *Learning to Heal*, 207–218; and Rothstein, *American Medical Schools and the Practice of Medicine*, 120.

62 Johnson, *Schooled Lawyers*, 154. Stevens also discusses the process of using university-based programs to make law an "intellectual profession": Stevens, *Law School*, 199. On medical education, Ludmerer argues that by the 1920s medical schools "served an educational rather than egalitarian role": Ludmerer, *Learning to Heal*, 255.

63 *Teachers College Report of the Dean for the Year Ending June 1932* (New York: Teachers College, Columbia University, 1932), Gottesman Libraries; Cremin, *A History of Teachers College*, 142.

64 Payne and Hug, *Response to Change*, 45.

65 Speech by Dr. Swift, Inauguration of James Michael Kieran as Third President of Hunter College of the City of New York, March 26, 1929, box 128, Division of Programs in Education Collection, Hunter College Archives.

66 Education Survey, 1931–1932, 8, Collection of New York University Surveys, NYU Archives.

67 U.S. Bureau of the Census, *Fifteenth Census of the United States: Occupations, by States* (Washington, DC: Government Printing Office, 1933), 1100.

68 U.S. Bureau of the Census, *Fifteenth Census of the United States*, 1100.

69 Clyde Miller, *Bureau of Educational Services: Report of the Director*, in *Teachers College Report of the Dean for the Year Ending June 1932*, 104, Gottesman Libraries.

70 May B. Van Arsdale, *Introducing Teachers College: Some Notes and Recollections* (New York: Bureau of Publication at Teachers College, 1948).

71 Committee on Teacher Education, *Report to the Dean and Faculty of Teachers College*, Columbia University, May 1936, Gottesman Libraries.

72 *Summer in New York, 1941*, Papers of Chancellor Harry Woodburn Chase, box 38, folder 2, NYU Archives.

73 *NYU Summer School Bulletin*, 1939, NYU Archives.

74 Rugg et al., *National Survey of the Education of Teachers: Bulletin 1933, No. 10*, vol. 3, *Teacher Education Curricula*, 436–440.

75 *New York University School of Pedagogy Bulletin*, 1900, NYU Archives.

76 *New York University Summer School Bulletin*, 1932, NYU Archives.

77 Lucas, *American Higher Education*.

78 *NYU Summer School Bulletin*, 1939, NYU Archives.

79 Forrest E. Long, Memorandum to Prospective Students in the Department of

Secondary Education, May 1, 1941, Papers of Chancellor Harry Woodburn Chase, box 38, folder 2, NYU Archives.

80 Long, Memorandum to Prospective Students.

81 *Teachers College Report of the Dean for the Year Ending June 1932*, 52.

82 *Teachers College Report of the Dean, 1938* (New York: Teachers College, Columbia University, 1938), 9, Gottesman Libraries.

83 *Teachers College Report of the Dean for the Year Ending June 1932*, 8.

84 U.S. Bureau of the Census, *Fifteenth Census of the United States*, 1100.

85 Solomon, *In the Company of Educated Women*, 63.

86 George Shuster, Hunter College Presidential Inaugural Address, October 10, 1940, Alumni Association Collection, box 181, folder 4, Hunter College Archives.

87 Clyde Miller, "Be Good-Looking, and Let Who Will Be Clever," *Newsweek*, August 3, 1935, 35, as quoted in Jonna Perrillo, *Uncivil Rights: Teachers, Unions, and Race in the Battle for School Equity* (Chicago: University of Chicago Press, 2012), 28.

88 Jackie M. Blount, *Fit to Teach: Same-Sex Desire, Gender, and School Work in the Twentieth Century* (Albany: State University of New York Press, 2004), 59–79.

89 Committee on Teacher Education, *Report to the Dean and Faculty of Teachers College*.

90 R. Freeman Butts, *New College for the Education of Teachers in Teachers College, Columbia University: Educational Plan and Announcement, 1937–1939* (New York: Teachers College, Columbia University, 1939), Gottesman Libraries.

91 *New College for the Education of Teachers in Teachers College*, 7.

92 *New College for the Education of Teachers in Teachers College*, 10, 26.

93 In 1936, the School of Education counted 415 Doctor of Philosophy students and 314 Doctor of Education students: "Statement of Registration Showing Student Classification for the Year 1936–1937—School of Education," in *RG3 Report of the Chancellor*, 52, NYU Archives.

94 Minutes of Subcommittee on Higher Degree, New York University School of Education, October 17, 1934–November 18, 1935, NYU Archives; Payne and Hug, *Response to Change*, 61.

95 Committee on Teacher Education, *Report to the Dean and Faculty of Teachers College*, 24.

96 *Teachers College Report of the Dean for the Year Ending June 1936* (New York: Teachers College, Columbia University, 1936), 7, Gottesman Libraries.

97 *Announcement of Teachers College, School of Education, School of Practical Arts, for the Winter and Spring Sessions, 1934–1935*, 71, Gottesman Libraries.

98 P. W. Wilson, "Educators Are Divided over Plan for New Teacher Requirements," *New York Times*, October 18, 1936, N5.

99 "Teachers Attack New License Plan," *New York Times*, October 7, 1936, 30.

100 "Asks National Study of Teacher Training," *New York Times*, November 23, 1936, 5.

101 "Hawkes Reports Teacher Plan," *New York Times*, October 29, 1939, D5.

102 Correspondence between Dean Baer and F. C. Borgeson, October 25, 1935–January 22, 1936, Archives H, School of Education, NYU Archives.

103 Payne and Hug, *Response to Change*, 45.

104 *Teachers College Report of the Dean, 1938*, 114; *Teachers College Report of the Dean for the the Year Ending June, 1930* (New York: Teachers College, Columbia University, 1930), 82, Gottesman Libraries.

105 Committee on Teacher Education, *Report to the Dean and Faculty of Teachers College*, 114.
106 *Teachers College Report of the Dean for the Year Ending June 1932*, 13.
107 Committee on Teacher Education, *Report to the Dean and Faculty of Teachers College*, 10.
108 Committee on Teacher Education, *Report to the Dean and Faculty of Teachers College*, 14.
109 *Annual Report of the Assistant Superintendents on Schools, School Year 1937–1938* (New York: Board of Education, 1938), 51.
110 *Annual Report of the Assistant Superintendents on Schools*, 14.
111 *Annual Report of the Assistant Superintendents on Schools*, 16, 17, 22, 25.
112 *Annual Report of the Assistant Superintendents on Schools*, 26.
113 Debate between Dr. Lefkowitz and Mr. Reigelman, March 26, 1936, collection 5279, box 6, folder 16, Kheel Center.
114 Rubin Maloff, Statement on Teachers' Salaries, December 20, 1948, collection 5279, box 6, folder 19, Kheel Center.
115 Charles Eichel, *The Principal and the Problems of Teacher Personnel*, 1938, collection 5279, box 6, Kheel Center.
116 Charles Linville to George Ryan, January 23, 1936, United Federation of Teachers Records, WAG 022, box 4, Tamiment.
117 Teachers Guild, *Teachers Stand in Line: Analysis and Forecast of Teacher Unemployment in the New York City School System*, ca. 1935,United Federation of Teachers Records, WAG 022, box 11, folder 4, Tamiment.
118 William Woolfson, Teachers Guild Sponsored Radio Speech, February 24, ca. early 1940s, United Federation of Teachers Records, WAG 022, box 8, folder 31, Tamiment.
119 Teachers Guild, Guild Song Sheet, ca. 1942, United Federation of Teachers Records, WAG 022, box 9, folder 29, Tamiment.
120 Executive Board Minutes, February 14, 1931, collection 5915, box 40, folder 8, Kheel Center.
121 Teachers Union, *The Situation in Local 5*, New York, August 26, 1935, collection 5015, box 25, folder 6, Kheel Center.
122 Lois Scharf, *To Work and to Wed: Female Employment, Feminism, and the Great Depression* (Westport, CT: Greenwood Press, 1980); Ruth Milkman, "Women's Work and the Economic Crisis: Some Lessons of the Great Depression," *Review of Radical Political Economics* 8, no. 1 (April 1976), 73–97; Winifred D. Wandersee Bolin, "The Economics of Middle Income Family Life: Working Women during the Great Depression," *Journal of American History* 65, no. 1 (June 1978), 60–74; Laura Hapke, *Daughters of the Great Depression: Women, Work, and Fiction in the American 1930s* (Athens: University of Georgia Press, 1995).
123 Scharf, *To Work and to Wed*, x.
124 Marjorie Murphy, *Blackboard Unions: The AFT and the NEA, 1900–1980* (Ithaca, NY: Cornell University Press, 1992), 131.
125 Henry Linville, *The History of Local 5's Factional Difficulties, The Situation in Local 5*, New York, August 26, 1935, United Federation of Teachers Records, WAG 022, box 15, folder 22, Tamiment.
126 Neill S. Rosenfeld, *The United Federation of Teachers: 50 Years* (New York: United Federation of Teachers, 2010). For more on the Union–Guild split, refer to Murphy, *Blackboard Unions*, and Perrillo, *Uncivil Rights*.

127 *100 Percent Americanism, Guild Delegate Assembly Minutes*, May 10, 1939, United Federation of Teachers Records, WAG 022, box 1, folder 4, Tamiment.
128 Teachers Guild, *Community Singing*, 1942, United Federation of Teachers Records, WAG 022, box 8, folder 31, Tamiment.
129 Gary Gerstle, "The Protean Character of American Liberalism," *American Historical Review* 99, no. 4 (October 1994): 1043–1073.
130 Diana D'Amico, "An Uneasy Union: Women Teachers, Organized Labor, and the Contested Ideology of Profession during the Progressive Era," *LABOR: Studies in Working-Class History of the Americas* 14, no. 3 (September 2017): 35–54; Nancy F. Cott, *The Grounding of Modern Feminism* (New Haven, CT: Yale University Press, 1987).
131 Teachers Guild, *Community Singing*.
132 Blount, *Fit to Teach*; John L. Rury, "Who Became Teachers? The Social Characteristics of Teachers in American History," in Warren, *American Teachers*, 9–48.
133 Evenden, Gamble, and Blue, *National Survey of the Education of Teachers: Bulletin 1933, No. 10*, vol. 2, *Teacher Personnel in the United States*, 62.
134 H. M. Lafferty, "Young Men Wanted," *Phi Delta Kappan* 21, no. 3 (November 1938): 91–92, 100–101; Edwin Lee, "Selecting Young Men," *Phi Delta Kappan* 21, no. 3 (November 1938): 65; E. A. Collins, "Young Men for the Profession," *Phi Delta Kappan* 20, no. 5 (January 1938): 149.
135 Edwin A. Lee, *Teaching as a Man's Job* (Homewood, IL: Phi Delta Kappa, 1939), 8.
136 "Married Teachers Held Inferior by Medical Examiner of Schools," *New York Times*, January 9, 1938.
137 Jackie M. Blount, "Spinsters, Bachelors, and Other Gender Transgressors in School Employment, 1850–1990," *Review of Educational Research* 70, no. 1 (Spring 2000): 83–101.
138 Cheryl Lynn Greenberg, *To Ask for an Equal Chance: African Americans in the Great Depression* (Lanham, Md.: Rowman & Littlefield, 2010).
139 W. N. Huggins, "The Negro Teacher and the Student Go to School," *New York Amsterdam News*, December 22, 1934, A7.
140 "Backs Opposition to Negro Teachers," *New York Times*, January 22, 1939, 18.
141 "Westchester Has Its First Negro Teacher," *New York Amsterdam News*, July 16, 1938, 4.
142 *Annual Report of the Assistant Superintendents on Schools*, 102, 101, 109–110, 117.
143 John Dewey, "Those Who Aspire to the Profession of Teacher," in *The Later Works of John Dewey, 1925–1953*: vol. 13, *1938–1939*, ed. Jo Ann Boydston (Carbondale: Southern Illinois University Press, 1988), 342–346.
144 *Annual Report of the Assistant Superintendents on Schools*, 92.
145 Elsa Becker, "The High School Turns Parents," *Bulletin of High Points in the Work of the High Schools of New York City* (hereafter cited as *High Points*), February 1935, 5.
146 Alfred Vogel, "The Role of Education in Reconstructing Society," *High Points*, April 1933, 15.
147 Vogel, "The Role of Education in Reconstructing Society," 15.
148 Daniel Krane, "The Parent–Teacher Relationship," *High Points*, April 1931, 7.
149 Helen Fried, "Character Training," *High Points*, January 1933, 24.
150 Educational Policies Committee, Teachers Guild, *Report on Working Conditions and Teacher Morale, 1945*, United Federation of Teachers Records, WAG 022, box 246, folder 38, Tamiment.

151 Andre Fontaine, "An Address to Parents," *High Points*, December 1933, 35.
152 Krane, "The Parent–Teacher Relationship," 7.
153 H. G. Shapiro, "Social Education in the New York City High School," *High Points*, May 1933, 40–43.
154 Becker, "The High School Turns Parents," 5.
155 Becker, "The High School Turns Parents," 5.
156 Shapiro, "Social Education in the New York City High School," 41.
157 Fried, "Character Training," 24.
158 Shapiro, "Social Education in the New York City High School," 40.
159 Vogel, "The Role of Education in Reconstructing Society," 19.
160 Shapiro, "Social Education in the New York City High School," 41.
161 Krane, "The Parent–Teacher Relationship," 7.
162 Mary Denson, "Pupil–Teacher Relationships," *High Points*, October 1933, 67.
163 Amy M. Gardin, "Shorthand and Americanization," *High Points* (February 1932): 63.
164 Teachers Guild, *Are We Orchids or Vegetables?*, ca. early 1940s, United Federation of Teachers Records, WAG 022, box 13, folder 52, Tamiment.
165 *Public Opinion Is in Overalls*, Teachers Guild, ca. early 1940s, United Federation of Teachers Records, WAG 022, box 13, folder 52, Tamiment.
166 Teachers Guild, *Are We Orchids or Vegetables?*
167 Teachers Guild, *There's No Madness in our Methods*, c. early 1940s, United Federation of Teachers Records, WAG 022, box 13, folder 52, Tamiment.
168 The Guild Teacher, December 4, 1936, United Federation of Teachers Records, WAG 022, box 5, folder 23, Tamiment.
169 *Guild Book of Fun*, c. 1942, United Federation of Teachers Records, WAG 022, box 9, folder 29, Tamiment.
170 Teachers Guild, Invitation, ca. 1939, collection 5279, box 3, folder 20, Kheel Center.
171 Teachers Guild Social Committee, *Representative Tea Party*, February 17, 1942, United Federation of Teachers Records, WAG 022, box 9, folder 29, Tamiment.
172 William C. Chase, *The American Law School and the Rise of Administrative Government* (Madison: University of Wisconsin Press, 1982), 143.

Chapter 4 "The Enlistment of Better People"

1 Earl James McGrath, *Annual Report of the Federal Security Agency, 1949—Office of Education* (Washington, DC: U.S. Government Printing Office, 1949), 1–2.
2 Benjamin Fine, "Teacher Shortage Imperils Our Public School System," *New York Times*, February 10, 1947, 1.
3 Grace E. Storm, "Educational News and Editorial Comment," *The Elementary School Journal* 49, no. 1 (September 1948): 8–9.
4 Benjamin Fine, "Education Review: New York City School System, for the First Time in Many Years, Has a Serious Teacher Shortage," *New York Times*, March 18, 1945.
5 Ernest O. Melby, "We Must Have More and Better Teachers," *New York Times*, May 12, 1946, 92.
6 Benjamin Fine, "School Reopening Emphasizes Crisis," *New York Times*, September 13, 1954, 17.
7 "Attracting New Teachers," *School Life* 31, no. 1 (October 1948): 1–2.

8 Grace E. Storm, "Educational News and Editorial Comment," *The Elementary School Journal* 49, no. 1 (September 1948): 8; Clyde V. Martin, "Teacher Shortage Again!," *Journal of Teacher Education* 8, no. 2 (June 1957): 198–200.

9 Andrew Hartman, *Education and the Cold War: The Battle for the American School* (New York: Palgrave Macmillan, 2008); Ellen Schrecker, *Many Are the Crimes: McCarthyism in America* (Boston: Little, Brown, 1998).

10 James Wallace, "Negro Migrants: Lured by Jobs, Schools, Negroes Flock North; Tension Speeds Move," *Wall Street Journal*, July 26, 1956, 1. Also refer to Nicholas Lemann, *The Promised Land: The Great Black Migration and How It Changed America* (New York: Vintage Books, 1992).

11 Nathan Glazer and Daniel P. Moynihan, *Beyond the Melting Pot; the Negroes, Puerto Ricans, Jews, Italians, and Irish of New York City* (Cambridge, MA: MIT Press, 1970), 93.

12 Ansely Erickson, *Making the Unequal Metropolis: School Desegregation and Its Limit* (Chicago: University of Chicago Press, 2017); Kevin Michael Kruse, *White Flight: Atlanta and the Making of Modern Conservatism* (Princeton, NJ: Princeton University Press, 2005); Kevin M. Kruse and Thomas J. Sugrue, eds., *The New Suburban History* (Chicago: University of Chicago Press, 2006); Jim Cullen, *The American Dream: A Short History of an Idea that Shaped a Nation* (Oxford: Oxford University Press, 2003); Elaine Tyler May, *Homeward Bound: American Families in the Cold War Era* (New York: Basic Books, 2008); Kenneth T. Jackson, *Crabgrass Frontier: The Suburbanization of the United States* (New York: Oxford University Press, 1985).

13 Glazer and Moynihan, *Beyond the Melting Pot*, 25.

14 Benjamin Fine, "School Woes Laid to Puerto Ricans," *New York Times*, March 3, 1954, 15.

15 Lee Bobker and Lester Becker, *Crisis in Levittown, PA* (Dynamic Films, 1957), https://archive.org/details/crisis_in_levittown_1957.

16 Earl James McGrath, "Crucial National Problems in Education," *School Life* 35, no. 7 (April 1953): 99.

17 *Statement by Dr. Abraham Lefkowitz at the Delegate Assembly of the New York Teachers Guild on Wednesday Afternoon, September 17, 1947*, United Federation of Teachers Collection, WAG 022, box 10, the Tamiment Library/Robert F. Wagner Labor Archives, New York University (hereafter Tamiment).

18 "The 1957 Teacher Supply and Demand Report: Research Division National Education Association," *Journal of Teacher Education* 8, no. 1 (March 1957): 17–31.

19 *Teacher! Are These Your Children?* (New York: Board of Education of the City of New York, 1946), vii.

20 Joanne Brown, "A Is for Atom, B Is for Bomb: Civil Defense in American Public Education, 1948–1963," *Journal of American Public Education* 75, no. 1 (June 1988): 68–90; Paul S. Boyer, *By the Bomb's Early Light: American Thought and Culture at the Dawn of the Atomic Age* (Chapel Hill: University of North Carolina Press, 1994).

21 Lester Kirkendall, Irvin R. Kuenzli, and Floyd W. Reeves, *Goals for American Education* (Chicago: American Federation of Teachers, 1948), ix.

22 Willard Elsbree, "Next Steps for the Teaching Profession," *Teachers College Record* 47, no. 4 (January 1946): 247.

23 Dorothea Blyler, "Certification of Elementary-School Teachers in the United States," *The Elementary School Journal* 45, no. 10 (June 1945): 578.

24 Fund for the Advancement of Education, *Teachers for Tomorrow* (New York: Fund for the Advancement of Education, 1955), 4.
25 Melby, "We Must Have More and Better Teachers," 92.
26 Benjamin Fine, "Teacher Shortage Biggest on Record," *New York Times*, June 29, 1946, 22.
27 Fine, "Teacher Shortage Imperils Our Public School System," 1.
28 "Million Teachers Needed," *School Life* 31, no. 3 (December 1948): 2.
29 McGrath, *Annual Report of the Federal Security Agency, 1949*, 2.
30 Fund for the Advancement of Education, *Teachers for Tomorrow*, 4.
31 "Ideas for Teacher Recruitment," *New York Times*, November 27, 1955, 221.
32 "Attracting New Teachers," *School Life* 31, no. 1 (October 1948): 1.
33 Fund for the Advancement of Education, *Teachers for Tomorrow*, 27.
34 McGrath, *Annual Report of the Federal Security Agency, 1949*, 4.
35 U.S. Office of Education, Federal Security Agency, *Statistical Summary of Education, 1943–44* (Washington, DC: United States Government Printing Office, 1949), 27.
36 Fund for the Advancement of Education, *Teachers for Tomorrow*, 21.
37 "The 1957 Teacher Supply and Demand Report," 17–31.
38 Dorothea Blyler, "Emergency Teaching Permits for Elementary-School Teachers," *The Elementary School Journal* 46, no. 4 (December 1945): 209.
39 McGrath, *Annual Report of the Federal Security Agency, 1949*, 3.
40 Charles Cogen, *Educational Policies Committee Report on Working Conditions and Teacher Morale*, 1945, 1, UFT Collection, box 246, folder 38, Tamiment.
41 Leonard Buder, "Nonwhite Pupils Increase in City," *New York Times*, May 11, 1961, 39.
42 *Teacher! Are These Your Children?*, vii, 43.
43 U.S. Bureau of the Census, *U.S. Census of Population: 1950*, vol. 6, *Special Reports*, part 1, chapter B, "Occupational Characteristics" (Washington, DC: U.S. Government Printing Office, 1956), 335–337.
44 For important background and context, refer to James D. Anderson, *The Education of Blacks in the South, 1860–1935* (Chapel Hill: University of North Carolina Press, 1988); Vanessa Siddle Walker, *Their Highest Potential: An African American School Community in the Segregated South* (Chapel Hill: University of North Carolina Press, 1996).
45 Adam Fairclough, "The Costs of *Brown*: Black Teacher and School Integration," *Journal of American History* 91, no. 1 (2004): 43–55; Michael Fultz, "The Displacement of Black Educators Post-*Brown*: An Overview and Analysis," *History of Education Quarterly* 44, no. 1 (April 1, 2004): 11–45; Linda C. Tillman, "(Un)Intended Consequences? The Impact of the *Brown v. Board of Education* Decision on the Employment Status of Black Educators," *Education and Urban Society* 36, no. 3 (May 2004): 280–303; Sonya Douglass Horsford and Kathryn Bell McKenzie, "'Sometimes I Feel like the Problems Started with Desegregation': Exploring Black Superintendent Perspectives on Desegregation Policy," *International Journal of Qualitative Studies in Education* 21, no. 5 (September 1, 2008): 443–455.
46 Samuel McClelland, *Analysis of Teacher Salaries and Schedules: New York Metropolitan Area*, Board of Education of the City of New York, publication 158, 1960–1961, New York City Board of Education Collection, Municipal Archives, New York City Department of Records (hereafter Municipal Archives).

47 Board of Education of the City of New York, *Staffing Our Schools Today and Tomorrow*, 1961, 16, folder 27, box 98, Administrative Files of the Dean of the School of Education, Daniel E. Griffiths, New York University Archives.
48 An Experienced Teacher, "Are Low Salaries or Poor Working Conditions the Main Reasons for the Teacher Shortage?," *American Teacher*, April 1946, 14.
49 Cogen, *Educational Policies Committee Report on Working Conditions and Teacher Morale*, 1–2.
50 Board of Education of the City of New York, "Chapter 3: Viewpoints about the Teaching Profession," in *Staffing Our Schools Today and Tomorrow*.
51 "Teachers Advised to Stop Self-Pity," *New York Times*, March 19, 1950, 38.
52 John White, "A Reconsideration of the Role of the Teacher in American Society," *Journal of Teacher Education* 7, no. 3 (September 1956): 223–224.
53 Elsbree, "Next Steps for the Teaching Profession," 246.
54 George Gould, *The Teacher and His Work: A First Course in Education* (New York: Ronald Press, 1947), 26.
55 Benjamin Fine, "Teacher Training in Need of Revision," *New York Times*, February 17, 1947, 21.
56 Paul Woodring, *New Directions in Teacher Education: An Interim Report of the Work of the Fund for the Advancement of Education in the Areas of Teacher Education and Recruitment* (New York: Fund for the Advancement of Education, 1957), 13–14, vii.
57 Fine, "Teacher Training in Need of Revision," 21.
58 Blyler, "Certification of Elementary-School Teachers," 578.
59 Daniel Davies, "The Teacher Crisis and Teacher Education," *Teachers College Record* 48, no. 8 (May 1947): 505.
60 For more on merit, refer to Joseph F. Kett, *Merit: The History of a Founding Ideal from the American Revolution to the Twenty-First Century* (Ithaca, NY: Cornell University Press, 2012); Lani Guinier, *The Tyranny of the Meritocracy: Democratizing Higher Education in America* (Boston: Beacon Press, 2015).
61 Fine, "Teacher Shortage Imperils Our Public School System," 1.
62 Edgar Dale, "Don't Feel Sorry for Teachers," *American Teacher*, April 1947, 11.
63 Benjamin Fine, "School Body Head Lauds Examiners," *New York Times*, October 13, 1954, 33.
64 State Board of Education, *Florida Requirements for Teacher Education and Certification* (Tallahassee, FL: State Department of Education, 1949), 7.
65 Blyler, "Certification of Elementary-School Teachers," 579.
66 Benjamin Frazier, *Relief of Teacher Shortages by State Departments of Education* (Washington, DC: U.S. Office of Education, 1943), 3.
67 Blyler, "Certification of Elementary-School Teachers," 580–587.
68 James C. Stone, "Seven Cardinal Principles of Certification," *Journal of Teacher Education* 7, no. 2 (June 1956): 155–157.
69 *New York Legislative Documents, One Hundred and Seventy-Third Session, 1950* (Albany, NY: Williams Press, 1951); William Viall, "Teacher Certification Reciprocity: A National Plan Is Needed," *Journal of Teacher Education* 9, no. 1 (March 1958): 33–36.
70 Letter from Charles Cogen to Max Rubin, May 7, 1963, UFT Collection, box 19, folder 50, Tamiment.
71 Press release, United Federation of Teachers, June 12, 1963, UFT Collection, box 19, folder 50, Tamiment.

72 "The Substitute Teacher Problem," *American Teacher*, March 1945, 10–11.
73 "Working Conditions," *American Teacher*, November 1946, 18.
74 "For a Better Teacher Examination System, the Guild Recommends . . . ," October 1946, UFT Collection, box 4, folder 33, Tamiment.
75 Harry B. Gilbert, "Discussion Comments in Response to 'Some Notes on the Measurement and Prediction of Teacher Effectiveness' by David G. Ryans," November 1, 1958, Educational Testing Services Invitational Conference, UFT Collection, box 8, folder 23, Tamiment.
76 "Schools Need 1,000 Who Speak Spanish," *New York Times*, June 11, 1951, 27.
77 Fine, "School Woes Laid to Puerto Ricans," 15.
78 Department of Education, *Annual Report, 1946–1947*, folder 2, box 1, Division of Programs in Education, Archive and Special Collections, Hunter College Library (hereafter Hunter College Archives).
79 *For a Better Teacher Examination System: Report of the Committee on Teacher Examinations of the New York Guild*, April 1946, 2, folder 1, box 8, collection 5279, Kheel Center, Catherwood Library, Cornell University (hereafter Kheel Center); Christina Collins, "'Ethnically Qualified': A History of New York City Public School Teachers, 1920–1980" (PhD diss., University of Pennsylvania, 2006), 88, Penn Libraries, University of Pennsylvania, https://repository.upenn.edu/dissertations/AAI3225443.
80 Daniel Griffiths, *Teacher Mobility in New York City: A Study of the Recruitment, Selection, Appointment and Promotion of Teachers in the New York City Public Schools* (New York: New York University Press, 1963).
81 Diana D'Amico, "Teachers' Rights versus Students' Rights: Race and Professional Authority in the New York City Public Schools, 1960–1986," *American Educational Research Journal* 53, no. 3 (2016): 541–573.
82 Letter from Samuel Moskowitz to Jacob Greenberg, June 12, 1956, Division of Personnel Collection, series 672, box 3, folder 2, Municipal Archives.
83 Interview with David Selden, 1986, United Federation of Teachers Oral History Collection OH 009, Tamiment.
84 Max Kline, "Preparing for an Oral?," *Guild Spring Conference Journal*, 1954, collection 5279, box 3, folder 26, Kheel Center.
85 Dr. George Friedlander, "Lecture-Demonstration in Preparation for Oral Interview—Elementary and Early Childhood," 1960, UFT Collection, box 6A, folder 32, Tamiment.
86 "Teacher Eligibles Scorn Job Offers," *New York Times*, February 28, 1945, 23.
87 Benjamin Fine, "Search Nation for New Blood in City Schools," *New York Times*, August 3, 1941, D4.
88 John R. Thomson, "Schools Here Act to Attract New Teachers," *Chicago Daily Tribune*, December 7, 1948, 19.
89 Office of Informational Services, Advertisement, February 13, 1959, Public Relations, series 565, box 25, folder 8, Municipal Archives.
90 Board of Education of the City of New York, "Teach in New York City—Cultural Center of the World," in *New York City's Expanded Recruitment Program*, 1963, UFT Collection, box 22, folder 5, Tamiment. Refer also to Board of Education of the City of New York, *Career for You in New York City Public Schools*; *Teacher! Teacher!*; and *The Future Teacher*, 1960, Municipal Archives.
91 Harold C. Hodgkinson, *Educational Decisions: A Casebook* (Englewood Cliffs, NJ: Prentice-Hall, 1963), 85.

92 For more on red baiting and the Feinberg Law, refer to Marjorie Murphy, *Blackboard Unions: The AFT and the NEA, 1900–1980* (Ithaca, NY: Cornell University Press, 1992); "The Feinberg Law," *Harvard Crimson*, March 8, 1952; Hartman, *Education and the Cold War*; Schrecker, *Many Are the Crimes*.

93 Murphy, *Blackboard Unions*, 175–195.

94 Michael Young, *The Rise of Meritocracy, 1870–2023: An Essay on Education and Equality* (Baltimore: Penguin, 1968).

95 Abraham Lefkowitz, "Analysis of the New Salary Law," March 14, 1947, UFT Collection, box 8, folder 22, Tamiment.

96 U.S. Bureau of the Census, *1950 Census of Population*, 335–337.

97 "Single Salary: A Dozen Reasons Why," ca. 1957, collection 5279, box 7, Kheel Center.

98 Advance on talk of Mrs. Rebecca Simonson, President, New York Teachers Guild, Local 2, American Federation of Teachers, at meeting of the League for Industrial Democracy, Tuesday evening, March 24, 1942, UFT Collection, box 9, folder 9, Tamiment.

99 Refer, for instance, to "Teacher Union Urges Raising of Salaries," *Chicago Daily Tribune*, August 21, 1956, 17; "Action Is Urged to End Education 'Mediocrity,'" *Washington Post and Times Herald*, August 21, 1956, 32; "Teachers' Fight Urged on School Mediocrity," *Los Angeles Times*, August 21, 1956, 12.

100 High School Teachers Association, *Crisis in New York City Public High Schools*, 1956, series 672, box 1, folder 1, Municipal Archives.

101 Benjamin Fine, "Education in Review," *New York Times*, April 30, 1950, E9.

102 High School Teachers Association, *Crisis in New York City Public High Schools*.

103 Mary Handy, "Boston School Budget Rises: Single Salary Rejected for Teachers," *Christian Science Monitor*, April 3, 1956, 6.

104 Michael Glassman, *Report on the National Education Association*, 1944, box 7, folder 4, Tamiment.

105 Letter from Rebecca Simonson to John Wade, January 18, 1946, UFT Collection, box 11, folder 17, Tamiment.

106 Letter from Jacob Greenberg to Rebecca Simonson, January 25, 1946, UFT Collection, box 11, folder 17, Tamiment.

107 "He Made Men . . . Out of Boys!," *American Teacher*, January 1946, 31.

108 Irvin Kuenzli, "Veterans as Teachers," *American Teacher*, February 1946, 10; Louis Kaplan, "More Men for Elementary Schools!," *Phi Delta Kappan* 29, no. 7 (1948): 299–302.

109 Kaplan, "More Men for Elementary Schools!"

110 Francis H. Horn, "Eat Your Cake, and Have It Too? What Stand Should We Take?," *Phi Delta Kappan* 31, no. 3 (October 1949): 82–85.

111 *March 4, 1947: An Act to Amend the Education Law in Relation to Teachers' Salaries. Article 33 B—Salaries of Teachers and Supervisors* [the Feinberg Law], Schenectady Federation of Teachers, reel 5, University at Albany, State University of New York, Special Collections.

112 "Teacher Standard Set Up in Report," *New York Times*, June 27, 1947, 23.

113 "Educators Debate Merit Pay Clause," *New York Times*, October 30, 1948, 21.

114 "Teacher Standard Set Up in Report," 23.

115 Wendall Wilson, "The Merit Rating Phobia," *High School Journal* 43, no. 8 (May 1960): 433–436.

116 A. S. Barr, "Merit Pay for Teachers?," *Phi Delta Kappan* 31, no. 1 (September 1949): 5–7.

117 Terrel Bell, *Effective Teaching: How to Recognize and Reward Competence* (New York: Exposition Press, 1962).
118 Wilson, "The Merit Rating Phobia."
119 Bell, *Effective Teaching*, 14.
120 W. L. Gragg, "The Controversy over Merit Pay for Teachers," *High School Journal* 43, no. 8 (May 1960): 411.
121 See, for instance, American Federation of Teachers, "Two Vital Issues," ca. 1958 UFT Collection, box 8, folder 23, Tamiment; Carl J. Megel, *Merit Rating Statement on the Christopher King Sounding Board National Radio Program*, 1957, box 8.23, Tamiment; Mary Herrick, *Merit Rating: Dangerous Mirage or Master Plan* (Chicago: American Federation of Teachers, 1958); Mary Herrick, *Merit Rating: A Dangerous Mirage* (Chicago: American Federation of Teachers, 1957), box 8.23, Tamiment.
122 Mary Herrick, "Subjective Rating of Teachers," *American Teacher*, April 1948, 9.
123 Herrick, *Merit Rating: Dangerous Mirage or Master Plan*, 11–12.
124 Megel, *Merit Rating Statement on the Christopher King Sounding Board*.
125 Herrick, "Subjective Rating of Teachers," 9.
126 *AFL Resolution and Statement against Basing Teachers' Salaries on Rating Scales*, October 1947, UFT Collection, box 8, folder 22, Tamiment.
127 John Eklund, "Promotion—The 'Super-Rating,'" *American Teacher*, April 1948, 12.
128 Rebecca Simonson, "Teacher Rating and Teacher Morale," *American Teacher*, April 1948, 8.
129 "If I Knew You Were Coming I'd a Made a Plan," *High Points* 32, no. 6 (June 1950).
130 Daniel R. Hodgon, "'Merit' System for Teachers," *Clearing House*, April 1948, UFT Collection, box 8, folder 22, Tamiment.
131 Herrick, *Merit Rating: A Dangerous Mirage*, 23, 3–4, 6.
132 Megel, *Merit Rating Statement on the Christopher King Sounding Board*.
133 Jay Belmock, "Why Teachers Fear Merit Rating," *Clearing House* 32, no. 1 (September 1957): 17–18.
134 Margaret Walsh and Harriet Pease, "'Merit' Rating—What's Wrong with It? New York's AFT Members Give the Answer," *American Teacher*, April 1948, 7–8.
135 "Report of Committee A" (ca. 1948), Schenectady Federation of Teachers, reel 5, University at Albany, State University of New York, Special Collections.
136 Belmock, "Why Teachers Fear Merit Rating," 17–18.
137 Herrick, *Merit Rating: Dangerous Mirage or Master Plan*, 39.
138 Herrick, *Merit Rating: A Dangerous Mirage*, 23, 6.
139 Schenectady Federation of Teachers, *The Story of Merit Rating in Schenectady, New York*, March 4, 1952, Schenectady Federation of Teachers, reel 5, University at Albany, State University of New York, Special Collections.
140 Schenectady Federation of Teachers, *Special Bulletin*, August 17, 1951, reel 5, University at Albany, State University of New York, Special Collections, 324.
141 Schenectady Federation of Teachers, *803 Board of Directors' Meeting, October 17, 1951—News Bulletin*, reel 5, University at Albany, State University of New York, Special Collections.
142 *Resolutions from Schenectady Federation of Labor Subject: Teacher Merit Rating*, October 2, 1951, UFT Collection, box 8, folder 23, Tamiment.
143 "News Item for Immediate Release by Secretary, Schenectady Federation of Labor," October 1951, UFT Collection, box 8, folder 23, Tamiment.

144 William J. Schoomaker, lawyer for SFT, writes to Mrs. Frank Zoller, president of the Schenectady Board of Education, November 1, 1951, reel 5, University at Albany, State University of New York, Special Collections, 345 (Schoomaker's oral argument is contained in the letter).
145 Department of Education, "Teacher Evaluation," Schenectady, NY, 1948, reel 5, University at Albany, State University of New York, Special Collections.
146 Schenectady Federation of Teachers, *The Story of Merit Rating in Schenectady, New York*, 6.
147 William J. Schoomaker, lawyer for SFT, writes to Mrs. Frank Zoller, president of the Schenectady Board of Education.
148 "Board Drops Merit Rating as Pay Raise Basis," *Schenectady Union Star*, February 27, 1952, reel 5, University at Albany, State University of New York, Special Collections.
149 John Theobald to Charles Cogen, October 14, 1958, UFT Collection, box 8, folder 23, Tamiment.
150 Telegram from Charles Cogen to John Theobald, October 20, 1958, UFT Collection, box 8, folder 23, Tamiment.
151 New York Teachers Guild, "News," October 21, 1958, UFT Collection, box 8, folder 23, Tamiment.
152 Charles Cogen, Letter to the Editor of the *New York Times*, October 22, 1958, UFT Collection, box 8, folder 23, Tamiment; Charles Cogen, "Teachers' Salary Program: Merit Rating Opposed as Adding to Demoralization," *New York Times*, October 27, 1958, 26.
153 Letter from Charles Cogen to Harry Van Arsdale Jr., October 23, 1958, UFT Collection, box 8, folder 23, Tamiment.
154 Letter from John Theobald to Charles Cogen, October 27, 1958, UFT Collection, box 8, folder 23, Tamiment.
155 Letter from Charles Cogen to John Theobald, November 5, 1958, UFT Collection, box 8, folder 23, Tamiment.
156 Letter from John Theobald to Charles Cogen, November 12, 1958, UFT Collection, box 8, folder 23, Tamiment.
157 Arthur Bestor, "How Should America's Teachers Be Educated?," *Teachers College Record*, October 1954, 16–19.
158 Paul Woodring, "The Ford Foundation and Teacher Education," *Teachers College Record*, December 1960, 224–231.
159 Woodring, *New Directions in Teacher Education*.
160 Woodring, *New Directions in Teacher Education*.
161 "Teacher Training Is Held Neglected," *New York Times*, October 28, 1949, 15.
162 *The Inauguration of Hollis Leland Caswell as President of Teachers College, Columbia University* (New York: Teachers College, Columbia University, November 21 and 22, 1955).
163 Alonzo F. Myers, *The Outlook for the School of Education*, March 1945, included with a letter from Myers to Chancellor Chase, March 5, 1945, folder 3, box 38, New York University Archives.
164 Van Cleve Morris, "Grades for Teachers," *Journal of Teacher Education* 7, no. 3 (September 1956): 246.
165 *Teachers College Dean's Report* (New York: Columbia University in the City of New York, 1947); Lawrence A. Cremin, *A History of Teachers College, Columbia University: The Bicentennial History of Columbia University* (New York: Columbia University Press, 1954), 213.

166 “NYU Dean Critical of Teacher Training,” *New York Times*, September 18, 1947, 17.
167 Merle Borrowman, “The Quest for a Discipline of Teacher Education,” *Teachers College Record* 55, no. 6 (March 1954): 329.
168 Karl W. Bigelow, “How Should America’s Teachers Be Educated?,” *Teachers College Record* 56, no. 1 (October 1954): 21.
169 *The Inauguration of Hollis Leland Caswell*, 33.
170 “Hunter College Faculty Survey,” 1954, 26–27, Division of Programs in Education, box 6, folder 1, Hunter College Archives.
171 Myers, “The Outlook for the School of Education”; Bigelow, “How Should America’s Teachers Be Educated?,” 20–24.
172 “Recruitment of Teachers for New York City’s Public Schools, 1958–1959: A Report of the Committee on Teacher Recruitment, Board of Education,” Public Relations, series 565, box 25, folder 9, Municipal Archives.
173 “A Guide for School and College Personnel: Student Teaching in the Elementary Schools,” Division of Elementary Schools, New York City, Board of Education, 1954, series 672, box 5, folder 5, Municipal Archives.
174 Marjorie B. Smiley and Arthur Sprague, “Professional Difficulties of Beginning Elementary School Teachers as Seen by Elementary School Principals,” November 1957, Office of Institutional Research, folder 10, box 4, Division of Programs in Education, Hunter College Archives.
175 Office of Education, *Proposed Minimum Standards for State Approval of Teacher Preparing Institutions*, circular No. 351 (Washington, DC: United States Printing Office, 1952), vi, 6.
176 W. Earl Armstrong, “#27: Education for the Professions,” in United States Office of Education, *Education for the Professions*, ed. L. Blauch (Washington, DC, 1955), 226.
177 National Council for the Accreditation of Teacher Education (NCATE), *Standards and Guide for Accreditation of Teacher Education* (Washington, DC: NCATE, 1957).
178 “The 1957 Teacher Supply and Demand Report,” 22.

Chapter 5 “A Brave New Breed”

1 Albert Shanker, transcript of speech delivered at Syracuse University, 1971, United Federation of Teachers Collection (hereafter UFT Collection), WAG 022, box 91, folder 45, the Tamiment Library/Robert F. Wagner Labor Archives, New York University (hereafter Tamiment).
2 *The People Who Serve Education: A Report on the State of the Education Professions by Harold Howe II, U.S. Commissioner of Education* (Washington, DC: Government Printing Office, 1968), 1–2.
3 Neil Cowan, “Albert Shanker Oral History—Interviewed in Preparation for the UFT’s 25th Anniversary Booklet,” 1985, American Federation of Teachers Presidential Files (hereafter AFT Presidential Files), Shanker Collection, box 10, folder 11, Walter P. Reuther Library, Archives of Labor and Urban Affairs, Wayne State University, Detroit, MI (hereafter Reuther Library).
4 Martin Mayer, “Close to Midnight for the New York Schools,” *New York Times*, May 2, 1965, SM34.
5 J. H. Duffy, “Radicalizing Education in New York City,” *New York Times*, September 6, 1975, 19.
6 Abraham H. Lass, “A Spoiled Apple for the Teacher,” *New York Times*, May 25, 1976, 28.

7 Board of Education of the City of New York, *Facts and Figures, 1969–1970*, UFT Collection, box 31, folder "BoE Pubs," Tamiment.
8 Mayer, "Close to Midnight for the New York Schools."
9 Marjorie Murphy, *Blackboard Unions: The AFT and the NEA, 1900–1980* (Ithaca, NY: Cornell University Press, 1992); Jon Shelton, *Teacher Strike! Public Education and the Making of a New American Political Order* (Urbana: University of Illinois Press, 2017).
10 Board of Education of the City of New York, "Salary Schedule," 1935, collection 5279, box 6, folder 16, Kheel Center, Catherwood Library, Cornell University (hereafter Kheel Center).
11 Teachers Guild, "What the Shouting's All About," 1950, collection 5279, box 7, folder 9, Kheel Center.
12 Benjamin Fine, "Teacher Boycott to Be Tightened," *New York Times*, February 7, 1956, 34.
13 High School Teachers Association, "Crisis in the New York City Public Schools," 1956, Series 672—Division of Personnel, box 1, folder 1, New York City Board of Education Collection, Municipal Archives, New York City Department of Records (hereafter Municipal Archives).
14 Rebecca Schneider, Letter to the Editor, *High School Teacher*, December 1956, quoted in letter from Schneider to Teachers Guild, January 1957, UFT Collection, WAG 022, box 3, folder 30, Tamiment.
15 High School Teachers Association, "Crisis in the New York City Public Schools."
16 Letter from David Selden to Sanford Gelernter, March 16, 1959, UFT Collection, WAG 022, box 6a, folder 44, Tamiment.
17 Letter from Emil Tron to Charles Cogen, May 14, 1959, UFT Collection, WAG 022, box 6a, folder 44, Tamiment.
18 Teachers Guild, "Elementary School Teacher: Newsletter," May 1959, UFT Collection, WAG 022, box 4, folder "Elementary School Committee," Tamiment.
19 Newspaper clipping, "Comment Phones to Helen Emory World Telegram," 1959, UFT Collection, WAG 022, box 6a, folder 44, Tamiment.
20 Letter from Rebecca Simonson to Charles Cogen, 1959, UFT Collection, WAG 022, box 6a, folder 44, Tamiment.
21 "UFT Is Moving," 1959, UFT Collection, WAG 022, box 6a, folder 44, Tamiment.
22 "Significance of the Promotional Increment," 1961, UFT Collection, WAG 022, box 21, folder 22, Tamiment.
23 "The United Federation of Teachers Presents: A Professional Approach to the Single Salary vs. Differential Dispute," 1960, UFT Collection, WAG 022, box 21, folder 22, Tamiment.
24 For more, see Murphy, *Blackboard Unions*; Jonna Perrillo, *Uncivil Rights: Teachers, Unions, and Race in the Battle for School Equity* (Chicago: University of Chicago Press, 2012).
25 Stephen E. Nordlinger, "Teachers Union Says Board Ignores Groups on Policy," *The Sun*, August 28, 1960, 24.
26 Fred Hechinger, "High Stakes Angry Teachers," *New York Times*, November 15, 1964, E7; Leonard Buder, "New Weapon for Teachers," *New York Times*, June 11, 1967, 205.
27 Richard Leger, "Militant Educators," *Wall Street Journal*, June 14, 1965, 1.
28 Gene Oishi, "Teachers Union Drive Snagged," *The Sun*, December 10, 1966, B18.

29 John F. Lyons, "American Federation of Teachers," in *Encyclopedia of U.S. Labor and Working-Class History*, ed. Eric Arnesen (New York: Routledge, 2007), 89.
30 Jerry Hart, *Collective Negotiations: A New Outlook in 1966* (Athens: Center for Educational Research and Service, Ohio University, 1966).
31 *The People Who Serve Education*, 1.
32 Dick Turpin, "School Strikes," *Los Angeles Times*, August 24, 1965.
33 Damon Stetson, "Teacher Union Loses Dues-Checkoff Right as a Strike Penalty," *New York Times*, October 14, 1976, 77; Leslie Maitland, "Teachers Union Is Fined $50,000 for Illegal New York City Public School Strike in 1975," *New York Times*, July 21, 1977, 21.
34 Richard Leger, "Militant Educators," *Wall Street Journal*, June 14, 1965, 1.
35 Charles Cogen, "The Impact of Collective Bargaining on Teachers," speech delivered at the Junior High School Principals' Association, March 23, 1963, UFT Collection, WAG 022, box 16, folder 49, Tamiment.
36 Letter from May Itkin to Charles Cogen, May 31, 1962, UFT Collection, WAG 022, box 21, folder 23, Tamiment.
37 Letter from Charles Cogen to May Itkin, June 22, 1962, UFT Collection, WAG 022, box 21, folder 23, Tamiment.
38 UFT Membership Committee, Minutes, June 14, 1962, UFT Collection, WAG 022, box 20, folder 2, Tamiment.
39 United Federation of Teachers, *Spring Conference Journal*, 1964, UFT Collection, WAG 022, box 21, folder 42, Tamiment.
40 Cogen, "The Impact of Collective Bargaining on Teachers."
41 Samuel Hochberg, "The Way to Achieve Professional Status," *United Teacher*, October 1961, UFT Collection, WAG 022, box 22, folder 26, Tamiment.
42 Interview with David Selden, 1986, United Federation of Teachers Oral History Collection OH 009, Tamiment.
43 Charles Cogen, "For Teachers Too: Collective Bargaining Works," October 1963, UFT Collection, WAG 022, box 16, folder 47, Tamiment.
44 Interview with Charles Cogen, 1985, United Federation of Teachers Oral History Collection OH 009, Tamiment.
45 Diana D'Amico, "An Uneasy Union: Women Teachers, Organized Labor, and the Contested Ideology of Profession during the Progressive Era," *LABOR: Studies in Working-Class History of the Americas* 14, no. 3 (September 2017): 35–54.
46 Interview with Charles Cogen, 1985.
47 Rene Epstein, interview with Rebecca Simonson, 1985, United Federation of Teachers Oral History Collection OH 009, Tamiment.
48 UFT Flyer, *UFT Is Moving!!!* (ca. 1959), UFT Collection, box 6a, folder "Merger with HSTA," Tamiment.
49 United Federation of Teachers and AFT-CIO, *The UFT Story*, 1966, UFT Collection, WAG 022, Tamiment.
50 United Federation of Teachers, *Spring Conference Journal*, 1963, UFT Collection, WAG 022, box 21, folder 41, Tamiment.
51 Cogen, "For Teachers Too."
52 Charles Cogen, "Denver Address: The Collective Bargaining Story in New York City," September, 1962, UFT Collection, WAG 022, box 16, folder 48, Tamiment.
53 Frederick Shaw, "How Teachers Get Injured," *High Points* 45, no. 7 (October 1963): 53–58.

54 Rebecca Simonson, talk delivered to the League for Industrial Democracy, March 24, 1942, UFT Collection, WAG 022, box 9, folder 9, Tamiment.
55 Eleanor Capson, "Seek and Ye Shall Find," *High Points* 42, no. 9 (December 1961): 43–45.
56 Irving Gerber, "In Defense of a Merit System," *High Points* 40, no. 3 (March 1963): 62–64.
57 James Cunningham, "The Best Teacher I Ever Had," *High Points* 40, no. 4 (April 1963): 58–59.
58 Letter from Charles Cogen to Michael Quill, August 8, 1963, UFT Collection, WAG 022, box 16, folder 31, Tamiment.
59 Letter from Charles Cogen to Genevieve Gideon, April 4, 1962, UFT Collection, WAG 022, box 18, folder 19, Tamiment.
60 Program transcript, April 7, 1962, UFT Collection, WAG 022, box 17, folder 1, Tamiment.
61 Letter from Joseph Giacobbe to Charles Cogen, April 18, 1963, UFT Collection, WAG 022, box 16, folder 31, Tamiment.
62 Letter from Charles Cogen to Joseph Giacobbe, April 25, 1963, UFT Collection, WAG 022, box 16, folder 31, Tamiment.
63 "Labor and the Intelligentsia," *United Teacher*, September 1961, 2, UFT Collection, WAG 022, box 22, folder 26, Tamiment.
64 Cogen, "For Teachers Too."
65 Lucia Mouat, "Teachers on the March," *Christian Science Monitor*, August 6, 1965, 1.
66 Administrative Committee minutes, October 1960, UFT Collection, WAG 022, box 16, folder 3, Tamiment; "Summary of Officers," *Spring Conference Journal*, 1964, UFT Collection, WAG 022, box 18, folder 42, Tamiment.
67 United Federation of Teachers, "Memorandum," December 21, 1960, UFT Collection, WAG 022, box 16, folder 3, Tamiment.
68 United Federation of Teachers, interview with Alice Marsh, 1985, United Federation of Teachers Oral History Collection OH 009, box 2, folder 12, Tamiment.
69 United Federation of Teachers, *Spring Conference Journal*, 1962, UFT Collection, WAG 022, box 21, folder 40, Tamiment.
70 George Gallup and Evan Hill, "The American Woman," *Saturday Evening Post*, December 22, 1962.
71 United Federation of Teachers, *Spring Conference Journal*, various years, UFT Collection, WAG 022, box 9, folder 42, Tamiment.
72 U.S. Bureau of the Census, *1960 Census of the Population, Classified Index of Occupations and Industries* (Washington, DC: Government Printing Office, 1960).
73 Board of Education, *Annual Report of the Superintendent of Schools, 1959–1960* (New York: Public Schools of the City of New York, 1960), Municipal Archives.
74 U.S. Bureau of the Census, *1970 Census of Population* (Washington, DC: Government Printing Office, 1971), table 171.
75 U.S. Bureau of the Census, *Classified Index of Occupations and Industries*; United Federation of Teachers, "District Chairmen," November 1, 1960, UFT Collection, WAG 022, box 20, folder 37, Tamiment.
76 Charles Cogen, TV program transcript, 1962, UFT Collection, WAG 022, box 17, folder 1, Tamiment.

77 Program transcript, August 25, 1963, UFT Collection, WAG 022, box 17, folder 1, Tamiment.
78 Nathan Levine et al., "A Program to Reestablish Teacher Morale," *High Points* 44, no. 8 (November 1962): 18.
79 United Federation of Teachers, Legislative Memo, January 28, 1963, UFT Collection, WAG 022, box 20, folder 38, Tamiment.
80 Quoted in Murphy, *Blackboard Unions*.
81 Letter from Patricia Halpin to Albert Shanker, October 23, 1975, AFT Presidential Files, Shanker Collection, box 13, folder 1, Reuther Library.
82 American Federation of Teachers, "Women's Rights Resolutions," 1981, AFT Presidential Files, Shanker Collection, box 10, folder 9, Reuther Library.
83 Charles Cogen, "A Professional Organization's Vision and Mandate," *Spring Conference Journal*, 1962, UFT Collection, WAG 022, box 21, folder 40, Tamiment.
84 Cogen, "The Impact of Collective Bargaining on Teachers."
85 United Federation of Teachers, "Recommendations for Recruiting and Retaining Teachers in the NYC System," 1963, UFT Collection, WAG 022, box 22, folder 5, Tamiment.
86 "Agreement between the Board of Education of the City of New York and the United Federation of Teachers Covering Classroom Teachers," January 6, 1964, UFT Collection, WAG 022, box 29, folder 7, Tamiment.
87 Charles Cogen, Graduation Address, June 19, 1962, UFT Collection, WAG 022, box 16, folder 2, Tamiment.
88 Interview with Charles Cogen, 1985.
89 Charles Cogen, "A Challenge to Administrators," speech delivered at the Experimental Society, November 1, 1962, UFT Collection, WAG 022, box 16, folder 48, Tamiment.
90 David Selden, "What Teachers Want," 1962, UFT Collection, WAG 022, box 21, folder 32, Tamiment.
91 *United Action*, June 1962, col. 11, no. 5, UFT Collection, WAG 022, box 22, folder 21, Tamiment.
92 United Federation of Teachers, "The Art of Shortchanging," 1961, UFT Collection, box 17, folder 7, Tamiment.
93 Albert Shanker, "Forty Years in the Profession," March 20, 1991, AFT Presidential Files, Shanker Collection, box 10, folder 15, Reuther Library.
94 United Federation of Teachers memorandum, "Supervision in the High Schools," ca. 1963, UFT Collection, box 16, folder 10, Tamiment.
95 United Federation of Teachers, "Theobald versus the Facts," October, 1960, UFT Collection, box 21, folder 37, Tamiment.
96 Charles Cogen, "The Teacher's Year of Decision," *Spring Conference Journal*, 1960, UFT Collection, box 9, folder 42, Tamiment.
97 Mouat, "Teachers on the March."
98 Albert Shanker, "The Making of a Profession," April 1985, 12, AFT Presidential Files, Shanker Collection, box 59, folder 34, Reuther Library.
99 Shanker, speech delivered at Syracuse University.
100 United Federation of Teachers statement on decentralization, ca. 1969, UFT Collection, box 57, folder 21, Tamiment.
101 Albert Shanker, speech delivered at Albion College, ca. 1964–1965, AFT-State Federations Collection, Shanker Collection, box 15, folder 25, Reuther Library.

102 Shanker, speech delivered at Syracuse University.
103 Shanker, "The Making of a Profession."
104 Shanker, "The Making of a Profession."
105 Letter from Roger Parente to Charles Cogen, January 20, 1961, UFT Collection, box 16, folder 10, Tamiment.
106 Letter from Albert Shanker to Murray Macy, January 4, 1965, UFT Collection, box 16, folder "American Federation of School Admin," Tamiment.
107 Mouat, "Teachers on the March."
108 Harry Bernstein, "Teachers Union Warns of Strike over Bargaining," *Los Angeles Times*, May 24, 1965, A1.
109 Jerry Hart, *Collective Negotiations: A New Outlook in 1966* (Athens: Center for Educational Research and Service, Ohio University, 1966).
110 "Union Hears Negotiator," *The Sun*, March 27, 1966, 18.
111 Board of Examiners of the City of New York, "Progress Report of the Board of Examiners," May 8, 1963, UFT Collection, box 32, Folder "BoExam," 62–63, Tamiment.
112 E. Blum, UFT memorandum on contract negotiations, June 22, 1967, UFT Collection, box 42, folder 2, Tamiment; Diana D'Amico, "Teachers' Rights versus Students' Rights: Race and Professional Authority in the New York City Public Schools, 1960–1986," *American Educational Research Journal* 53, no. 3 (2016): 541–572.
113 Marcia Reecer, interview with Albert Shanker, ca. 1980, box 10, folder 13, Shanker Personal Collection, Reuther Library.
114 "Donovan Charges City Teachers Lack Dedication," *New York Times*, October 25, 1967, 34.
115 D'Amico, "Teachers' Rights versus Students' Rights."
116 Preston R. Wilcox, "Teacher Attitudes and Student Achievement," *Teachers College Record* 68 (February 1967): 371–379, cited in D'Amico, "Teachers' Rights versus Students' Rights."
117 Heather Lewis, *New York City Public Schools from Brownsville to Bloomberg: Community Control and Its Legacy* (New York: Teachers College Press, 2013); Daniel H. Perlstein, *Justice, Justice: School Politics and the Eclipse of Liberalism* (New York: Peter Lang, 2004); Jerald E. Podair, *The Strike That Changed New York: Blacks, Whites, and the Ocean Hill–Brownsville Crisis* (New Haven, CT: Yale University Press, 2004).
118 As cited in D'Amico, "Teachers' Rights versus Students' Rights," 556.
119 D'Amico, "Teachers' Rights versus Students' Rights."
120 "School Muddle Thickens in Brownsville–Ocean Hill," *New York Amsterdam News*, June 22, 1968.
121 "Black Teachers to Stage Protest Rally at City Hall," *New York Amsterdam News*, October 15, 1975, A1.
122 "The New Teacher-Integration Plan," *Los Angeles Times*, January 8, 1975, C6.
123 Z. J. Browne, "U.S. Accuses NYC School System of Bias," *New York Amsterdam News*, November 13, 1976, A1.
124 A. Shanker, "Where We Stand: Last Gasp of Lame-Duck Bureaucrats," *New York Times*, November 14, 1976, 179.
125 A. Goldman, "New York's Schools in Accord with US on Minority Hiring," *New York Times*, September 7, 1977, 57. For more on the creation of this hiring plan and its consequences, refer to Diana D'Amico Pawlewicz, Sonya D.

Hosford, and Andrea Guiden, "In Search of Black Teachers: The Irony of Recruitment and Hiring Policies Post-*Brown*," in *AERA Handbook on Teachers of Color* (Washington, DC: American Educational Research Association, forthcoming).

126 W. J. Dawkins, "Hi Moynihan's Policy on Teachers," *New York Amsterdam News*, October 29, 1977, B1.

127 Edward Burks, "Moynihan Decries Plan to Assign New York City Teachers by Race," *New York Times*, September 24, 1977, 9.

128 "Shanker Alleges Some Teachers Hired by Boards Are Illiterate," *New York Times*, December 5, 1977, 45.

129 "Shanker Alleges Some Teachers Hired by Boards Are Illiterate."

130 A. Goldman, "HEW Weighs Suit to Affect Assigning of Teachers by City," *New York Times*, April 8, 1978, 21.

131 James Koerner, "How Not to Teach Teachers," reprint from *The Atlantic*, February 1963, UFT Collection, box 22, folder 10, Tamiment.

132 "Conant Sees Shoddiness in Training of Teachers," *New York Times*, February 20, 1964, 31.

133 Fred Hechinger, "Wisconsin Revolt over Education," *New York Times*, December 13, 1962, 6.

134 "Educator Finds an Era Is Passing," *New York Times*, February 14, 1963, 7.

135 National Council for the Accreditation of Teacher Education (NCATE), *Standards for the Accreditation of Teacher Education* (Washington, DC: NCATE, 1970), 2.

136 *The People Who Serve Education*, 2.

137 *Higher Education Amendments of 1967: Hearings before the Special Subcommittee on Education of the Committee on Education and Labor, House of Representatives, Part 1* (Washington DC: U.S. Government Printing Office, 1967), 28.

138 Education Professions Development Act, 1967, 90th Congress, Public Law 90-35, H.R. 10943, June 29, 1967.

139 Shanker, "The Making of a Profession," 20.

140 Letter from Nathan Brown to Albert Shanker, August 14, 1969, UFT Collection, box 29, folder 1, Tamiment.

141 Albert Shanker, "The Meaning of Accountability," UFT Collection, box 28, folder "BoE Accountability," Tamiment.

142 Shanker, speech delivered at Syracuse University.

143 American Federation of Teachers, "An Open Letter to the Deans of Teacher Education and Directors of Teacher Certification," 1974, UFT Collection, box 142, folder 17, Tamiment.

144 American Federation of Teachers, *Professionalism: It Should Be More than a Dream. It Should Be a Reality* (Washington, DC: American Federation of Teachers, AFL-CIO, ca. 1980).

145 Letter from Joseph Grannis to Albert Shanker, February 1, 1968, UFT Collection, box 44, folder 14, Tamiment.

146 Muriel Cohen, "New Harvard Dean Wants Changes," *Boston Globe*, February 25, 1973, 50.

147 Letter from Sandra Feldman to Max Rubin, June 15, 1972, Administrative Files of the Dean of the School of Education, Daniel E. Griffiths (hereafter Administrative Files), box 55, folder 10, New York University Archives (hereafter NYU Archives).

148 Letter from Daniel Griffiths to Eugenia Kemble, July 13, 1973, Administrative Files, box 55, folder 10, NYU Archives.
149 Frederick Rodgers, Memorandum Re: Financial and Program Progress Report of the New York University Teacher Corps Project, September 25, 1968, Administrative Files, box 99, folder 1, NYU Archives.
150 Letter from Arnold Spinner to Frank Arricale, June 6, 1978, Administrative Files, box 16, folder 8, NYU Archives.
151 Letter from Monica Blum to Daniel Griffiths, June 25, 1980, Administrative Files, box 16, folder 8, NYU Archives.
152 Mary Jordan, "U-Va to Offer 'Warranty' on Its New Teachers," *Washington Post*, September 26, 1984, C4.
153 School of Education, Health, Nursing, and Arts Professions (SEHNAP), "Futures Report," July 1980, Administrative Files, box 1, folder 28, NYU Archives.
154 Scott Moore, "Cal State to Merge School of Education," *Los Angeles Times*, July 1, 1971, C9.
155 National Center for Education Statistics, *The State of Teacher Education, 1977* (Washington, DC: National Center for Education Statistics, 1978).
156 United Federation of Teachers, "Proposal for a UFT Teacher Center," June 1973, Administrative Files, box 55, folder 10, NYU Archives.
157 Fred Hechinger, "Centers to Aid Teachers Imperiled," *New York Times*, March 30, 1982, C1.
158 AFT Advisory Group, *Teachers' Centers: A New Voice for Teachers in Teacher Education Reform* (Washington, DC: American Federation of Teachers, 1977).
159 Roy A. Edelfelt et al., *Lessons from the Teacher Corps* (Washington, DC: National Education Association, 1974), 393.
160 Cowan, "Albert Shanker Oral History."
161 Shanker, speech delivered at Albion College.
162 Richard D. Kahlenberg, *Tough Liberal: Albert Shanker and the Battles over Schools, Unions, Race, and Democracy* (New York: Columbia University Press, 2007), 2.
163 Duncan, "Elevating the Teaching Profession," *American Educator*, Winter 2009–2010, 3.
164 Shanker's biographer, Richard Kahlenberg, paints a picture of the union leader as a champion of American democracy and suggests that his vision fell short only because of others' reluctance. Shanker's "failure to convince fellow liberals to extend their support of democracy more broadly," Kahlenberg writes in *Tough Liberal*, "leaves open the question: what might society look like if we tried?" The history recovered in this book reveals another aspect of that narrative. At the core of Shanker's vision of democratic action was a fight for union power, his calls for reform inseparable from the union's institutional interests around growth and the preservation of hierarchical power structures. Embedded in Shanker's vision of democratic governance was a paternalism grounded in racialized and gendered ideologies.
165 Shanker, "Forty Years in the Profession."
166 Cowan, "Albert Shanker Oral History."
167 Albert Shanker, "A Call for Professionalism," National Press Club speech, January 29, 1985, AFT Presidential Files, Shanker Collection, box 10, folder 18, Reuther Library.
168 Reecer, interview with Shanker; Shanker, "Forty Years in the Profession."
169 Shanker, "The Making of a Profession."

170 Reecer, interview with Shanker.
171 Cowan, "Albert Shanker Oral History."
172 Shanker, "The Making of a Profession."
173 Cowan, "Albert Shanker Oral History."
174 United Federation of Teachers, "In-Service Education for Teachers," 1968, UFT Collection, box 29, folder 1, Tamiment.
175 Shanker, speech delivered at Albion College.
176 Shanker, "The Making of a Profession," 24.
177 Letter from "Former Admirers and Soon to Be X-Union Teachers and Secretaries" to Albert Shanker, September 29, 1967, UFT Collection, box 43, folder "Contract Neg 67/69 Contact Work Stoppage," Tamiment.
178 Letter from Albert Shanker to UFT members, September 1967, UFT Collection, box 43, folder "Contract Neg 67/69 Contact Work Stoppage," Tamiment.
179 Telegram from Seymour Samuels to Albert Shanker, September 1967, UFT Collection, box 43, folder "Contract Neg 67/69 Contact Work Stoppage," Tamiment.
180 Telegram from Lilian Marks and Frances Rose to Albert Shanker, September 1967, UFT Collection, box 43, folder "Contract Neg 67/69 Contact Work Stoppage," Tamiment.
181 Letter from Mark Durbin to Albert Shanker, 1975, UFT Collection, box 43, folder "Contract Neg—Strike 1975 Correspondence," Tamiment.
182 See, for instance, letter from Walter and Rhoda Burd to Albert Shanker, August 25, 1975, UFT Collection, box 43, folder "Contract Neg—Strike 1975 Correspondence," Tamiment.
183 Letter from James Friedman to "Mr. Al Sell-Out Shanker," September 16, 1975, UFT Collection, box 43, folder "Contract Neg—Strike 1975 Correspondence," Tamiment.
184 UFT form letter from Ned Hopkins, 1975, UFT Collection, box 43, folder 15, Tamiment.
185 Board of Education of the City of New York, *Facts and Figures, 1969–1970.*

Epilogue

1 Dan C. Lortie, *Schoolteacher* (Chicago: University of Chicago Press, 1975), xvii.
2 Lortie, *Schoolteacher*; Amitai Etzioni, *The Semi-Professions and Their Organization: Teachers, Nurses, Social Workers* (New York: Free Press, 1969); Richard Ingersoll and Gregory J. Collins, "The Status of Teaching as a Profession," in *Schools and Society: A Sociological Approach to Education*, ed. Jeanne H. Ballantine, Joan Z. Spade, and Jenny M. Stuver, 6th ed. (Los Angeles: Sage, 2018), 199–213.
3 Lortie, *Schoolteacher*, 236.
4 Lortie, *Schoolteacher*, 244.
5 U.S. Department of Education, "Working toward 'Wow': A Vision for a New Teaching Profession, Remarks of Arne Duncan, National Board of Professional Teaching Standards," July 29, 2011, https://www.ed.gov/news/speeches/working-toward-wow-vision-new-teaching-profession.
6 Jo Guildi and David Armitage, *The History Manifesto* (Cambridge: Cambridge University Press, 2014); Sonya Douglass Horsford and Diana D'Amico, "The Past as More than Prologue: A Call for Historical Research," *International Journal of*

Educational Management 29, no. 7 (2015): 863–873; Michel-Rolph Trouillot, *Silencing the Past: Power and the Production of History* (Boston: Beacon Press, 2015).

7 United Federation of Teachers, "UFT Responds to Janus Decision," June 27, 2018, http://www.uft.org/press-releases/uft-responds-janus-decision.

8 Pearson Assessments, "edTPA," July 25, 2018, https://www.pearsonassessments.com/teacherlicensure/edtpa.html.

9 Diana D'Amico et al., "Where Are All the Black Teachers? Discrimination in the Teacher Labor Market," *Harvard Education Review* 87, no. 1 (Spring 2017): 26–49.

Index

Note: Page numbers in *italics* indicate figures.

About the Author

DIANA D'AMICO PAWLEWICZ is a historian of education reform and social policy and assistant professor in educational foundations and research at the University of North Dakota, supported by the Elnora Hopper Danley Professorship. Her articles and essays have been published in *American Educational Research Journal*, *History of Education Quarterly*, *Harvard Educational Review*, the *Washington Post*, and the *San Francisco Chronicle*, among other outlets.

Printed in the United States
By Bookmasters